# *Transforming the Parish:*
## *Models for the Future*

# *Transforming the Parish:*
## *Models for the Future*

**Thomas P. Sweetser, S.J.**
**and**
**Patricia M. Forster, O.S.F.**

SHEED & WARD
Franklin, Wisconsin

As an apostolate of the Priests of the Sacred Heart, a Catholic religious order, the mission of Sheed & Ward is to publish books of contemporary impact and enduring merit in Catholic Christian thought and action. The books published, however, reflect the opinion of their authors and are not meant to represent the official position of the Priests of the Sacred Heart.

1993, 1999

Sheed & Ward
7373 South Lovers Lane Road
Franklin, Wisconsin 53132
1-800-266-5564

Printed in the United States of America

Cover design: Karen Y. Jones
Images © Copyright 1999 PhotoDisc, Inc.

**Library of Congress Cataloging-in-Publication Data**
Sweetser, Thomas P.
    Transforming the parish : models for the future / Thomas P.
Sweetser and Patricia M. Forster.
        p.  cm.
    ISBN 1-55612-654-9
    1. Parishes—United States. 2. Pastoral theology—Catholic
Church. 3. Catholic Church—United States—Government.
I. Forster, Patricia M.    II. Title.
BX1913.S938 1993
250'.8'822—dc2O                                      93-24332
                                                        CIP

# Contents

*To our parents
and brothers and sisters
who have provided the background
of faith, support and love
that have given us
the courage to face the future
of local church with
courage, expectation, hope and relish.*

# *Foreword*

CHURCH HAPPENS IN THE PARISH. THERE THE WORD IS proclaimed, sacraments are celebrated, community gathers as the people of God and the mandate is given to permeate all of life with the values of the Gospel. How well our faith is celebrated depends upon multiple factors. Father Thomas Sweetser and Sister Patricia Forster have drawn on personal experience and much research in charting out how parish life is being transformed and what the future might hold in store.

During the past two years I have visited sixty parishes. Some were small in size, less than two hundred units. Others were large and well-staffed. Some common themes emerged: a hunger for spirituality and meaningful liturgies, a confusion over inner and outer mission, stress in the area of finances and how to allocate limited resources, frustration as to how to involve inactive Catholics, excitement over some well-designed sacramental programs, commitment of teachers and catechists in sharing the faith, concern over the future and the ability to staff our parishes, the struggle of pastors to adapt to a changing Church and its new and numerous demands. Most inspiring of all was to witness in our parishes the deep faith of the community and its commitment to the Lord and his kingdom.

The key to any transformation, be it of oneself, one's parish, or even a nation, is vision. All depends upon the paradigm, the model, the imagined goal. Father Avery Dulles offered six models of the Church some years ago and those paradigms have had and continue to have an impact on parish life. His balanced presentation points out the strength and weakness of each model.

In *Transforming the Parish: Models for the Future*, the authors project a church that in five years (2004) will have a married clergy, ordination of women, the return of resigned priests. A process for the transition of a pastor is carefully designed. Much more emphasis will be given to creating a positive image of the parish. Small communities involving intense reflection will alter the celebration of weekend liturgies. Finally, all parishes will be kept open—no closing.

Some will dismiss this scenario and its underlying ecclesiology as rapidly as Girzone's *Joshua* and its Christology. Here is where the controversy will take place: is the model for the future that will transform parish life consistent with Catholic theology and the documents of Vatican II? Only those with a strong historical sense and an appreciation of the universality of the Church can answer this question.

While I think that the 2004 scenario will not be realized, for both theological and pragmatic reasons, I find the other chapters in this text to be most helpful. The question of spirituality is well-addressed; the crisis of leadership is urgent and demands immediate attention; people are yearning for liturgies that will both inspire and transform their lives; small faith communities are needed if we are to share meaningfully the faith given to us. In chapter after chapter we are given statistics and analyses of what is happening and what would be done to enrich our faith journey.

A small fear creeps through my heart as I ponder the complex issues of our world and the complexity of our church and family life. The fear is that the message of the Gospel, the good news of God's love and mercy in Jesus, might lose its focus in our minds and hearts. Goethe wrote many years ago something to the effect that not to know this, to die and so to rise, is to be always a troubled guest in the dark earth. Parish life is about the paschal mystery about dying and rising daily with the Lord. That is why *Transforming the Parish* gives spirituality such a prominent role.

Who will benefit from this book? The pastor ordained 35 years, who is looking for a new framework and a better understanding of what is happening today in the Church; parents who hunger for God and want to share their faith more fully; single people looking for community and how they might volunteer more effectively in the life of the Church and civic community; leadership personnel at all levels-bishops, catechists, principals, parish council members, boards of education, all those involved in shaping the future. A good read here that will cause intense and stimulating conversation.

—Robert F. Morneau
Auxiliary Bishop of Green Bay

# *Preface to Original Edition*

IN THE EARLY 1970S, THOMAS SWEETSER, SJ, FOUNDED THE Parish Evaluation Project (PEP). It was the result of a doctoral dissertation study on the Catholic parish. At the time there was hardly any emphasis on the local church and even less written on the subject.

Much more attention was on the universal and national church. The Second Vatican Council and the upheavals of the 1960s were still fresh in people's minds. The country was in the midst of Watergate and the pullout from Vietnam. Local church did not seem important.

The Catholic parish, however, was in trouble as it struggled to adjust to a new way of being church, one that stressed a joint ownership of priest and people.

The struggle still continues today, of course. The optimism and naiveté of the 60s and 70s have given way to the sobering realism that partnership and collaborative ministry is no easy task. How to be church on the local level is still very much a mystery. It is a hit-and-miss, two steps forward and one step backward affair.

What has changed since the start of the Parish Evaluation Project is that parish is now *the* focus of church. Countless books, studies, articles and entire magazines are devoted to the study and implementation of parish life and ministry.

If that is so, why the need for this book on *Transforming the Parish*? Because we feel we have a unique vantage point from which to view the present and future parish. We at PEP keep running up and down the hill, part of the time looking at the larger picture and the rest of the time immersed in the concrete reality on the ground level.

Each weekend for the last 20 years, except for a few weeks in December, July and August, we have spent on the local scene working with the staff and lay leaders, surveying parishioners' attitudes and talking at the weekend Masses. Most of all, we have listened to the stories about the successes and failures of parish life as we have tried to guide the parish toward a more meaningful future.

As our PEP process developed, we spent more and more time with individual parishes; at the present moment we contract with a parish for at least two years that includes six weekends of intense interaction between ourselves and the staff, leaders and parishioners.

In between these weekends of hands-on experience, we return home to our office in Des Plaines, Illinois and climb back up the hill to get a wider view of the local church landscape. We study our surveys of Catholic parishioners' opinions, we interact with students and colleagues at the Institute of Pastoral Studies of Loyola University in Chicago and the Divinity School of the University of St. Thomas in St. Paul, Minnesota.

We also try to put into writing our discoveries about parish life and ministry, as well as offer insights about what might work in the future, based upon concrete experiences of what is already working in local churches. So far we have published three books and numerous articles based upon our experience with parishes. We do this to help the parish leaders become more responsive to their people and to the Spirit's urgings and direction.

This book is unique, however. We have tried to go beyond what is the present situation and look to what might become of the local parish, or rather, what we would like it to become. If we had not ·been directly involved with parishes, we might have been tempted to go farther in our dreaming. The real always has a way of tempering our wish lists. Change in the church is a slow process and the next millennium is only a few years away. We have hopes but we also have an awareness of what is possible. What will work is our concern. Much of what we have written about in this volume is already working in a parish or two somewhere in this country. We also want to test the limits, so we have gone beyond our experience and shared some of our dreams as well. The rest is up to you, you who are the practitioners of local church. You are in the trenches. You are being stretched and drawn from many quarters to make parish come to life. Whether you are a priest, staff professional, dedicated leader or pastoral minister, this book is meant to touch the desire and fire for local church that lies within.

If your vantage is from outside the parish as educator, consultant or chancery official, our advice is to use this book as a way of getting in touch with local church. It is a start, but it is no substitute for direct involvement. Local church is where Christ is present to the people, whether it be an organized parish with all the trappings, or a small faith community that is reflecting on the Word and trying to put the Word into action. Local church, large or small, is where the action is these days. It is Christ walking alongside "the folks." Our hope and prayer is that this book on *Transforming the Parish* will help the parish community on its journey.

We have many people to thank for bringing this volume to completion. One is our publisher, Robert Heyer of Sheed & Ward, who agreed to republish our last book, *Leadership in a Successful Parish* by Thomas Sweetser and Carol Holden if we would think about starting a new book on parishes. That got us started.

We also are indebted to Carol Holden who has been the co-director of the Parish Evaluation Project since 1980 and has helped develop many of the ideas and strategies contained in the chapters that follow.

Mary Borowicz, our PEP office administrator, has typed and retyped our manuscript more times than we can number. Our thanks to her and to our special readers who gave us valuable feedback, Katie Hage, Ann Leadon, Jim Flaherty, SJ, Clara Stang, OSF, Elise Saggau, OSF, Mary M. Yaeger, OSF and Jim Ewens, SJ.

Chapter Nine was not written by ourselves but by Fr. Vincent Donovan, C.S.S.p. We have included it because it says so much about future church and the place of small faith communities in the life of the church. We deeply appreciate his willingness to let us republish an edited version of his original article that appeared in *Chicago Studies,* August, 1992. We thank Fr. George Dyer, the editor of *Chicago Studies,* for granting permission to include that article as part of this book.

Thomas Sweetser wrote a number of articles in the early 1990s that appeared in various publications. The gist of these articles appears in various parts of this volume, as well as a joint article by Thomas Sweetser and Patricia Forster that was originally published in the August, 1992 issue of *Chicago Studies.* We thank the publishers of these magazines for allowing us to use portions of our articles in the chapters that follow. The articles and publications are listed below.

"The Parish of the Future: Beyond the Programs," *America,* March 10, 1990.

"The Money Crunch: Why Don't Catholics Give More?," *Chicago Studies,* V. 30, No. 1, April, 1991.

"Managing the Parish," Copyright 1991, *Church Magazine,* Winter, 1991. Used with permission.

"The Flip Side of the Priest Shortage," *St. Anthony Messenger,* July, 1992.

"Scarcity and Abundance in Parishes," *Review For Religious,* V. 51, No. 4, July-August, 1992.

"Parish Leadership Versus Parish Management," *Human Development,* V, 13, No. 3, Fall, 1992.

"Fostering Spiritual Growth Through Parish Structures," *Theology Review,* V. 5, No. 4, November, 1992.

"A *Festschrift* on Small Faith Communities," *Chicago Studies,* V. 31, No. 2, August, 1992. Sweetser, Thomas & Patricia M. Forster.

# Preface to Updated and Revised Edition

WE HAD NO IDEA WHEN WE FIRST WROTE THIS BOOK THAT IT would meet with such success. For this we are grateful. It received the first place book award from the Catholic Press Association in 1994. It has been used in classes on pastoral ministry, workshops on leadership and management and in countless meetings of staffs and parish leaders as they try to respond to the needs of their people and to the call of the Spirit. One difficulty with this popularity was that all the printed copies were sold and a second edition became necessary. The question was whether an entirely new book needed to be written or whether it should be reprinted in its original form.

In looking over the material that the book covered, most of the chapters are still relevant, having held up well in years since the first writing in 1993. There is still, for instance, a crisis of leadership in parishes today (Chapter Four). An underlying spirituality is still a major theme, not only in churches, but in the American culture as well (Chapter Three). Discovering structures that are freeing and not restrictive is still a worthwhile endeavor for parish communities (Chapter Six). The search for meaningful liturgies, the effort to form small communities of faith, the recruitment and coordination of volunteers are still major concerns in current Catholic parishes (Chapters Seven, Eight and Twelve).

Chapter Five entitled "A Change in Pastors" became so important that we experimented with the process we outlined and used it as a pilot project in three dioceses as a new method for the placement of pastors. The results were so positive that we published the process in a book called *Changing Pastors* (Sweetser and McKinney, Sheed & Ward, 1998.) Another book, *Spiritual Companioning,* expanded on the theme of spirituality found in Chapter Three (Forster, Mexican American Cultural Center, 1997).

One chapter did need revision and updating. Chapter Two on "Parishes Today" contained statistics based on our surveying of Catholic parishes throughout the United States. We have continued to gather information

xiii

about the attitudes and desires of Catholic parishioners since the first printing of this book. These new figures have replaced the ones originally used in order to reflect Catholic opinion.

Another chapter had to be completely rewritten. The title for Chapter Thirteen, which was originally called "Looking Back from the Third Millennium," has been changed to "Parish for the Third Millennium." This change in title reflects new predictions for the future of Catholic parishes. These predictions name three issues that we hope will be addressed within the next ten to fifteen years. The topics include priesthood and Eucharist, a new focus that takes the parish to the people rather than the people to the parish, and a reconciling leadership that breaks down the barriers between peoples and concentrates on what religions have in common with one another rather than what divides them.

The choice of these issues that will be facing Catholic parishes in the future surfaced from repeated conversations with those in the center of parish life and those on the fringe, both within this country and south of the border. Some of these ideas found their way into an article written for *America* magazine entitled, "Taking the Parish to the People" (Sweetser, Sept. 13, 1997, pp. 23–27.) Other outlets included presentations at the Southwest Liturgical Conference in January of 1999 and at the Archdiocese of Los Angeles Religious Education Conference held in Anahiem, California, in February of 1999.

We have been gratified with the success of *Transforming the Parish* thus far and we hope that this new edition will provide new ideas for ministry and leadership to those interested in making parishes relevant to people's needs and respondent to the urging of the Holy Spirit.

—April, 1999

# CHAPTER ONE

# *Underlying Tension: Renew or Start Over?*

IN A LABORATORY, FROGS WERE PLACED IN SHALLOW PANS of room-temperature water. They were free to jump out of the pans at any time. Under each pan was a Bunsen burner, which heated the water very gradually. As the temperature rose, degree by degree, the frog adapted to the new temperature. Unfortunately, regardless of how hot the water became, the frog never became uncomfortable enough to jump out of the pan. In fact, it stayed right there until the heat was so intense that the frog died. (Pfeiffer, Goodstein and Nolan, *Shaping Strategic Planning,* 1989, p. 1.)

Over the last 25 years that we have been studying parish life and operation, the question keeps surfacing, "Can the American Catholic parish be salvaged or should we throw it out and start over?" After many years of surveying, facilitating and consulting, the tension between these two options still exists.

On the one hand, we can spend large amounts of money, time and effort trying to renew the present structure. If we could just find the right pastor, help the staff function more effectively, sharpen leadership skills among council and committees, improve communication, strengthen the liturgy or education or outreach or youth program, then we would have something!

We have been working out of this assumption since 1973 when Thomas Sweetser founded the Parish Evaluation Project. Our motivation was to listen to the voice of the Spirit in the desires and expectations of the parishioners and then help the leadership respond to the people's needs. In this way the parish will succeed. This approach has had both exalted success and dismal failure.

A success story. A parish made up of African-American parishioners was about to close. There were no priests to serve it, no money to pay for its upkeep, not enough people showing up for weekly Mass to support it. The diocese said it must close.

A small band of faithful parishioners petitioned the diocese for one last chance at survival. With help from outside funding, the diocese and parish together hired the Parish Evaluation Project to see if there was any hope for the parish.

After two years of toil, the attendance at Mass doubled, new programs were established, a new sense of pride and ownership became evident among the people. One of the visiting priests who helped out on weekends was so impressed he asked to be assigned to the parish as its pastor. The diocese agreed and the parish not only stayed open, it became a model for others in the area to emulate. Renewal worked.

Not so for another parish that used our services. It started the program with great hope and promise. The pastor, staff and lay leadership were enthusiastic when they learned the needs and desires of the parishioners through the surveying process. They set up priorities based on the results and started responding to real needs, not ones they presumed people had. The parish was about to be inspired, set on fire.

Then the pastor was changed and the replacement had a different concept of parish, one that he controlled. Within a year the staff had all moved out, the pastoral council floundered, priorities were forgotten, parishioners' desires lost.

When we encounter such failures—and there are many—we begin to wonder whether the present parish structure can survive. Perhaps radical change is necessary. What might that change be?

## *Paradigm Shift*

A paradigm is a set of rules and regulations which we use to construct a model to place on reality in order to make sense out of it, to give it meaning and shape. A shift in a paradigm takes place when the model no longer holds water or doesn't fit the situation. These shifts can take place in large matters or small.

Joel Arthur Barker has produced a thought-provoking video and book called, *Paradigms: The Business of Discovering the Future* (NY Harper Business, 1993). In it he describes how businesses and organizations, as well as individuals, get stuck in ruts. They become blinded and self-satisfied by success. When someone suggests a new way of operating or a new insight, it is rejected as foolish, not productive, a waste of time and effort. Many examples are presented in the video, but the one that struck us the most was the quartz watch. It was invented by a Swiss worker who offered it to the Swiss watch industry. He was turned down. The Japanese discovered the invention and put it on the market. Where is the Swiss watch industry today? A shell of its former self. The Japanese revolutionized and captured the watch market in just a few years.

The quartz watch is one example of a paradigm shift, a leap over the way things are usually done and into a whole new way of operating. Barker gives 10 steps that take place when a group is ripe for a paradigm shift:

Step 1:  The established paradigm begins to be less effective.

Step 2:  The affected community senses the situation, begins to lose trust in the old rules.

Step 3:  Turbulence grows as trust is reduced.

Step 4:  Creators or identifiers of the new paradigm step forward to offer their solutions.

Step 5:  Turbulence increases even more as paradigm conflict becomes apparent.

Step 6:  The affected community is extremely upset and demands clear solutions.

Step 7:  One of the suggested new paradigms demonstrates ability to solve a small set of significant problems that the old paradigm could not.

Step 8:  Some of the affected community accepts the new paradigm as an act of faith.

Step 9:  With stronger support and funding, the new paradigm gains momentum.

Step 10: Turbulence begins to wane as the new paradigm starts solving the problems and the affected community has a new way to deal with the world which seems successful. (Barker, pp. 205–206).

Based upon these steps, it would seem that the American Catholic Church is ripe for a paradigm shift on many levels. The Hispanic experience of Church in the United States is one example. One of the authors lived in a Mexican section of Chicago from 1973 to 1990 and watched a paradigm shift take place firsthand. During that period, Mexicans poured into the area, many of them without proper documentation. They were lost in an alien land.

They went to the local Catholic church looking for support and identity, as did many European ethnic groups before them. Some found what they were looking for and became regular members of the parish, usually by becoming associated with Small Base Christian communities. Many others did not receive the help and support they needed. The parish was too big, too impersonal, too "white and Anglo-American." So they went around the corner to the storefront, Pentecostal church. There they found a small, caring, concerned, inviting community of Mexicans who understood their fears and alienation.

This shift from Catholic institution to small community is taking place all over the country. It is a different way of being Church. Renewing the Catholic parish was not enough. Even adding Christian base communities didn't do it. Too little, too late. The Protestant sects knew the need and responded. Now their numbers continue to grow in Hispanic communities. A paradigm shift is taking place.

Sexual mores is another area of a paradigm shift in Catholic parishes. It comes as a surprise to the leadership that their parishioners have such lenient attitudes on sexual issues. The official Catholic teaching is that birth control, divorce-remarriage, premarital sex and abortion are not permitted. They are serious sins.

Parishioners, both active and inactive, old and young, have made up their own minds as to what is sinful or not. Their conclusions are a great distance from the "party line." Twelve percent of a typical Catholic parish membership consider artificial means of birth control for married couples to be wrong. It is a non-question for most Catholics. The matter is settled. This includes parish staffs and leaders as well.

Fifteen percent feel divorce and remarriage is always wrong. Much depends on the circumstances surrounding the first marriage. In some cases, a second marriage could be a blessing rather than a sin, even when annulment is impossible. Less than half (49%) feel pre-marital sex is wrong and 58% feel abortion-on-demand is wrong. The Catholic membership is not willing to go through gradual adjustment. As the frog was unable or unwilling to do, many Catholics have jumped out of the pan in the area of sexual ethics. The Church no longer speaks their language so they make up their own minds. They still consider themselves good Catholics, although their attitudes and behavior may be at odds with official Church teachings.

## Two Options for Parishes

What follows in these pages is a struggle between two options for Catholic parishes. Can they be renewed under the present setup and conditions or will the system have to be junked and a new one set up in its place? Is it possible to adapt and adjust, as does the frog, or is it time to jump out of the pan and start over?

At first glance, renewing the present system looks to be the easier and more promising course to follow. Yes, there are huge problems to surmount, but all the building blocks for renewal are in place. All that is needed is some remodeling, knock out a few walls, put in some new rooms, add some plaster and paint.

But what do we have after the remodeling? Perhaps a structure that is not up to the demands of the people. In the words of Joel Barker, the "turbulence increases even more as paradigm conflict becomes apparent." Maybe we should tear it down and start over. Some sign posts are pointing in that direction. The shortage of priests and religious is one. Why is the Vatican digging in its heels and insisting on a male, celibate clergy? Could it be the Spirit forcing on us a paradigm shift?

Reading the signs of the times is a difficult venture in any field. This is especially true with religious issues involving radical thinkers and false prophets, as well as true reformers and Vatican Councils. What is happening to parish life? What do we need to do now to prepare for the future?

This book will address this struggle from many angles. The attempt will be to point out areas of weakness and stress, as well as offer ways for strengthening them and provide avenues for growth and renewal. Underlying these suggestions, however, will be that nagging question, "Are these adjustments and adaptations enough to do the trick?" Should we, perhaps, let the parish institution die of its own weight and spend our energies creating a more viable, lasting, rewarding structure for the future life of the Church?

Perhaps the Church of Central and South America is the example to follow. Two parallel religious structures exist. One is the official Church structure of diocese and parishes. The other is the *Comunidad de Base* structure that has captured the hearts and energies of the *camposinos.* They and their leaders have experienced much persecution from both Church and government. Through it all they have hung tough and are changing the face of their own countries and the larger church.

Is this the route we American Catholics should follow? This is the tension we feel in working with parishes, teaching classes and writing this book. Are we merely prolonging the death pangs of an institution that must collapse so that the phoenix can rise from its ashes, or are we helping create a renewed parish structure that will rekindle the hearts of its members and fulfill the desires of its lifeblood, the Spirit of the Risen Christ?

## How Shifts Happen

As another way of looking at the tension, consider how paradigm shifts take place. Max Weber, a sociologist who lived at the turn of the century, describes the progression. *(Economy and Society,* eds. Guenther Roth and Claus Wittich. NY: Bedminster Press, 1968, pp. 212–271.) The process starts with the status quo, the accepted tradition. This is represented in Figure I as a triangle. The ones in charge are at the top and the membership is spread out across the bottom.

The pre-Vatican II Catholic Church was one such institution made up of many time-honored traditions. The paradigm stressed uniformity with clear codes of obligation and conduct. The ordained clergy were the leaders at the top of the triangle. They "owned" the Church, top to bottom. If a person wore a Roman collar, and all the priests and bishops did, that person was given the authority, no matter one's ability or personal traits.

Every institution or organization develops a tradition. "This is the way we do things around here." It could be a mothers' club, choir or prayer group on a small scale, or it could be a church, school or business on a large scale. This tradition fits those associated with the group. At the same time, it leaves others out on the margin.

Such was the experience of the African slaves brought to the southern United States. The dominant paradigm was the Baptist religion. The slaves were expected to follow this same religious format. It didn't fit them, however. They were on the margin. As a result, they created their own religion, a blend of their native experience and the Scriptural heritage of their owners. One outgrowth of this adaptation was Gospel Spirituals, a fresh type of music that is now part of standard religious musical repertoires.

The marginalizing trend is represented in Figure I by the sections at the far ends of the triangle that are cut off and floating on their own. Such is the experience of people who no longer fit in with the dominant paradigm. They are hungry for a change, for something new, for whatever will fill the vacuum and give them meaning. Jesus described such people as "sheep without a shepherd." (Mk. 6:34)

This is an unstable situation. Not, of course, to those in the institution. They feel secure and satisfied. But it is unstable to those who are adrift, especially if their numbers grow. Many Catholics felt too confined and "boxed in" by the uniformity of the pre-Vatican II Church. The Council provided the spark and gave individuals freedom to reach out to people on the margin and form what in the 1960s was called "underground churches." Priests who had trouble with the clericalism of the institutional Church gathered people into small faith communities and celebrated Mass in classrooms, dormitories and homes. These Masses included many practices not yet approved by the Church, such as unauthorized English prayers, real bread for Eucharist and communion in the hand.

At this stage of the process, those who are on the margin flock to a leader who touches their hearts and speaks to their needs. The leader provides an experience that is new and exciting, one that is so unlike what they encounter in the institution.

In the African-American experience, preachers gathered the slaves in secret and spoke to their longings and dreams of freedom. In the decade following Vatican II, the leaders were primarily religious order priests who were studying new theologies related to the People of God as Church and Christ present in the assembled community. At the present time, many people are attracted to leaders who provide security in the literal interpretation of Scripture and in a support network for people experiencing addictions, poverty or alienation.

Figure 1 represents this stage with the marginated people drawn in around a central figure who has a charismatic personality that can spark interest, touch hearts, bring out dormant longings and speak to new dreams and hopes. These charismatic leaders fill up the vacuums people on the margin have been feeling. This is leadership more by heart than by the role a person fulfills. Women and men who founded religious congregations were such figures, as were despots such as Adolf Hitler, Jim Jones and David Koresh.

**Figure 1**
**Changing Leadership**

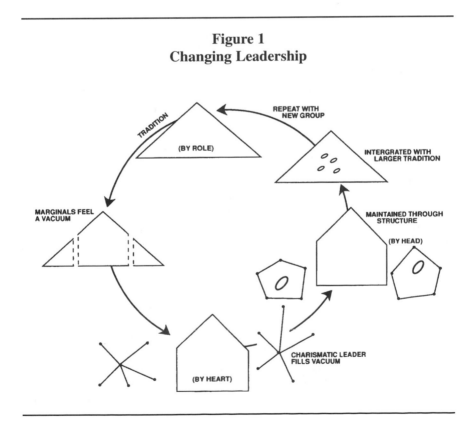

The traditions built up in these marginal gatherings depend upon the inspiration, gifts or whims of the leader. The leader provides the life, nourishment and vision for the group. Codes of right conduct, belief systems and rules of behavior are established by the leader and may change as the leader adapts to changing situations. The life of the group is at once exciting and dynamic, as well as fluid and adapting.

Then there comes a moment when the leader is no longer present. The soul of the group has vanished. The group is in crisis. The disciples are left looking up to heaven as Jesus leaves them. The theologian-priest finishes his studies and moves to another city. The charismatic leader is shot and killed, or indicted for income tax fraud or censored by authorities. The center of the group's life and meaning is no longer present. Now what?

This is a critical stage in a paradigm's life and future. The new ways of acting were thrilling, spoke to people's inner longings. Now the source of that life is gone. Some movements collapse at this stage. The followers pack up and go home, like the two people leaving Jerusalem for Emmaus after Jesus' death. The new paradigm dies when the leader leaves.

Other paradigms survive because the followers pull together and tell stories about what it was like when the leader was with them. They start to organize and structure the paradigm. They make it into an institution that has a more logical and ordered existence.

Thomas Sweetser was sitting in a large auditorium at Notre Dame University in the middle 60s at just such a moment. The meeting was a gathering of people in the "Spontaneous Prayer Movement." The founder of the movement was no longer present and the participants were debating as to how to organize the spontaneous prayer movement. What an irony trying to *organize* spontaneous prayer. But it had to be done if it was to have a future.

All new paradigms, all new ways of acting and operating, no matter how fluid and dynamic, must do the same. Figure 1 shows this by groups linking the members together through leadership of the "head." This is a rational process. Founders of religious groups write a "Rule" to give the group life after they die. That's the origin of Scripture, an account of what is expected of us in this in-between time, the time between Christ's first and second coming.

As the new leaders of the paradigm try to organize, codify and concretize the dream and vision of the original leader, they make the dream more intelligible and less threatening to the original institution.

For example, the underground churches started to gain credibility as they became less radical and avant garde. Communion in the hand or under both species of bread and wine became accepted by the mainstream church. They were accepted as part of the new status quo. These practices were now legitimate traditions. Other practices sought after by those on the margin have not as yet been accepted by the Church. These include a married clergy or women priests. These new practices are being organized in small circles. Eventually they will be accepted into the tradition as part of the new paradigm.

As Figure I indicates, the cycle becomes complete as the new paradigms are accepted into the institution and incorporated into the practice of the mainstream. Once the radical fringe is given a rationalization and stability through leadership of the "head," the larger institution is not so threatened by the radicalism. It begins to see the advantages of the new paradigms and seeks to incorporate them into its own life because they speak to the needs of the people to a greater extent than did their own way of acting.

This does not always happen, however. Some small, organized traditions remain split off from the larger tradition and continue to float free. This happened in the early Puritan churches that splintered into a number of independent religious sects. Some of these have regrouped as national churches, others have remained separate.

In other situations, the larger institution rejects the splinter groups, is blind to the momentum and energy the new paradigms contain and is left behind as the new model becomes the dominant tradition. For example, Christianity replaced the Greco-Roman paradigm while borrowing heavily from its philosophy and organizational insights. The Reformation was another example: two religious movements survived in a parallel coexistence. American industry is now struggling with the same dynamic as it tries to figure out how to adjust to new world trade realities.

The cycle of change continues. Many people feel on the margin of today's Catholic Church, especially at the local level. New paradigms are being discovered and tried out. As they develop, will the institutional Church incorporate them and be renewed, or will it reject them and be left behind as the People of God create a new way of being Church?

Before delving into the local experiments of church, we must first become aware of people's attitudes on the local level. This is the stuff out of which paradigms spring.

## Questions for Review and Reflection

*Hopes and Fears*

What aspects of your parish or area of ministry give you hope for the future? Who are the key people who keep this hope alive? What aspects cause you concern or make you wonder if the present structure can or should survive?

*Paradigm Shift*

Are there any ruts your parish is stuck in at the present moment? One way of identifying a movement out of ruts is turbulence. Where is there turbulence in your parish or pastoral ministry? What is the cause of the turbulence? Besides confusion and frustration that the turbulence creates, does it point the way to a new way of operating, to a new paradigm?

*Changing Leadership*

Using Figure 1 as a reference, what traditions lie at the heart of the parish? Which groups or programs are on the margins? Do those on the fringe have anyone to lead them or speak up for their needs and desires? Is there a way of allowing the marginal groups to have a positive impact on the parish as a whole?

## Prayer Ritual

*Music*

*Song of Hope* by John Foley, SJ (Portland, OR: New Dawn Music, 1985.) "1 know the plans I have for you," says the Lord, "plans of fullness, not of harm."

*Process*

Divide into small groups of three to six persons each. Give each group some building blocks and ask them to build the highest structure possible from the blocks. Allow each group to work on its own, out of view of the others. Once all the groups have finished, have everyone look at the results and see if different paradigms emerged from the way the structures were built. Were there different perceptions or different ways of viewing the task?

*Reading*

Read aloud the journey of the disciples to Emmaus (Luke 24:1330) and spend a moment quietly reflecting on the story as it relates to different paradigms. Then read aloud the 10 steps of a paradigm shift found on page 3 of this chapter, each step read by a different person. How do these steps apply to the scripture story? How do they apply to your own or to the parish situation?

*Closing*

Allow time for discussion and close with a repetition of the song used at the beginning.

# CHAPTER TWO

# *Parishes Today*

WHAT DO YOU WANT FIRST? THE GOOD NEWS OR THE BAD news about American Catholic parishes? The good news? Okay, we'll start with a story.

"Hello, Ted. You got a minute? Something rather extraordinary has happened to me and I just have to share it with somebody. It took place just a few hours ago, this very Sunday morning.

After reading the paper, I got my coat on and went for a walk around the neighborhood. I didn't go my usual route, the one I use for jogging. I turned another way, lost in my own thoughts.

Without realizing how far I had gone, I walked past a church, a Catholic church, to be exact. I haven't been inside a church for a long time. Remember I mentioned to you that I grew up a Catholic. When I was little my parents didn't have a lot to do with church. They tried to get me to go to religion classes, CCD, as they called it. I went for awhile, I even think I got confirmed.

As soon as high school was over, that was it for me with church. It just turned sour for me. As you know, my wife is somewhat religious in her own way, but we don't talk at all about religion.

As I walked by this church, there were a lot of people going in. I had an urge to follow suit, just to sit for a while and get my thoughts together. Besides, I was getting a little chilly. My experience of church in my childhood was to go to the back pews and remain unnoticed.

That's not what happened to me this time. What I walked into was not the church proper but a gathering space. People were hanging up their coats and greeting one another. A woman came up to me and said hello. This really surprised me. I never experienced such a thing when I was growing up in the Catholic Church.

The woman, Mary Talcott, according to her name tag, was about my age. She wasn't pushy, just friendly. She recognized me as someone new and wanted to be sure I felt at home. I must admit that I did. I thought I would feel out of place but I didn't. She explained that today's Mass

11

would be a little different. She had no idea she was talking to someone who hadn't been to Mass for many years.

Mary told me that after the Gospel was read, everyone would have a chance to reflect quietly on its significance for the coming week and then share any insights with the person next to them. She could tell, I'm sure, that none of this was registering for me. She offered to go in and sit with me during the Mass to ease my uncomfortableness. For this I was supremely grateful. Part of me wanted to turn heel and run. Another part of me was curious enough to see the thing through. By this time I could hear the music starting and people moving into the church proper. I was hooked.

The church was large, but still homey. No pews, just chairs, arranged in a half-circle around the altar. Just as Mary mentioned, once the Gospel was read, the church fell silent. (The children had already left for their own Gospel story.) In a few minutes the priest invited everyone to share any insights with one other person. I could tell people were ready for this because the whole place erupted into active conversation.

The Gospel was about a sick person whom Jesus healed. The sick person couldn't get in through the door so his companions lowered him down through the roof. My mind was a blank at first, but with some encouragement from my companion I started to say things I never knew were there.

I found myself talking about what significance this story had in my life. I couldn't believe it. All of a sudden I realized I had not entered into any of this church stuff because there was no way of getting through. There were all sorts of rituals and customs and rules and obligations, set ways things had to be done. It just felt like the door was always crowded with all sorts of other people who knew how to act so that I just couldn't get through the opening.

On this Sunday I felt I was now coming into church by another way, through the roof as it were. This Mary that I was talking to was doing the lowering of me through the roof and it felt good. I was coming down into this church in spite of myself, into a church very different from my previous memories.

Mary told her story about feeling the same way, that she was doing the lowering and it was an important moment for her as well. I could tell it wasn't just something I was saying to her. We were both caught up in the power of this strange happening.

In what seemed like a very short time, the priest broke in on our conversation and spoke a few words of his own about the Gospel. Then the Mass continued. The collection basket was passed around and I dropped in $20.00. I felt this whole thing was amazing. My $20.00 stood for the exhilaration I was feeling. Mary Talcott, sitting next to me, was enjoying my enthusiasm.

There followed some quiet reflection time which I needed. Mary invited me to join her as she went up to receive Communion but I refrained. I had received so much already.

When Mass was over and everyone went out to the original gathering space for coffee and donuts, I thanked Mary for guiding me through this wonderful experience and she gave me a hug in response. "Would I be coming back?" she asked. "Not sure," was my response. "I may have to bury my wife instead. She'll drop dead once I tell her about what happened here today."

When I got back home I didn't know where to turn. That's why I called you. It's too soon to relate this experience to my wife. She would hardly know what to make of it. It will take some time for me to absorb it myself before I try to pass it on to her.

I know I am not the same person. I don't know where all of this is leading but I do feel like I'm being lowered down through the roof into something fresh and wonderful. It's more than I had hoped or imagined or fathomed. I'll let you know what happens. Thanks for listening, see you after work next week. Bye."

This story is good news. It could happen anywhere, in any church, Catholic or otherwise. Someone is led by the Spirit and experiences a conversion through a chance encounter with a caring person. It's an invitation of grace. The bad news is that this happens all too rarely.

Think of your own church. What would happen to a person who comes in from the cold just to sit in the back and be absorbed into the service? Would he or she be greeted, be welcomed into the liturgy, find a companion, have a chance to tell his or her story, be thrilled by the Gospel's relevance, be drawn to communion, be excited enough to come back again? If your answer is yes, you are indeed blessed. The more usual answer is "No, I'm afraid not." Why is this? There are many reasons, some lying inside and some outside the Church or parish.

## Church Consumerism

Our American culture does not encourage active involvement, especially in religion. We are a consumer, individualistic society that wants to enjoy what is already made to order. Television, microwaves and car phones have taught us well how to get what we want when we want it. Religion does not fit that mold well. Finding time to be quiet and reflect on what gives our lives meaning goes against this pressure to "shop till you drop." Sharing personal reflections with others goes against the drive to be self-sufficient and self-directed.

People come to church, if they come at all, with this mind-set of consumerism and individualism. "I'm here to be filled up with God, to feel good, to be uplifted. Then I'll go home, have breakfast, read the paper and go to the mall." This, of course, is a caricature, but it has a subtle impact on our religious behavior. No matter what a particular parish might do to invite and encourage active involvement and response, the pressures of the culture and personal life patterns are great obstacles to overcome. At special moments in people's lives they are forced to interpret these patterns and face new realities. No latest product or even one's own ingenuity will show the way. These new realities could be unemployment, the breakup of a marriage, the start of a family, serious sickness, an accident, addiction, a move, or the death of a loved one. It is at these moments that our consumer, individualistic selves lose control and are forced to stop and take stock of our lives. Most often we are not able to do this by ourselves. We are humbled by our own powerlessness. We reach out to others for help and support.

This is when church and religion come to mind. When recessions hit, churches grow in attendance, not in membership but in attendance. We go back to old patterns, looking for insight and assurance until we get some control and order back into our lives. Then the individualism begins to take over once again and we settle back into being self-sufficient consumers once again.

In our surveys of Catholic parishioners across the United States over the last 25 years, we have found that in a typical parish the majority (65%) attend church with some regularity, at least every other week. The remaining 35% are marginal members, that is, people who come once a month to never. Not counted in these figures are the 30% or more of all baptized Catholics who do not belong to any church. They may live within the confines of a Catholic parish but their names are not on the membership list. That means that of all baptized Catholics who attend Mass regularly, this amounts to about 45% of the total Catholic population. For those between the ages of 18–35, the attendance rate is half that number. Churches swell at Christmas and Easter as the inactive Catholics make an appearance. Attendance figures return to "normal" the following week. Nothing that the parish does will make much of a dent on this syndrome. It comes from people's connections with the dominant American culture.

Such was not always the case. When Catholics identified more with their place of origin than their citizenship, they attended church in greater numbers. The local parish was a focus for common customs and familiar patterns, whether Polish, Italian or Filipino. Most Catholics are no longer outsiders to the American culture, however. Even the more recent arrivals from Asia, Eastern Europe or south of the border become assimilated quickly into the dominant culture. They feel less of a need for a church social center than those who emigrated earlier. Television, consumerism, and the push to be self-sufficient forces newcomers to become independent. It cuts them off from support structures and centers of identity, leaving them adrift to fend for themselves as they seek "the good life." Attending church is not part of their push for the American dream.

The surrounding culture touches each one of us. It takes discipline, inner conviction, and a support system to break out of the mold. That is one reason parishes, as they are presently structured, don't speak to people's needs or stir their interest. But it is not always the parish's fault. What is demanded of the individual is too great. Except in crisis moments or times associated with nostalgia, church for most Americans, Catholics included, is not a "cool place to be."

That's one side of the coin for nonattendance. The other side lies with the Church, especially the leadership. Think back on our original story. What made the experience unique for our visitor? It was not one thing but many. The space for gathering before Mass, the greeter who took an interest, the chance to share one's reaction after the readings, the welcoming environment, good music, friendly people, to name a few. How did the Mass become so inviting and appealing to the newcomer? Someone, perhaps many, had some imagination about what liturgy could be and then put it into effect.

Imagination is so important and yet so rare in Catholic parishes. In most churches all the weekend Masses follow the same, often deadly, routine. People know just what to expect and are seldom surprised by creativity or challenged by fresh patterns of prayer and worship. Even those who come to Mass with enthusiasm, ready to celebrate, are all too often squelched and forced to give into the routine of the lowest common denominator.

While we were working in a parish one Sunday morning, a younger man came to us as we were saying goodbye to people at the end of Mass. He asked if we knew of a good liturgy in the area, one where he could feel celebrative and revived. We knew the area fairly well but could not suggest a single place where he could go for nourishment and meaning. What an indictment of our church. So many of our liturgies are dead. No imagination. How much longer can we survive this vacuum?

The church, however, is not dead. The Spirit of the Risen Christ is alive and well. What will bring the Church back to life? Imagination.

Envision a new future. Look for a new paradigm. Take a quantum leap into the unknown. It's here, right in front of our noses. It is up to us to discover what God is offering us for the next millennium.

## People's Attitudes

In order to discover new paradigms for the local church, we must first look at what we have to work with. Who are the people that are now members of the Church? What do they reveal about a new way of being parish?

Since 1973, we have been surveying the opinions of Catholic parishioners as an initial step in our parish evaluation process. During these years we have processed over 30,000 randomly-selected surveys from all types of parishes throughout the United States. This is what we have discovered.

When people go to church on the weekend, and the majority of Catholics still do attend Mass at least monthly, almost everyone (86%) receives communion. They like to have music at Mass, although they themselves are reluctant to join in with the singing. Only 21% said they favored a quiet Mass with no singing. They listen attentively to the readings. When asked what was the primary reason they go to Mass on the weekend, 32% said it was out of a sense of obligation. But the highest choice (37%) said they came primarily to hear the Word of God. For most Catholics this is the only contact they have with sacred scripture. Only 34% of Catholic parishioners read the bible any more than on rare occasions. Two-thirds of the registered members in a parish, in other words, experience the Word of God only at Mass. All the more reason to have well-trained lectors who can speak the Word clearly and with authority.

As for the homily, attitudes are mixed. Most are willing to give the speaker the benefit of the doubt. Taken as a whole, 78% of Catholic parishioners said they liked most of the homilies they hear at the weekend Masses.

The comments we receive in connection with this question are long and varied. Most ask for more than just a repetition of the theme from the scriptures. They want something that touches their lives and is related to their everyday experience. What follows is a sampling of the reactions we receive in response to the homilies.

"There are very few sermons I can relate to in daily life. One of my biggest disappointments in the Catholic Church is lack of good speakers—parish priests should all be able to have this ability. I also resent a 15-minute sermon totally related to collecting money for one thing or another."

"Sermons need to be current, positive, inspiring and less than 10 minutes! (Preferably eight minutes.)"

"This is my current answer because of the current combination of "liturgy" and "preaching." Liturgy is a shambles and sermons/homilies are poor, as well as excessively long. It is most difficult to look forward to the Mass in such circumstances."

"There is little evidence that our homilists have kept up with what's happening in the Church or the world of morality, politics, psychology, or anything aside from sports."

"More of the sermons should relate to daily life and living as a Christian in the midst of it."

"I feel Father needs to relate the gospels to more everyday living for the people of our parish. I look around when he gives the homily and people are not paying attention. They look bored! When he explains new things, the people are more likely to listen. Most just come to fulfill their Sunday obligations, I think."

Part of a search for a new way of being church centers around the few moments people hear and respond to God's Word during Mass. What can be done so that it makes a difference in their lives? One parish, in response to a low-positive reaction to homilies, inaugurated a "homily helpers" project. Anyone who wished could join the priests and deacons for an hour each week discussing next weekends' scriptures. They provided insights to the homilist about the scripture's significance for everyday living. The story at the beginning of the last chapter provided another alternative. Once a month, at one or other of the Masses, people are primed to reflect with one another about the readings as these relate to their daily lives. At the end of the Masses on the previous Sunday, everyone is given a sheet with the scripture readings and a couple of questions to help focus their attention and reflection over the week. Parishioners are given a choice to attend Mass at another time if they don't want to be part of this shared reflection experience.

Such a simple gesture as reading the Gospel as the prodigal daughter rather than the prodigal son gets people's attention and peaks interest.

Those parishes that have fostered small faith communities discover people coming to Mass who are well-versed in the weekend scriptures. They have reflected on it during the past week in their small groups. This puts demands on the homilist to go beyond the clichés and platitudes. It demands getting at the meat of the Word and its implications in people's lives. What a parish does with this weekly scripture points the way to bringing the parish as a whole to life. Perhaps a shift in the way the reflection of scripture is handled at Mass is the start of a new paradigm for parishes.

Three out of four Catholic parishioners (76%), both old and young, favor the greeting of peace at Mass. Favoring a practice such as this and making it a meaningful experience are two different things, however. Most parishes have settled into a routine so that when the moment comes, everyone shakes hands with those close by and the Mass continues. That's a start but is it enough? What imaginative alternatives are possible?

Introducing one another at the start of the Mass is becoming more common. We have also heard people complain that this is just doing the greeting of peace twice. Other parishes have put the greeting of peace at another place in the Mass so as to heighten its impact. It could be done, for instance, after the petitions as a way of calling people into the liturgy of the Eucharist. One parish had the custom at the Prayer of the Faithful to read a few petitions as common to all and then invite people to turn to the one next to them and ask the person to pray for something special over the next week. Once this contact has been made with someone nearby, when the greeting comes, the wishing of peace has more significance.

As for communion, Catholics still have some difficulty with a few aspects of the service. Although almost all are favorable toward communion in the hand, about two-thirds favor lay ministers of communion, up 10% in recent years. Slightly less (60%) favor communion under both species, a response that has held steady in the last few years. Many people fear drinking from a common cup, so they pass it by when offered. The written comments that come back to us state that the risk of contracting a communicative disease is too great. Many ask for another way of distributing the wine, perhaps with separate disposable cups, as is the custom in many Protestant churches. Will that be part of a new way of being parish? If it is not, most parishioners will not have a chance to take communion in its fullest sense. The same is true for the use of bread rather than wafers. Communion speaks nourishment, giving the people their fill, with baskets left over, as signified in the miracle of the loaves and fishes. How is it possible to communicate this experience of nourishment with symbols that are so sterile? Words, greetings, music, bread, wine, candles—all speak of a deeper reality of God's self-giving, as well as our response to this offer of new life? What imaginative rituals will get this across at the weekend liturgies? We will offer some suggestions in Chapter Seven when dealing with creative rituals.

## Reconciliation

The majority of American Catholics still go to church on the weekend. Do they go to confession, that is, the Rite of Reconciliation? In a word, no. Less than one in five (19%) participate in the sacrament more than once a year, if at all. The reasons people give for not coming is that they don't feel sinful, they confess their sins to God directly and don't need a priest, they don't know the times it is offered or how to go about the new ritual. The sacrament, in other words, is falling into disuse as a private one-on-one experience. This is happening at the same time that there is an increase in people seeking professional therapy and personal counseling. Confessing sins is not enough. Healing, self-knowledge and personal growth is what people are seeking. Where is this happening in parishes? For some, communal penance services fulfill the need for healing and forgiveness. Fifty-nine percent of our Catholic respondents favor these services. Some parishes have inaugurated a simple gesture of sorrow, such as holding out a hand or a sign of the cross when approaching the priest for absolution. This frees people from needing to confess a list of sins and keeps the long line to a minimum when there is a large number. One parish we visited had a communal penance once a month after the last Mass on Sunday as a way of giving a larger number of people the chance to express sorrow and experience healing and growth.

People do feel the need for forgiveness. When we ask on our surveys whether parishioners are bothered about going to confession, 37% admit being concerned at the present time, either a great deal or at least somewhat. Even though the Rite of Reconciliation is a rare experience for most Catholics, over a third are still worried about it.

What could be done to ritualize forgiveness and help people feel healed from brokenness and wrongdoing? Perhaps no other area is crying out more for a new paradigm. The old way is dead. A revision in the sacrament was too little, too late. A new way of expressing sorrow for sin and experiencing forgiveness is demanded.

Some suggestions are surfacing. One focus is the weekend liturgy which contains initial rites for preparing people to celebrate worthily the sacred mysteries. So much more could be done to make this moment a deeper experience of healing and forgiveness. Another is the Rite of Initiation (RCIA), when people have a chance to share with each other their journeys of discovering God's call to faith and conversion. Those who have participated in small faith communities or those involved in 12-step programs related to overcoming addiction speak of the experience of healing and growth that takes place within a supportive community. These options touch only a small percentage of Catholic parishioners, however. What new ways of reconciliation lie open to American Catholic parishes? The answer may be right under our noses if we have the eyes of imagination to see it and the courage to give it a try.

## Parish Activities

How do Catholics react to their parishes and what activities do they like best? Seventy-five percent of parishioners are favorable toward their local parish, compared with 77% of the leadership, including staff and pastoral councils. Generally, the less active parishioners are more critical about specific aspects of parish life, be it liturgy, formation, decision-making or outreach.

As for activities that interest parishioners, only one out of five (20%) attends any parish function other than the weekend Masses once a month or more often. Despite this lack of attendance, most parishioners like most of the activities the parish offers. For instance, 87% favor recreational activities, such as sports, card games or dances. The leaders have a favorable reaction to these activities as well, with the exception of fundraisers. This may be from a theoretical bias that financial support should come from the offertory collection, good stewardship or tithing. Most of the leaders will admit, however, that the real reason they are ambiguous towards fundraisers is because these take a toll on the leaders themselves, both in planning and cleaning up afterwards.

The leadership in the parishes we work with are usually amazed that 82% of the parishioners favor adult religious education programs, such as bible study or discussion groups. "Where are the people when we offer these programs?" they ask. We explain that liking something and coming to it are not the same. Almost everyone may favor adult education, but only 4–6% come in a typical parish. Why is this? For one thing, people are too busy with other concerns related to job, home-life, children and leisure activities. Adult formation is far down their priority lists. When asked the primary reason they don't come, the responses range from too busy (38%), not interested (23%), not qualified (13%) (this is especially prominent among older parishioners). Other reasons include don't feel welcome (10%) and not asked or encouraged to attend (7%).

## Faith Formation

Adult education programs may not be the answer for dealing with formation and growth issues. Where else can Catholics learn about their faith and develop their spirituality? Consider our original story of the visitor passing the church and stopping in to attend Mass. He wandered in from the cold and got "hooked" by the experience. What paradigm of parish will "hook" people long enough for them to be opened up to the possibilities of new life and insights into their faith? Once they are "hooked," what will keep them coming back for more? That's the challenge for the next century.

At the present time, a little over half (59%) feel they have been helped by the parish, either through the homilies, discussion groups or personal counseling, in the formation of their faith and beliefs. Less than half (45%) said they had been helped in learning how to pray. It's not that they don't need help. Only 16–22% indicated they didn't need any guidance from the parish in these areas. Many don't feel they have been given guidance or assistance in these important areas of adult growth and development.

One place to look for adult development might be personal growth groups. These offer occasions for people to tell their story, feel connected, be healed from the woundedness of life's struggles. When we asked about people's attitudes to such groups as Marriage Encounter or self-help sessions, 63% said they were favorable, a number that has been steadily climbing over the past 10 years.

As for the education of children, 36% of American Catholic parishes have schools. *(Official Catholic Directory,* 1998 Edition.) In parishes we surveyed that had a school, many people could offer no opinion about the school. It was not part of their experience. More and more of the parishes we work with are associated with regional schools, ones that serve a number of parishes. Although this was done for survival in the face of rising costs and shrinking enrollment, it has drawbacks in the way it relates to a particular parish. The school's grounding is cut loose and it floats free amid the sponsoring parishes, belonging to none. The principal is not part of any one staff. The loyalties of the parents are split between parish and school. Those without children in the school often resent the parish subsidy that goes to the support of the school. Will the parochial school be a hallmark of the new parish paradigm as it was in the past, when the ethnic-oriented parish had its own subculture of school, social center and church? The answer might be right in front of us if we only had the eyes to see.

## Devotions

Seventy-two percent of the parishioners favor benediction of the Blessed Sacrament. This is another example of favoring an activity but not showing up when it is offered. We often hear the statement, "Every good parish should have benediction and novenas for those who want to come. Just don't count on my attendance." Even among older parishioners, attendance is not high. It does, however, point to a need people feel for getting in touch with the sacred or transcendent aspects of their faith. How does the parish speak to this need? Are there opportunities for people to experience quiet, uninterrupted prayer? What other symbols besides benediction, novenas and rosaries help people gain assurance that they are talking directly to God and that their prayers are being heard? Remember the nine first Fridays? Get to Mass and Communion on these days and you were assured of getting to heaven. Our theology has shifted since those days but our need for rituals that make a difference is still present. How to speak to that need and fill up the vacuum left behind by Vatican II changes? That's the paradigm question.

## Social Issues

Local church should do more than provide a haven for its own membership. It has a public mission as well, one that reaches out to the poor and needy. It has a responsibility to seek to change oppressive structures in the surrounding culture. How do parishioners react to this aspect of parish life? Answer: with apprehension.

Less than half (44%) favor parish groups or activities that deal with social justice issues, such as racism or sexism. A third (33%) favor the parish taking a stand on public issues. Fourteen percent of the parishioners in a typical Catholic parish do not think the parish should become involved in any way with social issues. Most of the others have ambiguous feelings about parish social involvement. In some areas, such as abortion, they favor parish involvement. In other areas, such as capital punishment, they resist parish involvement. Most parishioners want to keep the parish separate from public life. Keep it "religious" and not socially oriented, they urge. As one person remarked, "That just gets matters too sticky."

The problem with addressing public issues is that the parishioners themselves come with a wide variety of attitudes. Even talking about social issues gets their hackles up and stirs up emotional reactions.

Take abortion, for instance. Just over half of our Catholic parishioner respondents (55%) agreed that it was wrong for a woman to get an abortion. Thirty percent had mixed feelings or thought it depended on the circumstances of each case. Twelve percent did not feel it was wrong and 3% had no opinion. In contrast to this result, 71% of the parish leadership considered abortion to be wrong, no matter the circumstance. Only 6% did not feel it was wrong. The rest had mixed feelings on the matter.

Capital punishment is another area that shows a wide variety of opinions. Half (50%) felt the death penalty is a just sentence for a select set of crimes. Less than a third (31%) of the staffs and lay leaders agreed with this position. Twenty-eight percent of the parishioners had mixed feelings and 20% did not consider capital punishment to be a just sentence.

Welfare also prompted mixed reactions. Close to a third (31%) agreed that most people on welfare could support themselves, while 42% have mixed feelings and 21% disagree. The leadership itself was also divided in their feelings. Bring up this issue, in other words, and people will have opinions on all sides. No wonder the pastor, staff or council are hesitant about addressing social questions that people feel strongly about. It is sure to cause division in the ranks.

Such, however, is the essence of our Christian heritage. Jesus raised these issues and he received a prophet's reward: passion and death. How does a parish follow this example and still remain in one piece? Any new way of being parish cannot shirk this public mission. Addressing the plight of the poor or the demands of the larger world is part of being Church. Can this be done within the American milieu of the early 21st Century?

At the present moment most parishioners are not being challenged to reshape their attitudes in a way that reflects the social teachings of the Church and Gospels. When asked whether the parish had given them guidance, through homilies, discussions or counseling in social moral issues, only 31% felt that it had. This compared with 39% who considered the parish to be not much help one way or the other. Twenty-eight percent said they did not need any help from the parish in this area.

## Leadership

Throughout this discussion of parishioners' attitudes is the issue of leadership. The staff, lay leaders and especially the pastor, shape people's opinions. How do people react to their leaders?

The pastor is still the dominant figure. Even in the most collaborative settings, that pastor sets the tone and "gives permission" to the staff and lay leaders to act as a partnership and to share his authority. In almost every place we have worked, the parish seems to take on the personality of the pastor. If he is gregarious and fun-loving, this colors the liturgies, the homilies, the social events, the meetings and discussions. The parish catches the same spirit and becomes gregarious and outgoing. If the pastor is serious and academic, then this tone is felt throughout the life and activities of the parish. If the pastor is quiet and retiring, the energy level of the parish seems to slow down to that pace as well. This may change with future paradigms, but for now, the pastor still plays an essential role in determining the success or failure, the growth or decline of the Catholic parishes.

How do people react to their pastor? This varies both with the parish and with the personality, gifts and motivation of each pastor. As a whole, the majority (69%) like the way their parish is being run. The percentage is the same for the leadership itself. Only 50% of the people feel the priests, especially the pastor, are interested in them personally. For most respondents, the parish is too large and impersonal, the pastor too remote for people to experience his direct concern and care. This personal touch is now handled by others, whether by a staff member, leader or volunteer. Nevertheless, a pastor can create an image of being approachable and interested, even though his personal ministry reaches only a small percentage of the membership. We will speak about image in Chapter Four when dealing with the crisis of leadership.

## Church Authority

Image has much to do with how parishioners relate to the larger institutional church. Although 75% of the people and 77% of the leaders are favorable toward their parish, 58% of the people favor the institutional church as a whole. Parishioners question sending money to the diocese for special appeals because they feel the parish has needs of its own. They question the Pope's authority in regulating morality, especially in personal and sexual areas. When asked to react to the statement, "Catholics should follow the teachings of the Pope and not take it upon themselves to decide differently," 26% of the parishioners and 25% of the leaders agree. Thirty-seven percent of the people have mixed feelings and 34% disagree. The rest (3%) have no opinion. During the Pope's visits to the United States, the percentage who agreed went up 10%. As soon as he returned to Rome, it went back down to 26% once again.

As mentioned earlier, only 10% of the parishioners consider artificial birth control means for married couples to be wrong. Less than half (46%) consider premarital sex to be always wrong. Among young adults, less than a quarter feel it is wrong.

Both leaders and people are making up their own minds about these issues. Their conclusions are not in agreement with the institutional church. These are dedicated, churchgoing, God-fearing people, not marginal, inactive Catholics. Any new way of being church must take into account their discernment and informed conscience related to personal moral issues. The church and parish must enter into dialogue with these people about what God is calling us to as a People. Any appeal to an external authority that settles difficult questions from an *a priori* approach will not survive a new paradigm.

Parishioners still want and seek out guidance from the church on many of these issues. They want guidance, but not answers. They don't always get the guidance they seek. Thirty-one percent agreed that they received help, through homilies, discussions, and counseling, on personal moral issues, while 25% said they didn't need any help. This leaves almost two-fifths who said they needed help but either didn't get it or found the parish unhelpful in the guidance they received. This same pattern was apparent in the amount of guidance people received in family and marital matters—40% were helped, 27% didn't need any and 31% considered the parish ineffective or unhelpful.

Parishioners also questioned limits put on who is permitted to be ordained to the priesthood. Over half (56%) of the parishioners and 69% of the leaders agreed that priests should be allowed to get married and still function as priests. Two-fifths of the parishioners (40%) and 55% of the leadership agreed that women should be ordained to the priesthood. These figures keep climbing as more and more parishes face the challenge of their future without a resident priest. The figures from Gallup Polls are even higher because the surveys are conducted by phone and included all those who are Catholic, whether members of a parish or not. The more marginalized the Catholic, the more likely the person will favor a married clergy and the ordination of women.

Even among the mainstream, however, the percentage who desire a more inclusive priesthood is growing. This will affect, perhaps more than any other, the new way of being priest in the next century. Already smaller, mostly rural parishes, are experiencing a new breed of pastor. Ruth Wallace, in *They Call Her Pastor* (Albany, NY: State University of New York Press, 1992), documents the changes that have taken place when a woman is appointed the pastoral administrator of a parish and a priest comes from outside to preside at Mass and administer the sacraments. The parishioners take a more active part in the life of the parish, their contributions increase, their interest is heightened. The official title for the woman may be administrator, but the parishioners themselves consider her to be their pastor and that's what they call her.

The growing shortage of priests is putting pressure on bishops and diocesan personnel to keep plugging the holes with a shrinking supply of qualified priests. At the same time, the desire for quality pastoral leadership among the parishioners increases. Soon, the breaking point will be reached, if indeed it is not already upon us. The present way of being parish, the predominant paradigm, no longer holds water. What happens next? We look around for what is or might work. The old way is still operating and people are holding on despite feelings of misgiving. But there are some signs available to us that point in a new direction. This is what we wish to explore. We begin with a description of why parishes exist. In our minds it exists as a way of fostering a deeper spirituality among its members and in the world at large.

# Questions for Review and Reflection

*Welcoming Ritual*

What would happen to someone who walked into your parish weekend Mass from out of the cold? Would the person be welcomed, feel "at home," want to come back again? Have you visited a church for the first time and felt welcomed or accepted? Did you feel, instead, a stranger and alone?

*Consumerism*

Why do you go to church? Is it primarily out of obligation, convenience, to hear God's Word, experience community, talk to God, enjoy the music, hear a good homily? What excites you? What leaves you sad or depressed? Do you think you are typical of the majority of people sitting around you at Mass? Why do they come? What keeps others away, especially the young adults? Whose fault is it?

*Attitudes*

Which Catholic attitudes and opinions presented in this chapter surprised you and which ones were no surprise to you? Do you think these attitudes reflect the feelings of the majority of the parishioners at your own parish?

# Prayer Ritual

*Music*

*Gathering Song* by Marty Haugen (Chicago: G.I.A. Publications, Inc., 1982.) "Here in this place, new light is streaming ... Gather us in, the lost and forsaken."

*Process*

The leader invites everyone to go to the person he or she knows the least and give the person a greeting of peace and gather them into the room.

*Reading*

Read aloud the story of the person lowered through the roof to be healed by Jesus. (Mark 2:1–12) Quietly reflect on an experience of feeling a need for healing and not finding any help. Did help come from an unexpected source?

After a few moments, invite everyone to walk around the room and look for a symbol of healing, one that might apply to their own situation. Ask people to carry this symbol in their mind back to the group.

Encourage people to explain the symbol they brought to the group and how it spoke to them of healing.

Sum up the discussion with the following intercessions:

*Leader:* Loving God, bring forth your Spirit that we might recognize the stranger or the person in need of healing and gather them into our celebrations.

*All:* Jesus, we have gathered here to use our imagination and respond to one another.

*Leader:* We pray for conversion of heart and release from paralysis.

*All:* Jesus, we have gathered here to use our imagination and respond to one another.

*Leader:* We pray in gratitude for being healed and sending us unexpected means of new life and energy.

*All:* Jesus, we have gathered here to use our imagination and respond to one another.

*Spontaneous Petitions:*

*All:* Jesus, we have gathered here to use our imagination and respond to one another.

*Conclusion:*

*All:* God of the Gathering, we seek your creative imagination to bring life to our parishes and to one another. Make us open to new possibilities so that your kindom. 1 may know the fullness of life.

*Closing Song:* The fourth verse of the Gathering Song.

---

1. "Kindom" is an inclusive form for the Reign of God.

# CHAPTER THREE

# *Underlying Spirituality*

---

PARISHES DO NOT EXIST FOR THEMSELVES. THEY ARE VEHICLES.
The buildings, the staffs, the leaders, the liturgies, programs and ministries all exist for a purpose outside themselves. This purpose has two
dimensions. One is the spiritual growth of the membership. The other
is the needs of people in the larger community, those beyond the
parishioners.

Before we can deal with the parish in the next century, we must first
look at its purpose, both the inner and outer mission of fostering spiritual
growth.

To do this we will deal with spirituality from three perspectives, all
of which are interrelated and all linked to parish life and operation.

## *PERSONAL SPIRITUALITY*

The first dimension of spiritual growth is on the personal level, that
is, a person's unique relationship with God. Prayer is the first step in this
direction.

One of the essential tasks of a parish is to help people, both old and
young, learn how to pray to God in a way that fits them, one that is natural to each person's background, capabilities and inclinations.

When we ask about prayer in our parish surveys, we discover that
only 45% agreed that the parish had helped them, through homilies, counseling or discussions, to learn how to pray. Sixteen percent said they did-
n't need any help in this area, leaving almost 40% who said they had not
been helped by the parish. Some of these indicated that the parish had
actually been unhelpful in teaching them how to pray.

### *Prayer at Mass*

Reflect on your experience of parish life. Could you locate moments
parishioners have been introduced to various methods of prayer? Consider
scripture, for instance. For most parishioners the only time they experience the Word of God is at the weekend Masses. Twenty-nine percent in

a typical Catholic parish read the bible any more often than on rare occasions. If a parish would use the weekend Masses as a springboard, so much could be done to help parishioners foster a personal prayer life.

Consider, for example, inviting parishioners to bring a Bible to Mass. Perhaps once a month, at one Mass establish a tradition in which the homily becomes a learning experience. The presider would do a brief explanation of the context and significance of the passage, citing parallel passages and references. The people would be invited to continue reading the text during the coming week. The implication is that scripture is a living word that needs to be reflected upon both individually and as a family. This is a simple idea but one that could leave a profound impact on people's personal spirituality.

Sunday homilies could be used to explain alternative methods of prayer and meditation, encouraging parishioners to spend just a few minutes each day in quiet reflection. They could do this while driving to work, during their lunch hour, preparing a meal or in place of a television program. This presumes, of course, that the priests and staff members themselves have explored various methods of prayer and have prayed together regularly, both individually and as a group.

So many parish structures get in the way of growth in prayer. One is the Sunday Mass routine that does not allow for flexibility, both within the Mass and between Masses because of the pressure of time, shortage of parking spaces and a reluctance to shake up people with changes in worship. Preparation, explanation and formation are all necessary, but the effort to provide opportunities for spiritual growth lies at the heart of what is essential to parish life.

## *Praising God*

Developing a personal spirituality involves so much more than prayer, however. A second aspect is praise. This includes making time to stop and smell the roses, rejoicing in a sunset, treasuring a child's first steps, delighting in the return of a loved one. These are the ingredients of a deeply spiritual person who is aware of God's presence in nature, in people and within one's own being. A person who gives praise is thrilled by the outpouring of God's generosity, pressed down and overflowing. Part of the parish's role is to help people be attentive to and give praise for these blessings. The parish should be giving people the opportunity and occasion to give praise to so generous a God.

Is this happening? Priests are overworked, staffs run ragged, volunteers burn out. Parishioners see this and wonder if the purpose of parish life is to become overworked. The parish should be giving an alternative message, one that challenges the American syndrome of hyperactivity and overextension. The modeling must begin with the leadership itself. Meetings are the stuff of parish life, but must they be a burden, something to shun or regret?

Here are a few suggestions for redirecting energies. Consider the staff that took seriously the call to give praise to God through leisure and renewal. One day a month was put aside for stretching. Each "stretch day" was planned with care in order to give staff members a change of scenery, a chance to do some exercise, enjoy the outdoors, do extra reading, enjoy a meal together.

The parishioners were told of this day so that it both freed the staff from other meetings and parish commitments, and said to the people that they themselves should carve out of their busy schedules opportunities for leisure and relaxation. One result of the staff stretch day was a packet sent to all parishioners with suggestions and options for personal and family renewal days, options for praising God for gifts and blessings received, time out to enjoy life for a change.

In order to free lay leaders from a plethora of meetings, one parish settled on having only one leadership meeting per month. All commissions and committees that gave direction to parish events and ministries met on the same evening. They gathered together for a prayer service and separated into groups to do their business. They ended the evening with a brief report of what each group had decided for the month. This was followed by a social. Not only did this improve communication among the leaders, it also forced people who belonged to three or four different committees to refocus their energies and choose only one to work on at a given time. All of this helped emphasize the need to economize one's energies and freed people to devote more time to their own and their families' spiritual growth and well-being.

## Spiritual Direction

Having a sense of direction and purpose in one's life is another aspect of personal spirituality. People who are motivated to pursue personal goals in life, who have a sense of order and are led by a Gospel-centered set of priorities are deeply spiritual individuals. How could a parish help people develop personal goals that reflect their baptismal call of love and service? The weekend Masses might not be the best place to do this. They are too large and are limited to offering general exhortations and universal ideas for personal spiritual growth. Individual counseling, retreats and small groups are more effective means for assisting people in the development of Gospel directed personal goals.

We will touch upon small groups when dealing with societal spirituality, and again in Chapter Eight. Besides small groups, however, parishes that seek to develop people's spiritual growth must provide resources for personal counseling and spiritual direction. How is this possible, given the already overburdened staff and limited finances? It's a matter of priorities. The Rite of Christian Initiation for Adults (RCIA) was only a vague dream 20 years ago. Now it is a staple for many parishes, one that is given direction with paid professional staff and a large contingent of volunteers. Why not give the same attention to the regular membership that is given to neophytes? One way is to establish a tradition of regular spiritual direction and personal counseling to those parishioners who are searching for meaning and direction in their lives.

This would demand a restructuring of priorities, a reshaping of job descriptions and a change in emphasis in the parish.

The question, of course, is that once the restructuring takes place and counseling opportunities are provided, will anyone show up for spiritual direction? That's always the risk.

Suppose a parish committed itself to providing spiritual direction for all parishioners. Space is set aside for personal and family counseling and direction. A full-time professional person is added to the staff to cover this area of ministry. A minimum fee is charged for the service so that people realize its importance and help defray expenses.

If it is to succeed, the push must come from the pastor, staff, council and prominent lay leaders. The leadership, in other words, helps people see the value and importance of this service. The leaders themselves should experience spiritual direction, either within or outside the parish. Care must be used, however, so that this ministry is not seen as elitist, something for only the most active parishioners. It must be billed as a value for everyone, young and old, active and inactive alike.

Image is so important. At all the liturgies, education programs and parish activities, both through written materials and verbal encouragement, parishioners must be introduced to the option of spiritual direction and be shown how much they could benefit from this service. Every attempt is made to adjust the schedule to fit people's needs and occupations, providing opportunities for anonymity, babysitting and group counseling as well.

Slowly—and it will take at least a year for this to catch on—a tradition is established. Parishioners are given personal direction for their journey of faith. This is a simple concept but one that has far-reaching effects, both for the individual and the parish as a whole.

## Facing Limits

Personal spirituality also includes an awareness of one's compulsions, addictions and limitations. We all need help, forgiveness and assistance in dealing with these. We are willing to admit that we are not self-sufficient, not a world unto ourselves. We are not gods, in other words.

God is the source of our life and living, not ourselves. Our constant point of reference is outside ourselves, not within. Spiritual persons are acutely aware that they cannot survive by themselves, that is, "go it alone."

Our American culture preaches the opposite. We are self-sufficient. We can make it on our own. It's the old "pull yourself up by your own bootstraps" myth. Another countercultural movement is quietly sweeping the nation, however. It is the 12-step program used by recovering alcoholics and addicts.

The first two steps in the process are: (1) admitting the person is powerless over the mind-altering substance, that one's life has become unmanageable and (2) coming to believe that a Power greater than oneself could restore the person to sanity.

These two steps reveal an aspect of personal spirituality that is so difficult for those of us who live in an addictive culture to admit: we cannot save ourselves. Becoming a free, unrestricted, spiritual person is all God's doing. We must let go of the controls and be willing to be saved, instead of trying to do it all by ourselves.

The implications for parishes are far-reaching. It requires an admission by the leadership—pastor, staff, council, ministers—that we are all caught up in addictive behavior to varying degrees. We are, all of us, powerless to free ourselves from our addictions. It takes a Power far greater than ourselves. This does not mean, however, that the situation is hopeless. We can be freed from our compulsions through grace, conversion, hard work and the help of others who provide support and companionship on the journey.

The 12-step program initiated by Alcoholics Anonymous is one of many paths to recovery. We have already mentioned spiritual direction as another means. Other suggestions will be offered throughout the pages of this book.

At the same time, most Catholic parishes have not utilized the benefits of the 12-step program within their programs and ministries. Churches often provide space for 12-step groups to meet, but these have little connection with the life or operation of the parish itself. This is a loss of an opportunity for fostering personal spirituality among the parishioners as a whole.

Imagine what growth might happen if, over the course of a year, the weekend Masses might explain the 12-step process to parishioners, one step each month. 12-step groups already meeting in the parish would feel more a part of the parish, that their efforts at recovery were respected and valued. Care must be taken that people's anonymity be respected. On the other hand, admitting the pervasiveness of addiction in our lives and providing a path to recovery is a great service a parish could provide its membership.

## Personal Fitness

Fitness is another characteristic of personal spirituality. We don't often think of our personal well-being as linked to spirituality, but it is. This includes not only physical fitness, but emotional, intellectual and spiritual fitness as well. Such an emphasis on fitness flies in the face of addictive behavior. Caring for and feeling good about one's body is part of being a spiritual person, whether it be diet, exercise, rest or leisure. Our body belongs to God, but it is up to us to keep it healthy.

An emphasis on health and exercise can be overdone. A moderate care of one's personal well-being, however, demands a disciplined spirituality. Our American culture tries so hard to tear our bodies down, either through fast foods, excessive exercise, self-indulgent pleasure, drugs, stress or anxiety.

Fitness extends to mental and emotional well-being as well. A spiritual person finds time not only for rest and relaxation but for intellectual updating, retreats and continued human development. A spiritual person is a healthy person, one who is able to resist the constraints of our fast-paced society and remain whole in both mind and body.

Does belonging to a parish help foster one's physical, emotional and intellectual fitness? The ethnic parishes of the early and middle 20th-century did a much better job than present day churches. They provided gyms, social centers, even swimming pools for their people. The parish was an oasis for people trying to cope with an alien culture. It became an outlet that served the physical, emotional and relational needs of its "own people."

This is no longer the function of parish life. People look elsewhere to satisfy their personal needs. Might not the parish, however, still act as an example of health and well-being to segments of its population? For example, one pastoral associate held exercise classes twice a week before the "meals-on-wheels" program in the church hall. Staff members showed up and joined them at regular intervals. The seniors loved it and tried to outdo the "youngsters" on staff.

The story spread throughout the parish. Soon young mothers started coming. Some of the seniors babysat the youngsters, and in no time a community spirit was created around the exercising. Talk of diets and health foods followed. This changed the menus of the lunches. People's care of their bodies, in other words, led to a growth of spirit as well.

Many parishes offer a lending library as a means of updating parishioners. One parish went a step further and converted an unused confessional in the back of the church for this purpose. Because it was visible to churchgoers and easily accessible, more and more people began to use the service. Eventually video and audio cassettes were added. Parishioners were encouraged to use them for family discussions or while traveling to work in their cars.

Those parishes that wish to foster personal fitness might attend to the type of food and drink they offer at parish meetings and gatherings. Donuts, coffee and fried chicken are the staples. These could be replaced, or at least augmented, by fruit, juice, vegetables and low-fat, non-fried dishes.

Another example of personal spirituality is lifestyle. Parishioners pay attention to how their priests and staff members live: homes, furnishings, car, cuisine, clothes. All speak volumes about values and spirituality. The balance between an adequate means of support and a simplicity of lifestyle is not easily achieved. People notice flamboyant displays of wealth and privilege. They also notice simple, healthy appearances. These communicate. If a staff wants to be an example of a spiritually alive community that has an inner "soul," lifestyle is one ingredient that can't be overlooked. It is not an easy one, however. Even raising the topic demands much trust and understanding among staff members themselves. It is a source, however, of much grace and spiritual insight if members are willing to take the risk of discussing their own image among parishioners.

## *The Dark Side*

Going deeper into the personal aspect of spirituality touches upon what St. John of the Cross called the "Dark Night of the Soul." This experience is not reserved for mystics. It touches everyone's life one way or another.

We all experience periods in our lives when God is distant, invisible, absent. These moments may come as a result of personal tragedy, the death of a loved one or the loss of a job. They are associated with a general feeling of rootlessness and ennui. No one is exempt. Even the most faithful parishioners and most active members go through periods of searching for a God who is no longer present. One staff person described the feeling through a dream she had. "I was on a freeway, cars were whizzing past. I could not find my way. I was frustrated, started to cry, no one was there to help."

How does a parish help people through these anxious, trying moments? The first step is to acknowledge that parishes themselves go through dark nights when the future is uncertain and God seems far away. The loss of a beloved pastor through death, transfer or leave of absence can plunge a parish into darkness. A financial crisis, the closing of a school, tensions among staff members or conflicts between parishioners can do the same.

These moments force us to our knees and cause us to reevaluate priorities and refocus our energies. These can be blessed moments if responded to with faith and courage. At the time, however, all that is evident is darkness and suffering. The temptation is to give up and throw in the towel, to stop believing in a caring, loving God.

Acknowledging and accepting these dark nights of passage demand a deep level of spiritual growth. Helping people through them is part of what is essential to parish life.

Perhaps the greatest service a parish can provide is to be a support and crutch to lean on in times of darkness and distress. When a person finds it difficult to believe in God's presence, the parish community is willing to take on the role of believer until the darkness turns into light. When tragedy and crisis consume one's energies, the parish is a pillar of strength and sign of peace. Just being present to people, listening to their stories and offering words of encouragement and support is more important than programs or activities. Helping people hold on and endure the darkness is a great service in itself. Stephen's Ministry and The Befriender Programs are just two of many examples parishes offer as a way of holding out a helping hand to people who are experiencing the dark night of the soul.

## RELATIONAL/COMMUNAL SPIRITUALITY

The personal side of spirituality is one of three aspects. The relational side is also important. A person who has developed a deep relational spirituality is willing to be challenged by others and experience growth from others. We see this person as open to diversity, to new ways of relating, to fresh insights and ways of interacting. There is a willingness to grow and expand one's horizons because of diverse relationships with people unlike oneself. What a rich opportunity is provided by multicultural parishes, for instance, for this broadening of experience and interaction. How often these riches are squandered because every group remains in its own world.

We recently worked with a parish that was 60% Hispanic. The Anglos were in all the leadership positions. Half of the Masses on the weekend were in Spanish, but the Hispanics had no influence over the policy formation or decision-making of the parish. What was more surprising was that no one, not even the pastor, was aware of this discrepancy. He spoke Spanish and the entire staff was attentive to the needs of the Hispanics. The associate pastor, however, was the only Hispanic on staff. He alone handled the affairs of the Hispanic community. There were, in effect, two parishes, one Hispanic and one Anglo. The latter, although smaller in number, controlled the parish as a whole. This was happening on many levels: decision-making, finances, communications and programming.

We worked with them for two years, and during that time the situation began to change. The Hispanics and Anglos started to work together as a single parish, not two separate units. There are now a number of Hispanics on the staff, council and ministerial commissions. A parish office for Hispanic affairs has been established. Parish meetings are bilingual. All publicity and modes of communication are in two languages. How did this change come about? Primarily through a new awareness of structures that hinder and structures that help parish unity.

The process followed these steps. First, we took a survey of attitudes from a random sample of both Anglos and Hispanics in order to discover where the two groups differed and where they were similar. Many of the reactions from Hispanics revealed deep-seated feelings of alienation, inadequacy and frustration. The Anglos, on the other hand, showed more satisfaction with the parish but complained about the Hispanics not contributing to the parish or "doing their part."

Fortified with these findings, we gathered together the leaders from both groups and did a structure diagram of the parish. This diagram described not what was on paper, but what was actually happening. How did things get done? Who was linked to what groups? What were the lines of communication?

We discovered that most of the organizations and ministries of the parish were either "free-floating," that is, they were accountable to no one, or they fell on the shoulders of the staff. This was especially true of the associate pastor who dealt with the Hispanics.

The outcome of this revelation was a restructuring of the parish around ministries and not around ethnic origins. We established a worship commission that included both Hispanics and Anglos. When they held their meetings, they looked at the overall worship needs of the parish, English and Spanish together. Similar commissions were established for education, social service, administration and community-building. This last commission planned joint activities that brought together both the Hispanics and Anglos, while at the same time providing outlets for each group to celebrate on its own. The council itself was composed of both cultures, and decisions were made that respected the needs of each one.

The overall spirit of the parish has changed. It is now one parish. The people feel they belong to the parish, no matter what their language or background. It came as a result of a new awareness and a willingness to act on that awareness. We no longer hear, "Why don't they . . ." We hear instead, "Why don't *we* . . ." The parish has grown spiritually as a result of its diversity.

## Symbols

Ritual also plays a role in relational spirituality. A spiritual person knows how to celebrate, through symbols, poetry, music, dance and ritual, the important moments in one's life. We witnessed the ritual leave-taking of a niece about to be married. The family gathered together on the morning of the wedding. The parents and siblings talked about family events and how much she would be missed. But more, they wished her strength and support in her new life. The simple ceremony included a scripture reading, picture-taking and hugging. It ritualized an important moment for the family.

This ritual was not unique. The family has had a rich tradition of celebrating birthdays, holidays, anniversaries, weddings, leave-takings, graduations and special events. The parents, as spiritual people, have instilled in their children an awareness and sensitivity to ritual and celebration. When this family joins the larger congregation for Eucharist and sacraments, they know how to celebrate, how to symbolize through word, song and action deeper realities that can't be expressed directly.

A family of eight living on a farm in Minnesota has a ritual of dehusking corn each summer for the parish festival. Together they bless the corn and take it to the parish to feed the multitudes. The corn becomes a symbol of nourishment, freshly grown and quickly eaten. It represents sharing the fruits of the harvest, gathering together as a family to appreciate God's goodness and sharing one's blessings with others.

The question, of course, is how well does a parish help people ritualize important moments in their lives? Ritual is part and parcel of the weekend Masses, but does it have any effect on people's everyday lives or on their personal relationships?

One place to start is to bring into the Masses unique rituals that celebrate the lifecycle and rhythm of the parish itself. The parish Mission

Statement, for instance, could be used in place of the creed. This is what the leaders and people believe about themselves as a parish. Asking at the end of Mass who has a birthday or anniversary is another way of linking personal lives to parish rituals. Providing suggestions for family rituals is another help, along with a list of important personal and family moments that need celebrating. These include moves, leave-takings, promotions, mortgage-burnings, tree plantings, patron saints, birthdays, anniversaries, graduations, weddings, even anniversaries of deaths.

One parish ritualized the first Wednesday of every month as "at home" night. No meetings or activities were held in the parish and everyone was encouraged to stay at home and "fast from TV." Each month this announcement was read at all the Masses: "Spend this coming Wednesday night at home with your family or loved ones, just yourselves, with no TV, for a change. The Family Corner in the bulletin provides some ideas for family activities. No events or meetings are scheduled in the parish this coming Wednesday for that reason. If you have any insights on how best to spend the evening, let us know and we'll share these with others. If you live alone and are looking for some companionship, give the parish a ring. We have many options for you. This coming Wednesday, enjoy one another!"

## Partnership

Relational spirituality is also generative. Not only is a spiritual person creative in developing one's own talents and gifts, he or she is also creative in linking up with others in bringing to birth something that no one person could have produced alone. This is the aspect of spirituality that is collaborative. The person is willing to enter into partnership with others to fill up what is lacking in oneself and to complement the gifts, talents, motivation, desires and spiritualities of others.

This bonding together creates joint ministries. These manifest to others that God has called people together to interact with one another in mutual growth and companionship as they seek to minister to one another and to others. The bonding together for ministry creates offsprings that reveal the gifts and desires of each coworker. These unique qualities could never have been established if the persons worked independently of one another. It's like singing in two-part harmony. It just doesn't sound the same when done by oneself. It takes two hands to clap.

Americans have great difficulty developing a spirituality that is generative. We keep looking in the wrong places. Much depends on the local parish to provide the soil for growth in this area. The first place to begin is with leadership.

Some models of parish leadership, while efficient and well-meaning, hinder rather than help generative spirituality. An authoritarian style of leading, one in which all important decisions are made by the pastor, staff or select group of the "chosen" stymies generativity. For this reason it contradicts the essential purpose of parish life, the spiritual growth of its members.

Americans reject the authoritarian model as undemocratic, but they also seek after its pragmatic simplicity. It leaves them "off the hook." The temptation is to proclaim that "our parish is organized around a consensus model of leadership and decision-making," while in reality there are a few people who run the parish and call all the plays. This is not the way Jesus organized his Church. He prepared his followers and then got out of the way so they could take the lead. He sent them out two-by-two to proclaim the Good News and work miracles.

The miracle of our present age is generativity. Many pastors, staff and lay leaders are working together collaboratively rather than just doing their own thing. The medium is so much more important than the message, the medium of working together to create that which they could never do on their own.

So often we hear that parish leaders have trouble finding people to share in their ministry. It is always the same few people doing all the work. Seen from the pew, however, parishioners experience these capable people taking care of everything. These ministers do it so well that they themselves would never dream of volunteering. They could never do as good a job.

The challenge is to let go of the controls and to create vacuums. Don't rush in to save it. When a project is failing for lack of interest or motivation, the awareness of a vacuum is what convinces the less active people in the pew they really are needed and have something to offer. It not only uncovers new volunteers, it helps foster their own generative spirituality.

Other parishes go the opposite direction and foster a do-it-yourself structure. "We're all in this together, no one group is better than another." It sounds good on the surface, but underneath it can be a mess. There is no unifying structure or accountability, no common direction. Each ministry, group or organization builds its own kingdom. In an effort to be collaborative, the pastor and staff become *laissez-faire*. Whoever can shout the loudest or get the most attention carries the day. This is not the way to foster a relational spirituality that is generative. It doesn't take long before everyone is at each other's throats.

Parishioners need structure and organization, they need direction and facilitating leadership, they need bearers of the dream that lead the way.

What we have described are two extremes. On one side is a subtle, controlling, hands-on, dominating structure. On the other end is an abdicating, nondirective, hands-off style. Neither will foster a spirituality that helps people work well with others in creating something new, creative and exciting.

What's needed, of course, is a structure that is between these two extremes. This is a structure that challenges, gives direction, encourages the development of unique talents, fosters mutuality and is open to change and adaptation. Restructuring a parish around ministries is one way to find a balance between a controlling and a laid-back style. We will discuss this at great length in Chapter Six when dealing with freeing structures.

## Love and Care

One important aspect of relational spirituality is the balance between *loving* and *being loved*. Spiritual loving is the type that welcomes intimacy and deep sharing, with no trace of dominance or dependency, control or manipulation. The person presents the gift of self to another, whole and unencumbered, in vulnerability and strength. This is the root meaning of community. It comes from two Latin words, *cum* (with) and *munus* (gift or favor). We come together in community to be gifts to one another.

A more profound gift, however, is the willingness to be loved in return, to accept another's love, to cherish another person's gift of self. This demands a great and profound spirituality, not only to love another but to let that person love you. The spiritual person sees oneself as lovable, not in a manipulative way to achieve one's own desires, but as a worthy receptacle for another's love, attention, support, affection, concern and involvement.

Another aspect of relational spirituality is *caring*. This goes beyond loving and reveals the spiritual person as caught up in the concerns and needs of others. If someone is in pain, needs a friend, has a joy to share, wants an ear to listen, the spiritual person cannot help but respond. It takes loving to the next step of ministering. This is not a job or role or task to be performed but a way of life, a basic orientation, an automatic way of responding.

When people come into the presence of a person who manifests this level of caring and ministering, they feel they are accepted for who they are, not smothered, not taken for granted, not treated as a problem or a case study. They are, instead, befriended and made to feel worthwhile and valued as unique and special. This is spirituality that is at once freeing and also practical. The caring is not merely words of comfort and acceptance; it moves into action that alleviates the pain and seeks solutions to the problem.

## Communal

Fostering community is also a mark of relational spirituality. Some people have the gift of gathering people together into groups and creating a conducive environment for sharing. Others are not gifted in initiating community but help foster it once it has been formed. They do this through honest, open sharing. They are willing to risk revealing their own feelings, insights and ideas in the group, which in turn encourages others to share their experiences. It is this risk of personal sharing that brings groups to life. It reveals a spirituality that is willing to enter into group sharing. In this way it creates and maintains faith communities.

The hallmarks of community sharing are openness, risk-taking, honesty and loyalty. First, the spiritual person is willing to take part in the community and not sit back as merely a listener or observer. Secondly, the person is willing to be vulnerable to the group by sharing feelings of pain, joy, confusion and confrontation. This is a risk. Others may not rise to the same level of sharing and the openness falls on deaf ears. Third, the spiritual person is willing to be honest in giving feedback, in responding to other's comments, in confronting dysfunctional behavior, in bringing up minority positions or unwanted subjects. Finally, the person is loyal to the group by keeping confidences, protecting reputations, respecting individuals while at the same time confronting issues or abuses of control, power and authority.

What can a parish do to help people recognize and develop a relational spirituality that is loving, caring and builds community? The first step is to recognize the problem that most Americans are caught in a relational wasteland. Platitudes from the pulpit or a handshake of peace will never do the job. A concerted effort must be used to break into the apathy and touch a person's heart, one's relational center.

Consider the typical parish family, husband and wife, one teenage daughter, seventh-grade son and a preschooler. They come to church almost every week but that's the extent of their involvement. They have the potential for deep relational spirituality, but it lies dormant from a lack of invitation and challenge. What will stir their hearts?

The first step is what happens at the door of the church. One aspect of relational spirituality is building community. The ministry of welcoming, inviting people in and making people feel at home is what should meet this family as they walk in. Greeters are part of the solution; so is a warm environment and welcoming music. Even the celebrant and table ministers might extend a welcoming hand. Before the family sits down they feel loved, valued, important participants in worship, able to relax in the support of the community. This ritual of welcoming is an essential starting point for breaking through the cultural constraints of individualism in which everyone is supposed to be self-sufficient and private.

The second step comes not from the altar but from the pews, from people ministering to each other. It takes time to build up this tradition and custom of friendliness, but once created it is infectious. As soon as the family gets to their place, those around acknowledge their presence by a nod or smile or making room for them. Different Masses will have different mystiques, some quieter than others, but the atmosphere is the same. "We're happy to see you, glad to join in worship with you, we're interested in your hopes and joys, worries and celebrations."

How is this ministry from the pews fostered? People need to be invited, encouraged and challenged to minister to each other. Left to themselves they come to Mass to pray by themselves, follow the celebrant's actions or the musician's directions, go to communion and leave. But with some gentle persuasion and much good example, another environment of interaction can emerge.

The best place to start is with the period immediately following the Mass. A convenient gathering place with refreshments is essential to good socializing and community-building. Encouraging people to stay and talk to each other, either in church or close by, helps foster the ministry of interaction. People get to know each other and look forward to seeing one another again next week. Something special should be provided for various age groups. Using our sample family of five, the teenage daughter will be drawn in by people her own age, while the seventh grader may like the chocolate donuts and the preschooler the chance to run around the room a few times. The parents are drawn to the socializing after Mass not only by the announcement at the end of Mass, but by the personal invitation of those around them and the greeters at the door as they leave.

A second help is the example provided by the celebrant and worship ministers. Not only do the greeters invite people in, but throughout the liturgy the lectors, musicians, leaders of song, eucharistic ministers and especially the celebrant manifest by their actions and expressions that they are happy in their ministry. This provides a sense of joy and warmth to the assembled community. It is a manifestation of the generative character of relational spirituality that together they create something new, something with life and vitality, something not one of them could create on his or her own.

Small gestures, such as a welcome to newcomers at the start of liturgy, joining hands at the Lord's Prayer, even across the aisle, "wasting time" at the greeting of peace, acknowledging birthdays and anniversaries at the end, all speak volumes about how important and unique each person is to the life of the community and how glad people are with each one's presence.

Another help for fostering community at worship is to provide special emphases and occasions for various age groups. Perhaps our family has come to the monthly children's Mass without realizing it. At the Gospel, all the children under seven are invited up to the front of the church. The preschooler in our family, with some encouragement from the parents, goes up to hear the Gospel in story form and a special homily geared to the children. The parents and older children are drawn into the story as well. After the homily, the seventh grader sees schoolmates reading the petitions and leading songs. This gets his attention. The teenager hears about a hayride and dance coming up next week as part of the youth program. She looks in the bulletin for more information. The parents are happy to see their children getting interested in the Mass and activities.

The leader of worship is a critical person in a loving, caring community. The celebrant must be willing to risk loving and being loved, must speak out of a lived experience to the hearts of the people hungry for authentic and freeing relationships.

What a refreshing surprise to our sample family when they hear preached to them the good news of marital love that is freeing and not controlling or subservient. They hear about growing up in addictive homes and what affect it has on adult behavior. They're challenged to call into question the romantic illusions of loving found in the media and to endure the hard times through marital commitment. They hear others besides the priest talk of parenting and marriage, of friendship and how these relate to the words of Jesus. The language is down to earth and realistic, the ideas are challenging and life-giving. Imagine what an impact this would have on the family for the coming week. These are a few of the ways the weekend worship service could foster relational spirituality.

## SOCIETAL SPIRITUALITY

There is a third dimension to spirituality that is needed for a complete and integrated picture. If we only stressed the personal and relational aspects, we would be caught in a sectarian religion. The Church would be self-contained and would never reach out beyond its boundaries into the larger culture. It might provide a good model of holiness and community but never deal with the societal issues of poverty, injustice and social change.

Parishes, if they are to be followers of Christ, must challenge their members to develop the societal dimension of their spirituality. This includes an awareness that God is involved in ongoing creation. God did not wind up the universe and send it off on its own. God is part and parcel of all that happens and calls us to be partners in this unfolding creation. We are co-workers *with* God in this task. (See I Cor. 3)

## Protecting Rights

Part of our task as God's co-workers is to protect the rights of others. It is difficult to overcome our isolationism and be touched by the sufferings and injustices caused by selfish and oppressive structures. A person who has developed the societal side of spirituality first of all *sees* the injustices-so unlike the blindness most of us experience-and then *does* something to call attention to this social sin.

There is a delicate balance, one that demands a high level of sanctity, between working through structures and calling these same structures into question. Both are necessary. At times we must serve the structure, fit into the organization so that people can be helped. We all need a sense of order, continuity and predictability to keep society running smoothly.

Some aspects of the structures we live in do just the opposite, however. They oppress, dominate, establish favorites, cater to special interests. The person who exercises societal spirituality knows when to work through structures and create a more just system. The person also knows when to leave a structure and call it into question. He or she refuses to be usurped or co-opted by that structure.

The Los Angeles riots following the acquittal of Rodney King in 1992 provide one example of the dilemma people faced in either accepting the outcome of the trial and the miscarriage of justice it seemed to represent or stepping outside of the structure and challenging the system. That is not to say that the riots were justified. They did represent, in very graphic terms, the hard choices faced by those who seek to develop a societal aspect of spirituality.

## Ecology

Another example is care for our fragile world environment. A concerted effort is needed to bring nature back to health. It is dying and we are killing it. What is needed are coalitions of people who appreciate the urgency of this crisis, people who have developed a societal spirituality. The environment consumes their prayer life, their praise of God, their relationships and sense of community. All aspects of spirituality, in other words, go hand in hand. They reinforce and augment each other.

No one person alone can ever hope to have an impact on our society. We need each other. Together we can challenge people to let go of their vested interests and start caring for our troubled environment. This is one reason for a parish's existence, to provide occasions for people to come together and fill up what is lacking in their own spirituality, especially from the societal dimension.

## Starting Small

As we mentioned in the previous chapter, surveys of Catholic opinions show a great reluctance by Catholics to get involved in social issues. The people see this as "getting involved in politics." They stress the need to maintain a clean separation between Church and State. This is not an attitude that will foster societal spirituality, however. Some attempts at raising the people's social awareness have succeeded. One way is to concentrate on care for the poor and needy rather than confronting public policy or social issues directly. Asking for volunteers to staff a food pantry, spending a night at an overnight shelter, bringing baskets to the poor or helping victims of natural catastrophes have received a warm response when presented in a way that fits people's schedules and allows for flexibility. Linking up with a parish south of the border has also been well received, especially if the twinning parish becomes visible through pictures, artifacts or visits from those serving in the sister parish. Some parishes have sent volunteer workers to the sister parish for a few months as a way of concretizing their commitment.

These are all good and challenge, in small ways, people's individualism. They are, however, only stopgap measures. Perhaps the avenue that provides the most promise is the recent emphasis on small Christian faith communities.

On the surface, these look more relational than societal in makeup. Their emphasis is on building a sense of community among the 6–15 members of the faith community. If this is their only focus, however, they are not really faith communities so much as support groups. People come together solely to share stories that relate to their faith experience. This satisfies one dimension of parish life, that of serving the needs of its own parishioners. The other dimension is its public mission. This includes efforts to become aware of concerns in the wider community and to respond to these needs.

Some small faith communities have sprung up on their own. A group of people come together to share their experience, reflect on scripture and act out their faith in areas of social change and pastoral care.

In the last few years, Catholic parishes have been showing more interest in this movement and have restructured their priorities so as to foster the formation of small faith communities as part of the parish mission. In Chapter Eight we will describe in greater detail the process for developing small faith communities.

## Taking Stands

Some parishes are taking the risk of getting involved in social action. It usually begins with the pastor or a staff member who is concerned about areas of injustice or the needs of the poor and oppressed. This awareness is picked up by the lay leaders and a few concerned parishioners. One example is state lotteries. These exploit poor people because they raise unrealistic expectations. In one parish a committee did some research on what were the odds of winning the lottery and how people were using up their savings with little or no hope for return. Feeding this information back to the congregation helped raise the people's consciousness. It had timely impact because the city was contemplating the introduction of casino gambling as a way to raise revenues and create jobs.

Other topics related to societal spirituality include capital punishment, homelessness, greed in the marketplace, affordable day care for working mothers, more equitable funding for public schools. The need is great, the response is slow and faltering. Only when people have a chance to raise their awareness and plan action responses will these needs be addressed. This is best done in a supportive environment where people can speak their minds, reflect on scripture, pray together, share their fears and express their longings in a safe and supportive context. If it is to reach a majority of the parishioners, however, it has to fit easily into already-overworked schedules. The weekend liturgies can become an occasion for summing up one's experience of God over the past week and a challenge to live out Gospel values in the next. We'll discuss options on how this might happen when dealing with worship in Chapter Seven.

## Conclusion

We have touched upon the three aspects of spirituality—personal, relational and societal. We have also offered a few suggestions as to how a parish might restructure its liturgies, activities and priorities to foster spiritual growth among the parishioners in these three areas.

We live in exciting and yet risky times. On one side is limitation, shortage, scarcity, and want. On the other is possibility, opportunity, abundance, grace and newness. The local church stands in the middle between these two polarities, poised on the edge. It could fall—as many do—into the crevice of routine, rote response, business as usual, do what is expected, fulfill the minimum. Or it could—as many others are trying to do—meet the challenge and soar to new heights of spirituality, one that touches individual hearts, draws people together into community, effects change within and outside its boundaries.

We live in that dialectic. Which side will it be? The first place to look for an answer is to the leadership.

## Questions for Review and Reflection

*Personal Spirituality*

How has your parish helped you to pray? Have you learned different ways to pray, different ways to praise God? What kind of plans would you need to make as a parish so that spiritual direction and individual counseling might be available to your parishioners? How does fitness relate to your spiritual growth? Does it ever get addressed in the parish? Have you felt the support of your church in moments of darkness and distress?

*Relational Spirituality*

Name a few of your family rituals while growing up. How many of these do you still do? How does the parish relate to these family rituals? In what areas of the parish is partnership most apparent? Where is it lacking? How do people in the pew minister to one another? Is it better at one Mass than another?

*Societal Spirituality*

Catholics are reluctant to get involved in social issues, but they will respond to people in need. How does your parish encourage helping the needy? Are there ways parishioners are encouraged to challenge the causes of poverty and inequality as well? Are they given any guidance from the parish in this area?

## Prayer Ritual

*Process*

Begin in small groups of 3–6 people. Read aloud the story of Jesus calming the storm. (Mark 6:45–52) Ask each person to reflect quietly on how this story reveals some of the ways Jesus was a spiritual person, including the three aspects of personal, relational or societal spirituality. Looking just at the personal side, invite people to write down on an index card what more they need in order to foster their own personal spirituality.

As a way of experiencing relational spirituality, ask people to choose a group they are part of, preferably in the parish, and draw a symbol of that group's interaction. Are there any aspects of the scripture story that relate to this group's interaction? Invite people to share in the small group their symbol and what the symbol represents.

Ask people to pair up with one other person and spend some time talking about their own personal and relational spirituality. Ask people to spend 10 minutes in these pairs and then gather together as one large group to reflect on societal spirituality.

As a single group, brainstorm all the ways the parish is now helping people grow in societal spirituality. List these on newsprint or on a board. Identify those areas of the parish that best reflect this aspect of spirituality and those that do it the least. What more can be done? List ideas on newsprint or on a board.

Ask each person to formulate a petition related to one aspect of spirituality as this relates to the parish, and invite people to voice these petitions out loud, each person in turn.

*Closing Prayer:*

Dear God, You are the source of all life. Grant us the serenity to accept the things that we cannot change, the courage to change the things we can, and the wisdom to know the difference.

# CHAPTER FOUR

# *A Crisis in Leadership*

WE MENTIONED EARLIER THAT THE PARISH REFLECTS
the personality of the pastor. This is most apparent when there is a change
in leadership. Those who fit in with the style and direction of the outgoing pastor wait to see if they can relate to the new one. If not, they will
pull back and wait him out or take up membership in another parish.
While this is going on, other parishioners will come forward. These are
people who like the new pastor's emphases and choices. They become
more active and involved in the parish and its leadership.

As a whole, Americans tend to favor a participative, facilitating style
of leadership, one that listens to their thoughts and suggestions and allows
them a voice in important decisions and choices in the parish. They get
upset with an autocratic style of pastoring, one that is controlling and unilateral in its approach.

Pastors themselves react the same way towards the bishop and diocesan policies if they have not been consulted, if their suggestions are not
solicited or taken seriously. If pastors are not treated with respect by their
superiors and peers, they are not likely to give the same respect to their
people.

The crisis in leadership, then, is a systemic one.

It flows not so much from one individual pastor but from the entire
way the system operates. Consider the way in which new pastors are
assigned. A parish is in need of a pastor. This is listed on a sheet that is
passed around to priests who might be interested. Individual priests submit their names to the personnel board. The board makes a judgment as
to which of those who said they were interested would be the best person
for that parish. Members of the personnel board visit the parish to get a
firsthand impression of the place and to listen to parish leaders and
parishioners about issues important to consider in selecting a new pastor.
The final recommendations are sent to the bishop for approval. The priest
who is chosen is notified and the announcement is made to the parish and
to the diocese as a whole, usually through the diocesan newspaper. At no

time is there a chance for the priests who show an interest in the parish to sit down with the parishioners or the leadership to talk about what each has in mind. It is up to the personnel board and the bishop to make a good match between priest and people. That is the way the system works.

The problem is that there are no longer enough priests to fill all the vacancies. Parishes are lucky to get an ordained pastor at all, no matter his qualifications, inclinations or motivation. Eventually, almost everyone who is ordained will become a pastor, many of them within a few years of ordination and with limited pastoral experience. We facilitated a group of 30 priests who had been ordained five years or less. Many of them were already pastors and in charge of a parish, even though they themselves admitted that they were hardly dry behind the ears.

## Exploring Alternatives

We did have another experience in the selection process for pastor that did not fit this system. It took place in a parish staffed by a religious order. The pastor who served the parish found it a trying experience. He knew that no matter how hard he tried, he did not fit the needs of the people nor did they make him feel comfortable serving them. In one rather sudden gesture, he asked for a transfer and in the space of a weekend was gone. The religious order superiors were grieved by this experience and wanted to find a better match of pastor to people. They asked a few priests if they would be willing to become pastor. One person agreed to give it a try. Before being appointed, the Order asked the priest to spend a weekend in the parish. He attended a meeting of the leaders and as many of the parishioners who were able to attend. At this meeting the prospective pastor related his previous experience and spelled out his gifts and limitations. He tried to describe his dream for the parish. The people did the same. What followed was a month of discernment in which the priest and the parish sent to the Order's superiors their impressions of the meeting and whether they thought it would be a good match. In the end, both sides were happy with what they experienced. The provincial named the priest as pastor of the parish. This happened a number of years ago and he is still happily serving as pastor in a contented parish community. The only one upset by the process was the local bishop. He caught wind of what was happening and told the religious order how upset he was. "If other places hear about what you did in that parish, they will all want to do it and I can't let that happen."

What this story reveals is two options for dealing with the impending shortage of priests. One is retrenchment. "Circle the wagons, boys. Here they come!" The other is with imagination and expansiveness. As the motto of Star Trek states, "To explore new worlds where no one has gone before."

Retrenchment is a temptation in times of shortage. All that is apparent is scarcity and limitation. This approach must be resisted, however, if we are to have any hope of finding a new way of being church in the next century. We find the same temptation of retrenchment when a parish is experiencing a limited amount of funds. "Pull back, eliminate costly items, terminate staff positions, cut services," is the immediate reaction. What is the result? The budget is balanced, at least for a while, but the people suffer. The same dynamic happens when the shortage of priests is dealt with in a limited fashion. Requirements for entrance into seminaries and for ordination are relaxed. Priests are brought in from foreign lands. Pastors are kept on beyond retirement. Problems with addiction and poor delivery of services are tolerated. In the end, all people suffer.

The first reaction is that the people get mad. When anger does no good, they begin to give up and lose interest. Finally, they stop coming. The end result of retrenchment is worse than the beginning.

Facing the shortage in an expansive mood, on the other hand, is risky business. It is the only one, however, that points to a new paradigm, to a new way of being parish. A crisis in the number of priests or the amount of funds can be an occasion for evaluating resources and reinvesting in the future. The excitement this can generate will prompt people to contribute to the future life and growth of the parish and its leadership.

A few dioceses have taken this risk and stated in their guidelines that not all priests are gifted or called to be a pastor. Just because someone is ordained does not automatically mean they will someday lead a parish. This opens the lid and lets people think of new ways for providing leadership in a parish. It gives courage to other gifted men and women who may not be ordained but who are either active in the parish or attracted from outside to be leaders of the parish. Many parishes are now "pastored" by someone who is not ordained. This frees the priests to be sacramental ministers. They don't have to worry about taking care of other pastoring duties that they may not be equipped or motivated to perform. The diocese may call these nonordained pastoral leaders by many names, such as pastoral administrator, parochial vicar or pastoral minister. The people themselves know them to be their pastor.

## Expansion Amid Scarcities

Expansion is more growth-oriented than retrenchment for many reasons. For example, when parishioners get turned off or become angry at parish leadership, they not only stop contributing and eventually drop out themselves, they also influence others, both family and friends. It has a ripple affect. To stem the tide, three areas of expansion are necessary.

First, bishops, diocesan personnel and pastors must expand the boundaries of decision-making. They have to be willing to let go of control and empower others to contribute their wisdom and insight. No longer can they make unilateral decisions related to areas that affect other people's lives. When dealing with shortages, the leaders must gather the people together, as a family would do when facing a crisis. They must let the people's discernment dictate possible options and alternatives. They must be open to letting the people choose the best avenue to follow. When this happens, the results are immediate. People feel they belong, their contributions count, they become partners in the search for the new paradigm.

Second, the leaders must look to the system as a whole and see where it can be expanded, where new ways of acting can be initiated. It is not always necessary to throw everything out. Reshape, realign, reimage, renew. As Americans, we are great inventors. We throw out last year's models and start from scratch. Planned obsolescence, it's called. This approach feeds consumerism, but it doesn't help create a new future.

Consider the retrenchment vs. expansion option in parishes. Expansion does not always mean throwing out the old and starting over with all that is new. It means using what we have to best advantage, perhaps in new ways and with a new purpose. That is why we must keep drawing on the creative experiences we have already seen at work in present-day parishes. These experiences point the way to the paradigms. We build our future on the shoulders of the present.

Consider the current parish staff, for instance. Perhaps there are some talents and gifts that are not being used to the best advantage. Rather than terminating a position to save money, new ones might be established using existing staff members. Fr. William Bausch's book, *Hands on Parish* (Mystic, CT: Twenty-Third Publications, 1989) mentions three staff positions he considers crucial: a director of Volunteers, a psychological counselor and a parish spiritual director. That is expansion into new directions but with perhaps the same personnel, not new ones.

## *People Focus*

Third, the leadership must discover what people want and then respond to their wishes. Imagine what it would look like in a Catholic parish if the leaders adopted a motto similar to that found in businesses: "The parishioner is always right." What if a parish incorporated management techniques which included a monitoring process that kept in touch with the parishioners' level of satisfaction at Mass, during meetings, or at formation classes? What would happen if a parish held regularly-scheduled "parishioner review sessions" where people could voice opinions and give feedback? Parishioners could work on teams with the leaders to assess "performance shortfalls," as they say in management circles. Areas for assessment would include homilies, music, pastoral care, spiritual development. In this way the parish would expand, not limit, feedback options in order to discover what people really want and need. No longer would the leaders have to presume what the people desire. The leaders, along with the parishioners themselves, could then work out ways of meeting these wants and needs. Clusters of people could form "communication groups" (another management term) to monitor services in all areas of parish life.

What about the money that would be needed to pay for this expensive move? Who pays for all this? The answer is the parishioners, of course. They will pay for a service if it fits their needs, even to the extent of supporting a pastor who has a spouse and family. This is not the time to look back to what has been but to explore whole new worlds of what can be.

## *Leadership vs Management*

This exploring of new worlds is an essential aspect of leadership. Leaders and people alike must have a vision of what could be and then plan ways for realizing these dreams. Above, we used some terms familiar in management circles. The parish, however, is more in need of good leadership than good management. The two are not the same. Joseph C. Rost wrote an entire book trying to unravel the two concepts. The book is called *Leadership for the Twenty-First Century* (NY- Praeger Press, 1991.) According to Rost, "Leadership is an influence relationship among leaders and followers who intend real changes that reflect their mutual purposes" (p. 102). This means there is an interaction between leaders and people, both affecting each other. Both are part of the leadership mix. What they seek is change. The leaders and people inspire, encourage, challenge and lead each other to something new and different. They may never get there but that is what they intended when they entered into the leadership interaction. The changes they seek are in tune with their expectations, values, desires, purposes.

Take a look at Jesus and his followers. That was a leadership interaction. Not only did Jesus influence the people, they influenced him. This was especially true of the women: the one healed of hemorrhaging, the Canaanite woman who didn't give up, the woman at the well, Mary Magdalene.

Both Jesus and the people intended real change. The changes they intended were not always the same or well-articulated, but not only did Jesus want things to be different, so did the people. He brought a breath of fresh air, a new authority. The people longed for freedom, for less oppression, for a better way of life. Jesus offered a way out of the routine and boredom. Their purposes—Jesus' and the people's—were in sync.

So much for leadership. What about management? According to Rost, "Management is an authority relationship between at least one manager and one subordinate who coordinate their activities to produce and sell particular goods and/or services." (p. 145) This is not leadership. It does not include the notion of change. Instead, the focus is producing and selling something. There is an interaction that takes place between manager and subordinates. It does not have the same mutuality as leadership. Someone is in charge to see that a task is accomplished. Others help get that task done.

Jesus does not come to mind when thinking of management. Judas was the manager of the purse, but that didn't work out so well. The deacons who were chosen in the sixth chapter of Acts to help out the Greek widows might be a better example. The institutional church, taken as a whole, is a management concept. It is in the business of providing a service to people, both Catholics and others in need. It is an authority relationship between the hierarchy and subordinates in which the activities related to helping people are coordinated. There are leaders within the institutional Church, but they are about something other than management.

Leadership does not have the goal of coordinating the delivery of services. It is about the business of intending real change. Suppose a parish has to solve a problem related to its school and religious education. Ten years ago a new church was built a few miles from the original parish site. At the time there was not enough money for a new education building, so the old site continued to be used for the school and religious education. The old building is now in need of repair. Should they make the renovations or build a new facility at the site of the church?

From a management viewpoint, it is a question of coordinating the activities of those in finance and education to produce the most efficient and farsighted facility for the children. Those "in charge" come up with the best plan after consultation with the people involved, including parishioners, parents and the diocese. Once the plan is finalized, the managers convince the people to support and pay for the plan. Whether the result is renovation at the old site or a new building at the church site, the process of deciding is an example of good fiscal management: getting the most for one's money and, at the same time, providing excellent education for the children.

It may be good management but not good leadership. A second approach comes from the interaction of leaders and people to affect real change based on mutual desires and purposes.

Suppose the pastor, a gifted person of intuition and insight, submits the problem to the people and asks for creative alternatives. He emphasizes that this crisis is an opportunity for discovering what, as he put it, "we as a parish are being called to by the Spirit." A special committee is formed to discover creative alternatives. They research the facts and submit a proposal to the parish. The most logical solution would be to sell the old school and build an education center next to the church. Instead of selling, however, the committee recommends developing the old site for housing for the elderly and daycare for working parents. Eventually, it would be an income-producing property. But more important, it would satisfy a pressing problem in the area.

The pastor asks the parish to spend a month of discernment about this option, thinking up all the reasons for and against the proposal. The parishioners are given all the information they would need—enrollment, cost, building plan—for a good decision. At the end of the month, he asks for the results of their discernment on index cards. "Are you for or against the proposal and one reason why." The results go to a discernment group for a final decision.

Surprisingly, the discernment group discovers that the people will go along with the proposal with only minor changes. As one parishioner remarked, "When I first heard of this, I thought it was nuts. The more I thought and prayed over it, it wasn't so bad. Besides, I'm getting up in years and may just need a nice place to stay. I'd love to be around little children in my old age. The way we went about this decision makes such good sense, especially our pastor calling us to think about what we are being called to by the Spirit." Because so many people felt ownership in the decision, the new building and renovation of the old is paid for in five years. That's leadership, not management.

In a parish, *both* are necessary, but they are not the same. Management keeps the place well-functioning and running smoothly. The liturgies are well-planned, the music rehearsed, the readers are prepared and the ministers are on time and know their places.

The education is well-managed when children and adults have all the services they require. The school is up to par, the religious education programs are well-developed with enough trained teachers and sufficient materials and equipment.

There are groups in the parish to handle outreach to the needy, the Rite of Initiation for new Catholics, sports and recreational programs for the energetic, activities for youth and seniors alike. All these groups know who is in charge and how they relate to the parish as a whole.

These are all management issues. Without a well-managed parish, the services it delivers would be lacking and people would be up in arms. Surprisingly, a parish can get along better without leadership than it can without management. It can be maintained through management. It is changed through leadership.

Where does leadership happen in a parish? Remember that leadership is not just the leader but the interaction between leader and people. It seeks a real change. Here are a few examples.

The song leader gets up at the 9:30 Sunday morning Mass and inspires the congregation to sing their lungs out, first one side against the other, the men vs. the women, then the over-40 and under-40 crowds. They love it. That's leadership.

The youth director forms a youth council and encourages them to confront the drug culture in the local high school which everyone says "has no problem." The youth know differently. The 10 members of the council start a groundswell in the school, getting students to pledge not to sell, buy or use drugs for six months. Buttons appear on campus that read, "No way—Today!" Teachers are amazed. Students are feeling empowered. The youth council members are smiling to each other. The youth director continues to meet with the council every week for prayer and discernment.

The pastoral associate has a bag lunch twice a week for the elderly. Before lunch they all do exercises together and then, as one man said, "Collapse for lunch." It's getting to be such fun that some of the staff members are coming over for the "workout." This is leadership, not management.

What about the pastor? When is he involved in pastoral leadership? It happens whenever the pastor and people interact to intend real change. Based on the definition, many pastors are more often managers than leaders. There are moments of brilliant leadership, however.

At an Easter Vigil, for instance, leadership happens when the pastor and people pull off a stunning ritual of initiation for the new candidates. Everyone is moved.

Leadership happens at the finance meeting when the pastor challenges the committee to think of parish priorities and not just dollars and cents. He stretches their imaginations about what could be rather than what is.

At the annual "State of the Parish" townhall meeting, the pastor rallies the parishioners to accept the Hispanic community as part of the parish rather than the group that happens to use the church once a week for Mass.

At the semiannual staff outing, the pastor takes a risk and raises a conflict issue that everyone on staff was aware of but was afraid to mention. Amid much anger and tears the staff works through the conflict and pulls closer together as a group.

At the pastoral council meeting, he challenges the members to become more visible in the parish, so that everyone knows who they are. He encourages them to be open to new ideas and suggestions. This leads to pictures in the vestibule, inserts into the bulletin, a council table at coffee and donuts following the weekend Masses, a council-sponsored potluck supper. The parish is amazed at the change in the council members themselves. They become much more confident and energized.

These are leadership issues—pastor and people interacting to change the status quo. Both management and leadership are necessary in a parish, but they are not the same. To equate the two leaves the parish without a future. It may keep going for a while as a well-managed organization, but it lacks change because it has no leadership. It is like having a church without the Spirit of Jesus at its center. It's a body with no soul.

This is the crisis of leadership facing the church today on all levels. Some leaders want change but the people drag their heels. Many people want change but those in authority resist. The search for a new way of being parish involves both leaders and people working together for change. That change must reflect what they know lies ahead if they just open themselves to the Spirit. They must have the courage to say yes to the future.

## Shaping a Positive Image

Image plays a part in leadership. It helps leaders and people alike envision what could be. One parish decides it will try to create the image of a welcoming community and work toward that end. Another wants to be a haven for the marginalized and unchurched. It shapes its services and ministries around this desired outcome. A third parish might envision itself as oriented to young, single adults, while another sees itself as more family-oriented. Discovering what is the present image of a parish and what image it desires for the future helps move the leaders and people to a new way of operating.

We have used an exercise with staffs and councils that has been very revealing. We first asked them to write down on index cards, in a word or a phrase, what image they have of themselves and what image they have of the other leadership group, whether staff or council. In most cases the words are positive. The staff is seen as caring, hard-working, competent. The council is dedicated, generous, parish visionaries. We then ask both groups to put down what image the parishioners, that is, the ordinary people in the pew, have of them. A very different set of words appear. These include unknown, in-group, not needed, too expensive, doing their own thing, power group. It is not a very positive image. This is coming from the leaders' own admission of what the parishioners experience.

One parish we worked with had an image problem. When asked on the opinion survey, "What is your attitude toward your local parish?," just over half (57%) of both the staff and people were favorable. The national Catholic average is quite a bit higher (68%). Other statistics from that parish indicated that only 32% of the leadership and 46% of the people liked most of the sermons they heard at the weekend Masses. This was 20% below the national average. Other responses indicated that a third of the leaders and half the people agreed that, "In general, I like the way the local parish is being run." The national average is 61%. What was happening in this parish to cause such a low positive response?

In trying to understand the results, we looked first to the pastor. As we mentioned earlier, he is the tone-setter in the parish, the one whose personality has greatest influence on the mood and spirit of the community. We watched how he presided at liturgy, how he delivered the homily, how he greeted people before and after Mass. He had all the right intentions. He was interested in the people, was dedicated and well-informed. His manner, however, was withdrawn. He failed to reach out and make connections with people. He spoke at the people during the homily, not *with* or even *to* them. The message was excellent but the impact was lost in a poor delivery. He rarely smiled or reached out to meet people more than halfway. People had to make the first move towards him, not the other way around.

The staff was not visible to the people. Most had their own area of ministry and little contact with the parishioners as a whole. The council was an unknown quantity altogether. Each year it was impossible to find new candidates to fill vacancies, so council members picked their friends to replace them. It quickly became an inner circle of the "elect." No wonder the image among parishioners was so negative. The leaders had not attended to their image in the parish.

To turn their image around, we suggested three changes. The first place to start was with the pastor. He was unaware of his retiring, incommunicative manner. Painful as it was for him, he agreed to having his homilies videotaped. Once a month a few of his friends, people from whom he felt support and encouragement, sat down with him to review the videos. Over the space of a few months they were able to coax him out of reading from his prepared text and begin looking at the congregation. They got him to smile more and hold his head up so that he wasn't crouched over the microphone. The crowning achievement was the Sunday he put on the traveling mike and came out from behind the ambo and addressed the people with no boundaries between them. He surprised everyone by this move, himself included. He was beaming with pride. The people responded by giving him a hand after his delivery.

The next step was the staff. How could they improve their image in the parish? One simple way was to be seen together as a group. The logical place for this to happen was the weekend Masses. That's where the greatest number of parishioners gathered. One weekend in the fall they planned a commissioning ceremony at every Mass. Each staff member was introduced and blessed by the entire congregation for his or her ministry during the year. Once a month an insert to the bulletin featured a different staff person. It included a picture and a description of what the individual did. A group picture of the staff was added to the council photograph in the church vestibule. On Holy Thursday, the pastor washed the feet of the staff members who, in turn, went throughout the congregation washing the hands of the community as a gesture of service ministry. Slowly the parishioners became more acquainted with the staff and the contribution each made to the life and operation of the parish. The staff had a graphic indication of how much their image had changed in the parish. It came in response to a contest they sponsored in connection with the parish festival. The parishioners were to identify which baby pictures belonged to which staff members. So many correct answers were received that they had to hold a raffle to decide the winners. It pleased the staff no end to realize they were now recognized by the people, even when under tile age of two years old.

The third group was the council. To most parishioners, this was an unknown quantity. When asked on the survey whether the council was effective in solving parish problems, the highest response (42%) came from those with no opinion or "don't know." The council decided to change their "unknown" image with three projects. One was to put a table up at one end of the hall where coffee and donuts were served once a month. They put up a large sign behind the table that read, "We are your Pastoral Council. Ask a question. We will respond even if we don't know the answer." Some of the questions were hilarious, others very serious and thought-provoking. The message was getting across, however. The council belongs to the people, is made up from among the people. It's time it became responsive to the people and their needs and desires.

Step two was publishing the council's agenda in the bulletin before each monthly meeting, and the minutes following the meetings. Aware of the need to change their image in the parish, the council tried to make the agenda and minutes look interesting, provocative and relevant. They listed the priorities of the parish and which ones were getting the most attention at this time. They solicited ideas for a parish theme for the coming year, along with a tear-off section so people could more easily contribute their ideas. They tried to make communication interactive, in other words, not just one-sided.

Step three was the first annual "State of the Parish" convocation held after the last Mass one Sunday in May. They were afraid no one would show up so they facetiously gave as one topic to be discussed canceling the Masses on Memorial Day weekend and having a parade in the parking lot instead. Many people showed up just to find out if they were serious. They weren't, but it got people's attention.

After calming people's fears and anxieties, the council spent the next hour describing the activities of the council over the last year. The gathering then broke into small groups to assess the needs and desires for the coming year. The town hall concluded with a brief social and much acclaim from the participants. "We should have been doing this for years," one young adult noted. "It made me think seriously about being on the council in the years to come." His name was quickly noted by the council president.

What these experiences from a single parish demonstrate is that, in the words of Richard Nixon, "Image is everything!"

So little attention is given to fostering a positive image in parish life. It is a critical element in making the parish attractive to various age and interest groups. Targeting is a key ingredient for fostering a positive image. Businesses survey the public and try out various types of packaging for different groups. The same approach could be used in parishes.

The leadership begins the targeting process by auditing the clientele. What percentage of the parishioners are 18 to 30? What percentage are 30 to 55? What percentage are 55 and over? Each group will need a different focus and approach. Is there something to attract each age group at the liturgies, for instance, or the adult formation program or socializing, community-building events?

What about marital status or occupational interests? How many parishioners are single, single parents, widowed, have grown children, need baby-sitters? How many are in helping or service professions? How many in business or sales? How many full-time homemakers? All these sub-groups have different needs and expectations and desires. Shaping parish activities to attract particular backgrounds and interests will have much effect on the image of the parish. It means addressing concrete issues that fit various tastes or inclinations, or perhaps missing the mark entirely.

These are both leadership and management issues. Being attentive to image helps shape the future and bring about change. It also provides ways of eliciting support and backing for new proposals and directions.

## Complementarity

The area where image is most important is in dealing with the shadow side of leadership. We all have our limitations and shortcomings. Pastors, staffs and councils are not exempt. How to fill up what is lacking in our leading and turn the limits into strengths is no easy task.

In one parish the pastor's shadow side was his non-assertive, *laissez-faire* style of leadership. He was what Robert Dale described in *Pastoral Leadership* (Nashville: Abingdon Press, 1986) as a hermit pastor. He had great intentions but he was not equipped to inspire or motivate people to greatness. It was not his gift.

He admitted this shortcoming and asked his staff, as well as ourselves who had been invited in as pastoral consultants, what could he do to make up for his non-assertive behavior. We put our heads together and looked around for someone to share the leadership role with the pastor, much as Aaron shared this role with Moses in the Exodus.

Fortunately, one such person did exist, the associate pastor. He was a recent arrival from another diocese, gregarious and a crowd pleaser. Planning and goal-setting were not his strengths, but he held great promise for positive image-building in the parish. The people were immediately drawn to his friendly, cheerful demeanor.

Matching the two together was a natural. The pastor had the vision, the associate the charisma. They agreed to work as a team to create a warmer, more attractive image in the parish. Both served on the council, both greeted people after the Masses, both appeared at key parish events. They became known in the parish as the "Blues Brothers." The pastor wondered if this was an appropriate image to portray but he could see it was having an impact. People were responding with much more enthusiasm at the liturgies and activities of the parish. His shadow side was given light by the associate's outgoing manner. The associate's drawbacks were also being replenished by the pastor's wisdom and forethought. Together they provided a leadership in the parish that was both creative and appealing to the parishioners.

This leads to the one aspect of leadership that will take us into the next century. It's called partnership. No one person can hope to carry the weight of leading a modem parish by oneself. It takes a combined effort. The evidence of the need for partnership is all around us.

Even God is not a one-person show but a Trinity. The Gospel repeats over and over again that Jesus was not operating on his own. He kept referring to his Father. The Spirit does not operate independently of Jesus. It is the Spirit of Christ, after all. They work in partnership.

The story of creation shows that Adam was lonely and given a companion and helpmate. The two shared leadership in the garden.

In the Old Testament, Moses could not save the Israelites by himself. The story of the burning bush in the third chapter of Exodus shows this. Moses tried to get out of the task of leading the Chosen People out of Egypt. He pleaded with God that he was not a good speaker, that he couldn't do the job. "Get someone else," he insisted. Instead, God gave Moses Aaron as a partner to speak for him. It was a shared leadership. Later on, Moses was unable to keep his arms up over the parted waters of the Red Sea. He had to have help. He could not do it all by himself.

Jesus didn't go it alone. From the beginning of his public life he gathered companions around him. He formed them and sent them out in pairs, as partners, to share the ministry.

After a short training period, only three years, Jesus put the work of spreading the reign of God into their hands. He let go of the controls and gave the ministry over to these raw recruits.

The same story of partnership is found in the early church, as described in the Acts of the Apostles. The ministry of spreading the Good News is a shared ministry. Peter was not the only leader. He was in dialogue with many others, even Gentiles, about what following Jesus was all about. Paul had companions on his journeys, first Barnabas and then others.

From these accounts, it would appear that God wants us to operate in partnership as coequals. Only now are we getting back to this primary insight, that all baptized persons are called to be ministers, not just the priests or religious. The Second Vatican Council restored this insight and created a whole new way of operating, a new church, a new paradigm.

Underneath this shift is the rationale of partnership and shared leadership. We are made in the image of God. God is a Trinity, not one, or even two, but three persons, creating, saving, inspiring, renewing and above all, sharing leadership. That's the partnership of God we are called to emulate.

The evidence of partnership in the Church, especially on the local level is all around us. Parish staffs—pastors, religious, lay professionals—share as a whole the daily operation of the parish. When they meet as a group each week, the pastor is one among equals. Important decisions are arrived at through consensus. Each person takes a turn chairing the meeting and leading prayer. The pastor has not given up his role as pastor. His role, rather, is expanded as others enter into partnership with the pastor in providing for the pastoral needs and concerns of the people.

Pastoral councils, commissions and committees work together as ministerial teams. The finance committee, for instance, works hand-in-glove with the pastoral council to be sure the use of parish funds reflects the priorities of the parish as discerned by the council. Competition between groups gives way to a mutual search for what is best for the parish as a whole.

In this movement toward partnership, individual parishioners are taking initiative, sharing talents, dreaming dreams, filling up what is lacking in one another. They work collaboratively, creating something new, something far beyond what one person could do on his or her own.

This dynamic of shared leadership is happening in today's church, not only in the United States, but in Canada, Central and South America, Africa, Eastern and Western Europe, in the world at large. These are exciting times. Yes, there is a shortage of priests in many areas. There are not enough to pastor every parish in our own country, let alone other places where the shortage is much more acute.

But a Catholic parish can survive without a resident ordained person. It can do this to the extent that the parishioners catch on to this basic aspect of our faith: the Church is made up of a partnership of cobelievers. All believers—not just priests and religious—are responsible for its survival and future growth. It is on the shoulders of these partners in faith that the Church will be carried into the next century.

## Questions for Review and Reflection

*Retrenchment or Expansion*

What areas of your parish are growing, which ones are on a plateau and which ones are dying? What is the difference in leadership in each of these areas? Does your parish have any "parishioner review sessions" where people can give feedback and voice opinions? Would these sessions be of any help?

*Leadership or Management*

Leadership deals with vision and change, management with implementation. How much of your time is spent in pastoral leadership and how much in pastoral management? Are you satisfied with this ratio? Who are good leaders and who are good managers in your parish? Are their gifts being utilized?

*Image-making*

Is your image of the parish different from the majority's? How much attention has been given to shaping a positive parish image? Has there been any effort to pair leaders together as partners or cochairs so that what is lacking in leadership or management skills in one person is complemented by the skills of another? What steps would have to be taken to implement more partnership in the parish?

## Prayer Ritual

*Opening Prayer:*

Three people will be needed to read the following adaptation of Moses and the Burning Bush. (Exodus 3: 1–5, 4:1–5, 10–17) One person will be the narrator (N), one person Moses (M), and one person, perhaps a woman, God (G). Standing before the group, the three tell the following story:

N. One day as Moses was tending his fold, he saw a bush that wasn't burning up. He went over to investigate. All of a sudden he heard:

G. Moses.... Moooosesl

M. Who is calling me?

G. I am! Now listen, take off your shoes for you are on holy ground. I want to talk with you for awhile.

N. Moses took off his shoes and covered his face for he was afraid. Then the Lord told him:

G. I have seen the deep sorrows of my people and I have heard their great pleas for freedom. I have come to deliver them and I need someone to carry out my will. I was asking myself the other day as I was looking about my creation: "Whom shall I send? Someone good, not perfect, someone holy, with holes in his pockets, shoes, clothes, someone who has to struggle a bit with life, but is not overwhelmed by it." And do you know what? You came to mind. You are just the person to go and lead my people out of slavery. You are just the person to form them from a good people into a great people.

M. But, ah Lord, I am not the person for a job like that.

G. Moses, don't worry, I will certainly be with you.

M. What! Am I to go to the people and say "God has called me to lead you out of slavery, to become great people?" Do You think they will believe me? They won't. They won't do what I tell them. They will say, "God never appeared to you."

G. What is that in your hand? A walking stick, I see. Now throw it down.

N. Moses threw it down and it turned into a snake, a powerful creature. Moses then picked it up again and it turned back into a walking stick.

G. When the people see you using ordinary tools in such a way, when they see my power in you, they will believe and so, too, will their oppressors.

M. Oh, Lord! Get someone else. I am not a good speaker. I never have been, and I haven't become one since you began to speak to me. I have a speech impediment.

G. Who made your mouth? Is it not I, the Lord? Who makes a person speak or not speak, see or not see, hear or not hear? Now get along. Stop being afraid and saying that someone else is to do what I command. Free my people and form me a great people NOW, not tomorrow. I will help you speak and I will tell you what to say.

M. *(whining)* But Lord, please! Send someone else.

N. At this, the Lord became angry with Moses and said ...

G. Oh, all right! Your brother, Aaron, is a good speaker. You can speak to him and tell him what to say. I will help both of you to speak, and I will tell both of you what to do.

N. Still not sure of what it meant, Moses went off to lead God's People out of bondage.

At the conclusion of the story, the participants are invited to reflect on what this says about their own experience of leadership and the call to be a leader.

*Process*

Give each person two index cards. On one index card, ask people to write down, in a word or a phrase, how they would describe the image they have of their own leadership group, whether it is the staff, council, commission or committee. On the second card, ask people to write down what they think the parishioners' image of this group might be.

First, have people share their own image words or phrases. List these on newsprint or on a board. Then ask for the word or phrase that describes the parishioners' image of their group. List these as well. Discuss as a group the difference between the two lists.

Break into groups of three and discuss what is now going on in the parish that is helping create a positive image. List other options for improving the image of the parish itself and leadership groups within the parish. Choose one and present it to the large group for possible implementation.

*Closing*

Sing the Refrain from "We Praise You, O Lord," by Michael Balhoff. (Phoenix: Damean Music, 1978.)

Recite aloud the following prayer, each side of the group alternating stanzas.

> We are called to be ministers
> Faithful to who we are
> To our identity and graced history
> Choosing to live the present
> With an awareness of the past and
> An openness to the future
>
> Committed to collaboration
> And to change with the Church
> Realizing that no single person
> Or group has the whole truth
>
> The Spirit alone possesses the Church
> Inviting each of us to speak our word
> That the truth and wisdom of the whole body
> Be the basis for change and new life.

After the prayer, repeat the refrain from the song, "We Praise You, O Lord."

# CHAPTER FIVE

# A Change in Pastors

"The parish is doing very well just now, but I don't know what will happen next year when our pastor is changed."

"We're in the midst of a change in pastors. We don't know who the new one will be but we're hoping and praying it will be someone good."

"We just got a new pastor and we're holding our breath that all the progress we made toward collaboration and partnership won't go down the drain in the next few months."

"We're so happy with our new pastor, he's a breath of fresh air. Just what we needed right now."

"It's so sad. All we worked so hard for the last two years is gone. Most of the staff has left. The council and commissions are in shambles. I had no idea our new pastor could have so much affect on our parish in such a short time."

"Is there any way we can get ready for the transition in leadership? My turn as pastor is up. I want to help these wonderful parishioners through the transition."

These are some of the comments we hear again and again in our dealings with parishes throughout the United States. They reveal a number of issues. First, that people sense how critical a change of pastors is to the life, operation and spirit of a parish. In some parishes, the shift in style and approach of a new pastor is so radical that it becomes a new parish altogether. The liturgies change, programs dropped or added, staff come and go, new leaders emerge and old ones retire.

These comments also show how little is done in most parishes and dioceses to utilize the period of transition in a creative manner. It happens to a parish community, not with the community. This becomes more of an issue as fewer and fewer ordained clergy are available as pastors in Catholic parishes. The tendency, as the shortage becomes more acute, is to spend less time in trying to match the right pastor to a given parish. Instead, whoever might be available for appointment is assigned as the new pastor. This does a disservice to both the priest and to the parishioners.

Matching is the key. It is a delicate dance between the prospective pastor's likes, dislikes, dreams, motivations and aspirations on the one hand and the history, size, makeup, customs, culture and resources of the parish on the other. The two need to be in harmony as they come together to "make music" in the years ahead.

Sometimes the matching happens by chance. It is a union made in heaven from the beginning. Other times, because of the efforts of a sensitive diocesan personnel board and bishop, the match-up works like a charm. Other times, it is a disaster. Too much is left up to chance. So many opportunities for growth are lost.

The period of transition from one pastor to another is the most critical moment in the life of a parish. If handled with care and insight, it can be an occasion of growth for all involved. If not, the opportunity for new directions and new paradigms is squandered.

William Bridges in two books, *Transitions: Making Sense of Life's Changes* and *Managing Transitions* identifies these stages associated with every transaction. First comes the ending stage. This is the period before a change takes place. It has various lengths, sometimes as much as a year. This "ending" stage begins when the pastor either makes up his mind it's time for a change or is notified by the diocese that his time is up as pastor of the parish. He might be the only one aware of it, but at this moment the "ending stage" has begun. Whether of long or short duration, this stage is filled with termination, leave-taking, closure, disengagement, farewells, sadness, and finality. The pastor is leaving, no denying it.

The second stage is the "neutral zone" or "in-between time." This period overlaps with the first because people, in preparing for the transition, feel as if they are in limbo. They are uncertain, anxious, confused, unbelieving, at a loss. As the termination rituals for the departing pastor take place, staff, leaders and people are left with an unknowing feeling of "what next."

This in-between time does not come to an end when a new pastor arrives. It blends into the third stage of "new beginnings." As the new person assumes leadership, the uncertainty and anxiousness begin to give way to new experiences of "how this pastor behaves." People make comparisons with how he differs from the previous pastor, what's unique in his approach and emphasis, where is he the same and how is he different from what went before.

Slowly, the dance of pastor and people begins swaying to a new song. The transition comes to an end as the period of "new beginnings" becomes familiar to the pastor, leaders and people. Usually in six months to a year, the new ways of operating become predictable. Everyone settles into "this is the way we do things around here." Those who are attracted by and agree with the new style come forward with their support and affirmation. Those who find it not to their liking either withdraw, learn to live with the situation or "wait it out" until the next transition takes place.

In those parishes where the match of pastor and people was done poorly, the "new beginnings" stage is difficult. Instead of a gentle blending of the in-between phase into new beginnings, it becomes conflictual and confrontational. The entire organization is in turmoil. All suffer in the process, both pastor and people.

In order to prevent such a tragic situation from occurring, we suggest that more care and concerted effort be given to this period of a change in pastors.

## TRANSITION PROCESS

During an interview with Loren Mead, head of the Alban Institute in Washington, D.C., he mentioned that the six months before and after a change of pastor provided the most important opportunity for parish renewal. Once a pastor is appointed and settles in, not much substantial change will happen. Programs will come and go, liturgies shift focus, but the tone and overall direction will remain constant until there is another change in pastor.

We agree, and for that reason we suggest that both the local parish and diocesan offices pay close attention to this critical period before and after a change in pastor. If a diocese did nothing else but help a parish and pastor through this difficult transition, it would be doing a great service to the future life and vitality of the local church.

We will walk through a transition process as an example of what the ideal might look like. Suppose a priest has been pastor of a parish for 12 years. His tenure as pastor of the parish has come to an end.

### Endings

The diocesan personnel board contacts him, invites him to an "ending" seminar for all pastors undergoing a change in assignment. During this full-day conference, the pastor has a chance to reflect on his present pastorate, what worked and didn't work, what aspects of his leadership style he would like to repeat in his new assignment and what aspects not to repeat. He is given help in putting closure to his present pastorate and a chance to make choices for his new one. He is encouraged to think about giving himself time in the "neutral zone" before jumping into a new assignment, whether as pastor or in a new ministry. He learns about the stages of transition, both for himself and the parish. He is asked to form a transition team of parish leaders who will carry the parish through the change in pastorates over the next nine months.

Our pastor is surprised by how much enthusiasm he experiences at the workshop. It is a freeing experience. No longer does he feel overwhelmed or depressed by the prospect of moving. Rather, it is, according to him, "like taking a load of bricks off my shoulders."

He returns to the parish with a list of concrete, practical steps he will have to take during his last few months in the parish. First, he gathers the staff and council together for a joint meeting. He lays out the transition plan and asks for their wisdom and insight as to how best to proceed. He explains that many misconceptions and rumors will be flying around the parish. He wants all the leaders to have the same story from his own lips.

## Transition Committee

Next, he spells out the role of the transition committee and asks for suggestions as to who should be on it. Its job will be to handle the ending, in-between and beginning stages in the change of pastors. The committee will be meeting bi-weekly over the next nine months. A staff member and one council person agree to serve on the committee. Other names surface and are contacted. Eventually, a group of seven people is formed. Its first task is to decide when and how best to inform the parish about the loss of their pastor. The committee decides to call a special townhall meeting on Sunday afternoon following the noon Mass. They get the word out that an important announcement is to be made, one that will affect every member in the parish. The plan works. Over 500 people show up in the hall.

After an initial prayer for guidance, the pastor announces his departure, effective in two months. Most of the people are not surprised. They realized his tenure was coming to an end. They are sad because he led the parish well but are accepting of the inevitable.

The pastor then introduces the transition committee and describes the stages of transition that the committee will help facilitate in the parish. The pastor also describes his diocesan seminar on transition. He relates how the transition committee will be working in conjunction with the diocese to assure a smooth transition and find a suitable replacement.

One important insight gained from the seminar is that this period of change is a time for exploring creative options. In his words, it is a time to discover "what the Lord is calling the parish to become? What must we let go of and what create anew?"

The townhall then divides into groups of 20 each with a facilitator. The groups are to make up a history line of the last 12 years of the current pastorate. What significant changes have occurred, what were the high points and lows? What were pluses and what were minuses? At the end of the exercise, each individual is asked to write down on index cards two things the parish should hold onto and continue in the new pastorate, and one thing to let go of or discontinue.

When the 25 groups reassemble, they hang up the history lines on the walls for all to see. The index cards are collected and given to the committee for analysis and reporting back to the entire parish at a later date. The townhall concludes with a timeline for the transition process: when the farewell celebrations will take place, when the pastor will be leaving, how long the in-between phase will take, when a new pastor will arrive, how long the integration and "new beginning" stages will last. The meeting ends with refreshments and much discussion. The parishioners are happy that so much time, energy and forethought is going into this period of transition. Many crowd around the pastor, thanking him for his leadership, asking questions about what he will be doing next, wishing him well in all he hopes to accomplish.

The transition committee synthesizes the history lines and index cards from the groups and individuals. It publishes a report to the parish, explaining to those not at the townhall what is about to take place in the parish. The diocese also supplies a person from the Office of Transition to act as a resource to the parish and be a liaison between the diocese and the parish over the entire transition period.

The pastor himself is not part of the committee but is in constant contact with its work. He provides it with ideas and receives feedback in return. Both the pastor and the parish are in the "ending" phase, trying to find adequate and satisfying ways to say goodbye to each other, to put a fitting close to a wonderfully productive and blessed 12 years. It is a period of disengagement.

The transition committee spends its time helping the staff, council, commissions and parishioners say good-bye to the pastor and to the pastorate as a whole. Life in the parish will be different. This is the time to let go and face the future with new hope and expectations.

The committee plans ways for the various leadership groups, ministries and organizations to say good-bye to the pastor, to offer him gifts, not of material or economic value, but from one's experience of his pastoring. The staff, for instance, goes on an overnight and spends the time celebrating its ministry together. Each person gives a "wish card" to the pastor, something he or she hopes for the pastor's new life and ministry. The council has a potluck at one of the member's homes which includes all of the pastor's favorite dishes. The pastor is overwhelmed by the warmth and love he experiences from the people. The parishioners are thankful to be able to express thanks and gratitude for what he has meant to them. These sentiments came to a head at the farewell Mass and celebration a few weeks after Easter.

## The "In-between"

As the day of the pastor's departure, May 1, nears, the transition committee spends more of its time working on issues associated with the "in-between time." It prepares a preliminary "state of the parish" document that goes to the diocesan office of transition. This will help prospective pastors discover what type of parish it is and what form of leadership it requires, as well as its customs, traditions and plans for the future.

Once the pastor leaves, the parish will be without a permanent replacement for three months from the end of April to the beginning of August. During this time, the people are to consider their future and see what new directions might be desirable. No significant changes, of course, can be made until a new pastor arrives. This interim period, however, gives the parish community a chance to think creatively about its future.

The transition team sponsors three townhall meetings, one each month. The first one is centered on hopes for the future. What lies ahead for the parish? What issues must it face? What opportunities present themselves?

The second townhall is for uncovering ideas about what type of pastor will be needed in order to provide leadership over the next 6–12 years. Not only is the diocesan liaison person present for this second townhall but so are members of the diocesan Personnel Board, the ones responsible for finding a replacement.

The third townhall meeting uses the index cards from the March townhall. These cards revealed what people thought should continue and what to let go of in the coming years. The people divide into small groups to settle on the traditions they would like maintained, the ones they would like dropped and new ones they would like established. Attendance is high at all three townhalls. People feel an ownership in the parish. They feel their ideas are helping give direction to the parish. They begin to realize that their wisdom could have an impact on who will be appointed pastor of the parish. Their opinions and insights matter.

While this in-between phase is taking place in the parish, another dynamic is taking place outside of the parish. The Personnel Board and diocesan Office of Transition are making contact with those who are qualified and show interest in becoming the new pastor in the parish. The pool of likely candidates includes pastors who are leaving a parish, as well as other priests who might be interested in applying for the post.

The parish we have been using as an example will have an ordained priest for a pastor. Other smaller parishes may have a non-ordained administrator or a deacon couple as pastors with a nonresident priest serving as sacramental minister.

All those interested in becoming new pastors are required to attend a new pastors' seminar. This is where they learn about possible openings in the diocese and receive a summary report from each parish's transition committee that is undergoing a change. Prior to their workshop, each prospective new pastor, whether ordained or not, has become certified to be a pastor through a series of training sessions. The diocesan guidelines for pastors state that not all priests may be suited to become pastors. It is not a given, in other words, that ordination gives a person the right to be a pastor. Only those who indicate the desire and have the capabilities are allowed to pursue the immediate training required for new pastors.

In April, all those who are willing and able to become pastor in a new parish attend a full-day meeting. They learn which parishes are looking for pastors, what type of place it is, its traditions, aspirations and expectations for the new pastorate. They submit their names for their first, second and third choices. They are free to attend the townhalls held during May and June in each transition parish. They are encouraged to give their impressions and reactions to the Personnel Board about each parish they visit. By the end of June, the bishop makes the final appointments. Both the new pastor and the parish are notified of the decision before the third townhall in July takes place. This townhall is used as an occasion for the parish and new pastor to meet each other. All that is asked of the new pastor is to listen to what people feel should be kept and what let go of from the previous pastorate.

The pastor and the parish are still in the in-between phase, however. The pastor does not arrive officially until August. This gives both parties a chance to ease into the new relationship, to slowly join together as partners.

## *Beginnings*

August begins the third phase of transition, "new beginnings." The transition committee plans for the new pastor's arrival. Welcoming celebrations, an installation Mass and special gatherings and meetings are arranged. This gives the pastor a chance to become acquainted with all aspects of the parish, its leadership, ministries and organizations.

This does not conclude the work of the transition committee, however. They stay in existence until Thanksgiving.

In September they meet with the new pastor and alert him to the issues uncovered while the parish was in the in-between phase. These include the traditions and practices parishioners want to maintain during the new pastorate. The committee also describes a "wish list" people had for the future of the parish. They make clear that this is only a wish list and any new directions must be mutually agreed upon by pastor and people together.

The new pastor does not become a member of the transition committee. The committee tries to remain independent and objective during the integration period of the new pastor. Because of this, the parishioners are encouraged to give the committee any feedback or reactions about the new pastorate. Far better for the new pastor to know at the beginning whether there is a problem with his leadership than to discover later on that it is not a good match of people and pastor. Changes can more easily be made in the first few months rather than a year or two into the new pastorate.

In October, all the new pastors of the diocese assemble for a full-day seminar with the diocesan office of transition. At this time they are able to swap stories about what it was like coming into a new parish, how traumatic was the transition and what issues they might need help handling. Each new pastor brings along the feedback report prepared by the local transition committee. Only in rare occasions would a new pastor either ask for a new assignment or be asked to reapply for another parish. This could happen, however. The pain involved in relocating within the first six months is less than the years of frustration experienced by both pastor and people when there is an unhappy match. It bears repeating that not every priest is suited for the pastor's role. Not every parish is a good match for every pastor. This nine-month process of transition manifests how important is the effort to place the right leader with a given parish.

Thanksgiving marks the end of the transition committee's task, although the process of "new beginnings" continues for at least another six months.

One parish we worked with sponsored monthly Sunday afternoon dinners with the new pastor—35 parishioners at a time—so people could get to know him better. Participants were chosen according to how long they had belonged to the parish. All the forty-year-old veterans came one Sunday, all the five-year people the next. This continued until all who wished had a chance to dine with the pastor.

The last Sunday of the church year, the feast of Christ the King, is a time for affirming and appreciating the transition committee's work. This is also the occasion for the pastor to make a firm commitment to the parish, and the community to its new pastor.

The process outlined above may seem long and tedious. It is an intense nine months for all concerned, especially diocesan personnel. The payoff comes in the years following the transition process. The efforts at finding a good match of pastor and people will save hours of work later on. If the diocese were to spend more time whenever there is a change of pastor, it would have less to worry about once the pastor settles in and new patterns of behavior become established.

## *Other Transitions*

This same process of "endings," "in-between time" and "new beginnings" is present in any transition of leadership in the parish, whether staff, council or commission. If a key pastoral staff person is leaving and a new person hired, a transition committee should be appointed to help the parish through the change. This is more than a "search committee" whose task is to write up a job description, advertise for the new opening and interview candidates. A transition committee would also help the staff member and parish say good-bye to each other. It would help ministers and leaders explore what traditions to maintain and what new directions to pursue in that area of ministry. The committee remains in existence after the new staff person is hired in order to assist the person during the first few months of ministry and to provide feedback as to how well he or she is fulfilling people's expectations. This process should be included for all pastoral staff positions, including associate pastors and deacons.

For council or commission members, the transition process is not as involved. Some attention to the transition of membership is still necessary, however. Old members should have the opportunity to express their feelings about serving as leaders on either the council or commissions. What worked well for them, what was lacking, what more needs to be done? This would, in effect, be an exit interview conducted either by the body itself or a specially-formed transition committee. While new members are sought to fill vacancies, the council or commissions reflect on the wisdom of outgoing members and set new directions for the coming year. Those leaving the groups sit down with the new members and describe "how we do things around here," how meetings are run, how decisions are made, how crises and conflicts managed. Whatever time is spent on this transition process will save the council or commission countless hours in integrating new people into the group. From the very first meeting of the newly constituted leadership body, everyone is familiar with its purpose and way of operating.

## Conclusion

We have outlined a process in which transition can be an occasion for growth, especially when there is a significant change in leadership. This is the ideal. Unfortunately, few dioceses have realized the importance of planning ahead for this transition. They muddle through, hoping to place the right person in the right place. This is usually a hit-and-miss procedure based upon limited options and narrow vision.

Until a more systematic and inclusive approach is utilized, parishes and pastors alike will suffer through the mismatches and poor placement. That is not to say the people involved in assigning pastors to parishes have not tried their best. It's the system that needs revamping.

Until a new process for the change of pastors is realized, we encourage staffs and parish leaders to devote as much time and effort as possible to the transition stages of "endings," "in-between time" and "new beginnings." Ritualize ways of allowing people to let go and say good-bye. Allow for time in between the old and new so that people can assimilate change. Realize that it takes time to adjust to new people and situations. Establish transition teams and committees to handle important shifts in leadership. Above all, look upon transition as an opportunity for new vision and fresh growth.

Transition is part and parcel of all existence. Nature is filled with transitions, as the change in seasons manifests. Fall is ending time, winter a neutral zone. Spring provides the promise of new life and summer the settling into new patterns. The same progression is present in organizational life as well. Change is inevitable. Those who are unprepared suffer trials and frustrations of change. Those who are ready for it and make preparations are the ones who discover new life and promise in the transition.

## Questions for Review and Reflection

### Endings

Reflect upon the last experience you had of a change in pastors. How did the change take place? What preparation or involvement did the parishioners have in the transition? Reflect on a recent transition you yourself experienced, whether a change in location, a new position, a death of a loved one. How did you prepare for the change? What rituals did you go through for establishing closure and preparing for endings?

*In-between Time*

The time between the end of one phase and the beginning of another is the most creative period for both an individual and a parish. In your own transition, did you have any significant people to carry through the in-between time? What did they do to help? In the parish, whom would you name as good people to be on a transition committee? What functions would they perform? How much freedom would they have for their activity?

*New Beginnings*

What are some of the new things that happened to you as a result of a recent transition? What newness has occurred in the parish in the wake of changes? How open is the present leadership to change? Do they see it as an opportunity for growth? What scripture story gives you hope?

## Prayer Ritual

*Reading*

Jesus telling his disciples about his own transition and sending the Spirit to stand by his followers. (John 16:4–16)

*Process*

One person reads the following "givens" related to transition in a reflective manner:

- Change is ongoing.
- Change can include growth and growth is painful.
- Some change involves loss.
- When we experience loss and can express it, we can begin to grieve.
- One significant gift we can offer others is to accompany them on their journeys through change.
- We must acknowledge that people vary in their ability to accept change. Some are more flexible than others.
- Some do not want change. They want order. Change is experienced as a loss. For others, change is a challenge and provides new life.
- If there is trust in those leading people through change, they will move through it more easily.
- How do we perceive change? Is it a loss, a time to grieve, a period of growth, an investment in the future?

Note: The same initial reading and process is used for all three of the options listed below.

*Option I:*

Give people a worksheet with these three questions and a space to write their reflections. Allow about 15 minutes.

    I.   Recall a significant transition in your life.

    II.  What losses were you aware of?

    III. What were the "pearls" you gained from the transition?

Once people have had a chance to reflect individually, ask them to choose a partner and share their story of the transition with that person and listen to the other person's story. Ask them to look for common elements or similar experiences.

Return to the large group and discuss as a whole the common elements associated with transition uncovered by the personal stories. Conclude with the closing found at the end of Option III.

*Option II:*

Identify a transition that is currently going on in the parish, whether a change in pastor, staff, council or among the parishioners. In the large group, ask people to list on newsprint or on a board any insights they have about the transition that is now going on. Examples might include:

It takes longer than I thought it would.

I wanted to control it but was unable to do so.

It takes a lot of energy.

One door closed but another opened.

In order for people to be able to accept changes in the parish, certain steps are necessary. Ask one person to read the following steps and summarize them on newsprint or on a board.

*To accept change, people need:*

- All the pertinent information related to the change.
- To believe the information. Many may deny the facts.
- Time to digest the change and talk about implications.
- To negotiate both parish and personal losses.
- To ritualize the losses in order to help with the grieving process.
- To be called to let go of the past and face the future.

Divide into small groups of 3–6 people each and discuss:

> Where are we in this transition process? Are we still in the ending phase? Are we in the in-between time, or have we moved into the period of new beginnings?

> What is one action which will help us deal creatively with this transition? Bring this action back to the large group for discussion.

> Return to the large group and share the insights and actions of the small groups. Conclude with the closing found at the end of Option III.

*Option III:*

This option is best done when there is a change of pastors. Begin with the opening reading and process. Allow people time to talk about what the transition experience has meant to them.

Give each person a blank piece of paper. Ask people to write a letter to the pastor who left, stating what they had wanted to say to him but were unable to do so. Tell them to say whatever they wish. The letters won't be delivered. When finished, each person folds the paper and gives it to a representative of the parish. This might be the new pastor or a staff or council person.

The letters are then burned as a ritual exercise of "letting go" of the past and facing the future with greater freedom and acceptance.

The group then talks about ways in which to welcome the new pastor. What rituals, symbols or gestures might be possible and fitting?

*Closing*

Conclude with the continuation of the scripture used at the beginning from John 16:17–20.

# CHAPTER SIX

# *Freeing Structures*

PARISHES ARE SYSTEMS. THEY ENDURE CHANGES IN LEADERSHIP, membership, environment, ethnicity, makeup and size. They have a structure that is sometimes known and articulated. More often it is a system that is a mystery to both leaders and people. How do things get done around here? Who decides what issues? What groups are related to what other groups? The organizational makeup that is written down on paper is rarely a description of what actually happens in a parish.

## *Uncovering the Real Structure*

We have helped parishes uncover the real structure with a simple exercise. We first list in the center of a large piece of newsprint the leadership groups in the parish. These include the pastor, staff, council and any other groups or committees associated with the leadership. We then list around the sides all the groups, organizations and ministries that are going on in the parish. This includes lectors, servers, scouts, women's club, soup kitchen, religious education teachers, money counters, every recognizable group. We then ask the assembled staff, council and leaders, about 30 people in all, to connect the groups and ministries as each is related to the parish as a whole. What we discover is that many organizations and ministries are free-floating. They operate on their own and have no connection with anything or anyone else. Many others bypass the council or its committees and plug into the parish directly through the pastor or one of the staff members. Even the connection between the council and staff is hazy. "It's more of a dotted line than a solid one," one of our participants once remarked. As the exercise continues, we can see the leaders' awareness being raised. Many times they themselves, the ones who know the parish best, have no idea how it all fits together. When we finished in one parish, the pastor had to admit that all the important groups and all the important decisions passed directly to him. He had thought of himself as a collaborative pastor, and in many ways he was, but the structure diagram was an eye-opener to him. It confirmed what others on the staff were trying to tell him for some time: he's the boss.

In another parish, many of the lines coming from groups and ministries were connected to the pastoral associate. Her husband remarked as he saw the diagram developing, "I've been trying to tell her that the whole parish rests on her shoulders but she didn't believe me." It turned out to be a moment of insight for the pastoral associate and an occasion of growth for the leaders as a whole.

In a third parish, the exercise revealed a structure that bypassed the council and operated as a collection of "do-it-yourself" committees and subgroups. The council members began to exclaim, "No wonder we have such a hard time finding people to run for the council. We're not connected to anything else in the parish."

This is the first step towards establishing a freeing structure for the parish. After we did this exercise in a parish that called us in to help restructure the pastoral council, the pastor exclaimed, "We're not just restructuring the council, we're restructuring the whole parish!"

## The Parish As System

That is what happens when we begin to view the parish as a system of interconnected individuals, groups, ministries and organizations. Touch one part of it and the whole system is affected. That is what gives us hope that a new way of being parish is just ahead, perhaps is already here. A number of the parts in the system are being changed at this very moment. There are not enough priests to go around so tasks once done by the ordained are shifted to other staff members and parish volunteers. Parishioners who have volunteered to do various parish ministries are seeking extra training and are being hired on as staff members. Council members are learning how to share their wisdom together as a group. They no longer vote on issues but come to a consensus. Parishioners themselves are coming forward to be greeters and readers and communion ministers. Groups of people are spending their summers working in a sister parish in the central part of the city or in another country. The parish is sharing staff and school resources with other neighboring parishes. The system is being changed from bottom to top.

As this happens, two options lie open to the leadership. They can try to stand firm and keep the status quo. Eventually the changes will happen to them. Or they accept the inevitable and start taking a more active part in the changes that are happening to the parish system.

Over the last 10 years, we have been helping parishes restructure themselves in ways that utilize the best aspects of their own system. After helping the leadership uncover the existing structure through an exercise described above, we then help them cluster ministries, organizations and groups into a few recognizable categories. These usually center around areas of worship, formation, community building, administration and outreach. Each area is coordinated by a mini-council of volunteers which oversees that aspect of ministry in the parish. This mini-council includes a staff person who acts as a resource and a help to its work.

## Gathering of Ministers

The way these mini-councils are formed is through a gathering of ministers. Once a year all the people involved in any area of ministry or belonging to any parish group come together to size up what has happened over the year and to set a direction for the coming year. They gather as a single group for common prayer and orientation. They then divide into ministry groupings. All those involved in worship go to one area, all in formation to another. The same is true for the remaining three or four clusters of ministry.

If one person is involved in more than one area, then he or she must make a choice. "What do I want to concentrate on for the coming year?" This provides a vacuum for others to pick up the slack and get involved. It often happens that people who are not volunteers see the active ones doing such a good job that there is no need for them to get involved. "I couldn't get up and read as well as Jim does." "I could never teach fourth graders anything." "I would not know what to say if I brought communion to a sick person." If no one is there to fill in the vacuum, however, then people do come out of the woodwork to give of their time and share their gifts. This is one advantage of a yearly gathering of ministers. It forces people to refocus their efforts and provide room for new volunteers.

Once people gather in ministerial clusters, they share stories and offer suggestions about new directions for the coming year. Half of the people on each mini-council, (parishes call them commissions, committees, boards or teams) retire and new people volunteer to take their place. The total number on each mini-council varies from 5–12 people.

It is from these mini-councils that people are nominated to run for the parish pastoral council. Each year, two or three people are selected to represent one area of ministry on the council. The parish as a whole then has the opportunity to choose which one will be on the council for the next two years. Some parishes hold elections. Others are discovering that an alternate form of selection, one that takes place at the weekend Masses, works better. At each of the Masses, the three candidates for each area of ministry come forward and choose lots to see who will be on the council.

This is a process similar to that used in the early church as described in Acts 1:26.

More and more parishes are finding this to be a freeing structure. Each area of ministry has its own coordinating group, as does the parish as a whole, through the pastoral council. We originally described this structure in *Leadership in a Successful Parish* (Sheed & Ward, 1992, pp. 117–71) and have found it has held up well in many different types of parishes, both large and small.

## Sharing Wisdom

Three essential elements keep this system alive and functioning well. One is an underlying way of operating called a "Shared Wisdom" approach. Sr. Mary Benet McKinney, a Benedictine prioress from Chicago, wrote a book called *Shared Wisdom* (Tabor Press, 1986). In it she describes two ways of making parish decisions.

One is a parliamentary model in which people come together to decide important matters. The problem is analyzed, people line up on both sides of the issue, a vote is taken and the matter is decided. Well, not entirely.

Go out to the parking lot or tap into the phone lines and listen to the conversations. "Was I angry! I didn't say anything, but . . ." "I'm never going to open my mouth again, it never does any good." "How come we're always on the short end of the stick?"

What happens when another matter is put to a vote? The politicking and jockeying for power is more intense. Emotions and anger and tensions run high. Finally, someone or some group, usually those "in authority," call a halt to the conflict by a show of power.

There is, however, an alternative to this parliamentary model, one that is being used more and more often in parish settings. This method avoids voting in which there are winners and losers. It stresses dialogue and consensus instead.

The Shared Wisdom model follows three steps: information— prayer—dialogue. When an important matter comes up for a decision, those affected by the decision are given a chance to provide input and give feedback.

We worked with a parish whose church had become too small for its membership. Population patterns had shifted in recent years so that the parish was no longer centrally located. There was no question about building a worship site, but should it be on the present spot or at another location?

Before the leadership—staff, council and commissions working jointly together—came to a decision, they asked parishioners for their wisdom on the matter, both long-time parishioners and newcomers.

The second step, once all the pertinent information is gathered, is that the decision-makers spend time in prayer in order to come in touch with the movements of the Spirit within themselves, as well as the wisdom coming from the group as a whole. The predominant sentiment is, "What is God calling us to as a parish community in this matter?"

The decision-makers then talk about possible options and alternatives. This is where the sharing of wisdom is important. Everyone has a piece of the wisdom, but different pieces. No one has all the wisdom. If someone does not speak, then some wisdom is lost.

The dialogue continues until a solution that is acceptable to all is discovered. There are no winners or losers. The power of the group expands in the process because the power is in the group and not controlled by those in charge. In our example, the overall wisdom dictated staying put in the present location. It was owned by the people and not just by a few in leadership.

## *Covenant Booklet*

A second element that keeps this structure freeing is a covenant booklet. This document is common to all the mini-council and pastoral council members. Instead of a constitution written in stone, the covenant booklet is a loose-leaf notebook that contains these important sections:

1. The mission statement of the parish as a whole and the pastoral council's mission or purpose.
2. Long-range goal-statements for the pastoral council and for each mini-council. These goals should reflect the mission statement.
3. Criteria for membership on the pastor council and mini-councils.
4. The scope of activity for each mini-council and what groups come under each mini-council's ministry.
5. The timeline for when the gathering of ministers occurs each year, how and when the nominations and elections for the pastoral council takes place, the way new members are installed.
6. When and how the training of new pastoral council and mini-council members takes place.
7. The way meetings are conducted—the shared wisdom model, time for prayer and community building and rebonding.
8. Personal preparation for pastor, council and mini-council involvement, such as prayer time, reading, speaking up at meetings and listening skills.
9. Description of the decision-making process and how to solve conflicts when they arise.

10. The way the pastoral council funnels business items to the mini-councils asking for information, allowing the mini-councils to make decisions, holding them accountable.

It is a loose-leaf booklet so pages can be added or subtracted easily. It is called a covenant because it is the agreement that everyone in leadership, pastor included, makes with each other.

## Staff Resource

The third freeing element is staffing. Every mini-council has a staff resource person. The pastoral council itself has a staff representative, someone besides the pastor who serves as the link between the council and staff. The staff person acts not as the leader but as the resource to each mini-council. If the council members need help running a good meeting, need guidance in how to gather information about a new project, need insight into how to network groups, need options for setting goals or evaluating programs, the staff person is there to provide assistance, encouragement, expertise and support. The staff person also has the opportunity to carry back to the entire staff the plans and projects of each mini-council. A portion of each weekly staff meeting is set aside for discussion of the progress and concerns of each mini-council in the parish.

Structuring a parish by first networking together similar groups and ministries into clusters and then giving them direction through mini-councils is one way of fostering a system that is both freeing and spirit-directed. This may be only a pointer to a new way of being parish in the future. Other models may now exist or be found that work better. No parish, however, can operate without a structure. Otherwise, it flounders in a sea of possible options and varied suggestions like a ship without a rudder or a car without steering. It's bound for trouble.

In Chapter Four we discussed the difference between leadership and management. We described leadership as the interaction between leaders and people who intend real change. We also mentioned that all leadership and no management creates a parish that has great ideas for the future but no way of reaching its destination.

Discovering freeing structures for parish life is part of good management. So is keeping people happy who are involved in its ministries, as well as handling the inevitable power plays and conflicts that arise. Trying to put forth a good image or positive tone in the parish is also important. All of these are part of what it means to manage a parish well.

Suppose, for example, that you are a member of a parish staff—perhaps the administrator, director of religious education, liturgist, or pastoral associate. You have the responsibility for organizing, directing, and maintaining one aspect of parish life. What is the best way to go about it? How can you get the most out of your limited time, budget, and energy?

## Managing Structures

First you will want a plan of action and a framework for carrying out that plan. You sit down with people associated with your area of ministry, whether other staff members, teachers, volunteers, or ministers. You begin brainstorming ideas about what you want to accomplish in the ministry for which you are responsible. In the midst of the brainstorming, someone asks, "Why are we doing this ministry, anyway?" This is a wonderful question for any group to ask. In fact, if no one from the group asks it, you may want to raise the question yourself. It touches the underlying purpose or reason for the group's existence. You stop the brainstorming and spend time hammering out a statement of purpose. This provides an anchor for your plan.

From there you and your group work on specific goals for the next few years. You develop some signposts along the way to tell you whether or not you are still on the right track. You divide up the tasks and spell out the duties and action plans for each group or individual associated with your ministry.

For example, if you're the one in charge of liturgy, you help everyone agree about what kind of liturgies the parish should have over the next few years. You spell out what has to be done between now and then to reach the ideal. This may mean a new shift of emphasis in music, a way of providing feedback on homilies, the introduction of greeters, updating lectors, recycling eucharistic ministers. You make sure that every group associated with the liturgy knows what is expected and how each ministry fits into the whole plan for better, more responsive liturgies. In six months the planners reassemble to evaluate how well the plan is going. All this activity is associated with managing structures in a particular ministry.

Too often, however, when people think of management, managing structures is all that comes to mind. This, however, is only one-fourth of the distance one must travel to manage a parish well. Another fourth is directing the interaction among ministers.

## Managing People

Managing human resources includes helping people feel good about what they are doing. Managing "the workers" is paramount to keeping a parish and each ministry within it running smoothly. Human resources is about providing creative and productive working conditions for those carrying out the ministries. It means planning occasions for personal growth, greater commitment, and communication, fostering relationships and establishing a warm, supportive climate for parishioners.

A liturgist who is managing volunteers, for instance, is concerned about how the choir members are getting along with each other, whether the lectors are given enough support and affirmation, if the ushers feel valued now that they have to share some of their tasks with the new greeters, and that the Eucharistic ministers know where to pick up their schedules.

Suppose a volunteer comes up with a new way of doing a job. A good parish manager will want to affirm the person and, if appropriate, free up some of the liturgy budget to see the idea through. If individuals are under a strain or are confronting difficult issues, a manager of human resources gives them time off, throws a party, sends them helpers. The one in charge takes time to celebrate jobs well done rather than moving on immediately to the next task. All this is done in order to keep parish ministries running smoothly by keeping the workers and participants happy in their work.

## Managing Politics

Too often people working in church-related groups forget about politics. They forget that whenever there are limited resources, the temptation is to compete with one another over them, trying to wrest from competitors as much as possible for one's own work or ministry. The rhetoric of cooperation and sharing resources sounds lofty, but the reality is not unlike the competition and powerplays found in business, government and sports. "How much can we get for our team?" "Who has the power and influence?" "How can we get on their good side?"

Managing a parish well means managing the politics of parish life. The first place this comes into play is in dealing with the institutional church. Say, for instance, that the diocese sets guidelines for your particular area of ministry. They are good guidelines but they don't always apply to the concrete situation in your parish. As a whole, you follow them, but once in a while you bend the rules to fit the situation. You figure out how to guide your ministers around a sticky area, allowing the guidelines to remain unchallenged while also meeting people's needs. That's managing the politics of ministry.

Imagine that a conflict flares up between groups under your care. For instance, some of the most experienced teachers want to keep using tried-and-true textbooks, while other teachers would like to try a fresh approach along with new texts. Before the conflict gets out of hand, you call a meeting of the teachers and together work out a compromise. You are managing the politics of religious education.

The budget is going to be cut back. Staff members are starting to jockey for positions as they foresee a scarcity of resources for the coming year. At the next staff meeting you, as the administrator, give everyone the facts about what will be available so that there are no misconceptions. You assure people that there really is enough for everyone if people work together and do not build separate kingdoms or conflicting camps. In this way you start rebuilding trust and establishing calm amid the panic. Tensions relax and people begin thinking creatively about sharing resources. That's managing the politics of scarce resources.

Suppose the pastor is a wonderful man but he is not consistent. He talks about collaboration and partnership and really believes he is living it out in his pastoring. You see a different reality: he still controls the purse strings, has the final say about most areas of the parish, and subtly manipulates staff interaction-allowing some self-disclosure and airing of feelings, but only to a point.

As a staff member, you reduce some of your expectations and decide to live within realistic boundaries. You had hoped for more, but it won't happen here, not for the present pastorate, at any rate. The pastor is a loving, dedicated person, fun to be with and easy to know. So you manage your pastoral expectations and concentrate on what is possible, rather than on what you had hoped would happen.

Managing parish politics provides a realism and peacefulness in the midst of what could be an impossible situation. "Be clever as serpents," says the Lord. It does not make managing a parish easy, but it does make it less stressful.

## Managing Image

How well a parish or area of ministry manages its image through sign, symbol, ritual, and storytelling is important. If people are aware of and feel good about their parish, they tend to support and take part in its programs, projects, and services. That doesn't happen by chance. It must be planned and managed.

Perhaps the Mass in the downstairs chapel is not drawing the crowds it once did. The contemporary music is as good as it always was, the occasional dialogue homilies are still well-received, the level of participation is still well above what it is in the main church upstairs. But the image is getting tarnished. It is perceived as just for the young people, as having too many crying babies, and lasting too long. How does one change the image of that Mass to attract more parishioners?

Parish leaders meet to discuss the issue. Together they uncover the problem of "image" and devise a two-month plan of positive image-building. Since word-of-mouth works best in the parish, they begin by asking people who come to Mass in the downstairs chapel to "talk it up" with their relatives and friends, tell them how enjoyable this particular Mass is.

A special promotion of that Mass is focused around Fathers' Day. "Room for everyone at 10/50" is the slogan put on banners. Buttons with this saying are given out at Masses several weeks beforehand. The slogan means that the chapel has room for both young and old; it is not too crowded, as some who never came thought, and that Mass will start at 10 A.M. and will not last more than 50 minutes. A special insert in the bulletin describes the downstairs liturgy and promises free coffee and donuts on Fathers' Day. The goal of this promotion is to change the image of the downstairs' Mass by using signs, publicity, positive public relations, and storytelling.

Managing a good image is usually accomplished through nonrational, right-brain means. Notice how businesses sell their products through music, logos, suggestions, slogans and graphics. Jesus was a master at image-making through parables and stories. His actions made his image credible and attractive. Why not be imitators of Jesus by working on positive image-building?

In your parish you will have your moments of leadership, times when you and parishioners work together improving the status quo, creating new ministries, inspiring others with new visions and new directions. Much of parish ministry, however, is focused on management. This includes keeping programs and services alive, responding to people's needs, maintaining the faith community. Managing a parish is no easy task. It requires an ability to operate on many fronts at once—structures, human resources, politics, and image. It is not the whole answer to a successful parish, but it is an essential ingredient.

## DECISION-MAKING

One other aspect of freeing structures and good parish management is the way decisions are made. When we work with parishes we suggest five levels of decision-making, using the following exercise.

We ask the staff and lay leaders of a parish to list 5–7 examples of decisions that were made in the parish over the last six months, both large ones and small. The list might include such items as establishing a new staff position, starting a men's group, not having holy water at the entrance of church during Lent, forming a youth council, or buying a van for the seniors of the parish. We then present the five levels of decision-making described below. Once we finish, we ask each person to determine what would have been the ideal level for making each decision on the list. After doing this individually, we ask them to join together with two or three other persons and come to a consensus as to the best way to make each decision. When they have done this, we ask each small group to announce their results to the whole. This is matched with the way it actually took place. The ideal and the real often do not match. We'll provide a few examples later. First we will describe the five levels of decision-making.

### *Nitty-Gritty*

The first level is the simplest. We call it the "nitty-gritty" level. This means letting those who are responsible for a particular project, task or ministry make all the necessary decisions for that work. Stay out of their way as they do their ministry. No need to tie their hands so they can't do a good job. Give them the freedom to act and decide what's best. Tap into their wisdom and good judgment, in other words.

This sounds so simple, so logical, so obvious. It is not. Suppose a new music director is picking out songs for a parish anniversary. She gets suggestions from the choir and asks the priests and staff for ideas. When the event is only days away, the pastor suggests finishing the liturgy with "America the Beautiful." It's a lovely song but it doesn't fit the theme of the celebration. The anniversary booklets are already printed and ready to go. The first level of decision-making says, "Let the person in charge of that area of ministry make the decision." When the conflict arose, the music director had a talk with the pastor, explaining her dilemma. He saw the wisdom of her choice. She did agree, however, to use the hymn as an organ piece as the people were filing out of Mass. The pastor had to accept, however, that this was a nitty-gritty decision that belonged to the music director and not to him.

Pastoral councils often misunderstand their role as policy-setters and visionaries. They love to get their hands into issues that have nothing to do with them.

The youth group wants to go on a canoe trip. Some of the council members hear about it and wonder if it is a good idea. As parents of youth club members, they might question the youth director about safety issues or proper supervision. As council members, however, they should keep clear of this issue. It is a nitty-gritty matter for the youth group and its leaders to decide. It is not a council decision. If there are complaints made about how the trip is organized or carried out, then the council may need to hold the youth group accountable, but the original decision about whether to go on a canoe trip does not belong to the pastoral council.

## Voting

The second level of decision-making deals with smaller matters that require a vote of confidence or support from the group to which an individual or committee is responsible. We use the word "vote" on purpose because these matters are often settled with a show of hands or unanimous consent. A staff member is asked to research a place and date for the spring overnight. This is a yearly tradition at which the staff evaluates the year and sets up priorities for the coming months. He returns to the next meeting with a cottage on a lake that a parishioner is allowing the staff to use. The staff member also has three possible dates for the overnight. When the dates are proposed, people shift schedules and meetings until the group eventually votes on the best date. There is little emotion involved. It is a matter of what time is most convenient. The staff member feels affirmed in the work he did and the staff has decided as a group on a suitable date.

A subcommittee of the administration commission is given the task of gathering information about the best computer network system to install in the parish office. They do their homework and submit a recommendation as to which system will do the best job for the least amount of money. The administration commission looks over the report, decides that the proposed system meets all their requirements and votes to go along with the recommendation. This is a vote of confidence and support for a job well done.

## Consensus

Suppose, however, that the system the committee recommended was made by IBM. One of the persons on the administration commission is married to a person who submitted a rival bid. A few others on the commission are aware of this and are sympathetic to using "our own people." The vote is taken. It becomes obvious that it is no longer a vote of confidence and support. There is a division in the results and with it some obvious emotion. The matter can no longer be considered a level two decision. It jumps to level three, that is, to the level of consensus. Whenever those leading a meeting notice comments or body language that bespeak emotion, frustration or anger, then it is time to call a halt to the proceedings and ask the group to come to a consensus. This level of decision-making takes time and effort. Alternatives must be sought out and discussed, pros and cons explored, sources of emotion sought out. The group might even have to spend some quiet time in prayer and reflection as mentioned earlier in connection with the shared wisdom method of operating.

Certain requirements are necessary in order for a group to arrive at a consensus. First, the individuals must be willing to be guided by the Spirit and the wisdom of the group. Before they deal with the issue at hand, they must be willing to let go of their own vested interests and seek what is best for the parish as a whole. This is a difficult step because it demands much detachment and a high level of spirituality.

Secondly, people must have the freedom and the patience to explore alternatives until one is found that everyone can accept and support. The result may not be anyone's first choice. It does have a better chance of succeeding, however, because it is "owned" by everyone present.

We were working with one parish that was trying to decide on a new structure for the pastoral council. The group had narrowed the choices down to two. One was a council of ministries that operated out of a commission or mini-council structure described earlier. The other was a discernment council structure in which a few people were picked by the parish to be the discerners for the future with no connection to parish groups or ministries. We went around and around with the leaders, trying to come to a consensus. Time was running out and we had to catch a plane. Finally, the few people who were holding out for a discernment council were able to explain their concerns in such a way that the others could understand and incorporate those ideas into the proposed council of ministries structure. The process of coming to a consensus took almost an hour. All the details of who was going to do what to implement the new structure had not yet been discussed.

To our surprise, once a consensus was reached, all the tasks that needed to be accomplished for implementation were handled in only a few minutes. Volunteers came forward, jobs were defined and commitments to a timeline settled upon in record time. Why? Because by this point everyone had a much clearer idea of what the new structure would look like. They had been explaining it to each other for the previous hour while they struggled to come to a consensus.

What this experience taught us is that the effort spent at the information-gathering and decision-making stages is not lost time, no matter how long it takes. The implementation phase will happen much quicker and with greater commitment because everyone feels part of the decision and has greater ownership in the process.

When the administration commission had to stop and handle the decision about a computer network system, many were impatient to move on. Instead, the co-leaders of the meeting sensed the emotions of the group and tabled the rest of the agenda to leave time for this decision to be handled by consensus and not a show of hands. When people started to discuss the pros and cons of each system, it became evident that a combination of IBM and the local system might result in a better solution. The discussion and eventual consensus on a third option made the group feel happy with the result and gave the parish a better system. Consensus takes time and effort but the end result is usually better because of the discussion and probing for alternatives that it prompts. Consensus is the third level of decision-making. It need not be used in every situation. See if a nitty-gritty or a vote of confidence can be used instead. If not, if emotions are still present and a majority opinion will cause a division in the group, then clear the decks, set aside the agenda and settle down to a consensus form of decision-making.

## Problem-solving

The fourth level of decision-making is used when there are no options from which to choose. All that is present is a problem. The roof leaks, we're in the red, our church is too small, we don't have enough teachers, it's raining on our picnic. What are we going to do? This is when problem-solving, the fourth level of deciding, comes into play. It follows the five steps *Need, Ideal, What Now, Options, Choose the Best.*

The first step for problem-solving is to agree on the *need*. This is a difficult path for Americans to follow. We usually start with solutions, not needs. If the school is costing too much, close it. If the church is too small, build another. If it's raining, cancel the picnic. We jump to solving the problem before we spend enough time searching out what is really needed.

A parish staff called us in to figure out what to do about not enough space for activities in the parish. They wanted to build a new parish center. "Are you sure that's what's needed?" we asked. They were taken by surprise by our question. We then helped them formulate what they considered was the real need, not the solution. Community-building and faith-formation were the needs. There was no place for people to gather together and get to know one other. Nor was there space for people to learn about their faith. Once they agreed that these were the real needs, other options began to surface as a way of meeting the need. Fostering small groups in people's homes, for instance, might accomplish the same results. Eventually the parish did construct a new center but it had a different design because of our discussion around what were the needs in the parish.

Another parish was struggling with why so few people came to activities, why everyone rushed out of church when Mass was over, why the atmosphere was so cold among the parishioners. After talking about the problem for a while, the leaders finally agreed that the real need was to offer people more opportunities to get to know each other. That refocused the issue so that they were no longer emphasizing what was wrong with the people. Perhaps there was something wrong with what the parish was offering.

If a group can agree on what is the real need, they are over half-way to solving the problem. Often people who come together to settle an issue are trying to find solutions to different needs. In the example of people rushing out of Mass, some thought the need was better gathering space after Mass, others felt the need was to confront people on their coldness, still others wanted to offer more socializing activities. None of these got at the heart of the matter. What was needed was a more welcoming and friendlier spirit in the parish. How could they accomplish that?

Before offering ideas, the next step in the problem-solving process is to picture the *ideal* if the need were met. What would be happening in the parish if it were a more welcoming, friendlier place? When we get to this step in the process, groups come alive. They have no trouble coming up with a description of the "new" parish. "We would have to change our Mass schedule because so many people were staying afterwards to talk to each other that it would get in the way of the next Mass." "The greeting of peace would last half an hour." "The money would come rolling in because so many people would be enjoying our Masses and socials." "We'll have to enlarge our church because of all the new people coming into the parish." These were some of the comments people made as they envisioned the ideal. This step gets people thinking creatively and gives them something to shoot for. It broadens their horizons.

After expanding their vision, the next step is to ask what the parish is doing *now* that is helping it reach the ideal. This is an important step because it helps people realize that they don't have to start from ground zero. One parish was trying to deal with the need of making social ministry, especially care for the poor, more present to parishioners' minds. When they started listing what was going on now, they discovered there were many groups and organizations working on social concerns in the parish. These groups were all working on their own little project, mostly hidden from one another and unknown in the parish as a whole. This insight helped focus the response to the need of making social ministry more visible. All that had to be done was to publicize what was already happening and encourage existing groups to be more collaborative in their efforts at working more closely together.

Agreeing on the need, envisioning the ideal and stating what is happening now all lead to the fourth step in problem-solving. This step focuses on thinking up all the possible *options* for meeting the need and realizing the ideal. These are alternatives that take the parish beyond what it is now doing.

The staff that had the need for more space to do community building and faith-formation listed many more options than just a new parish center. Meeting in homes, renting space in a local school, sharing space with other churches, rearranging current meeting rooms, changing the Mass schedule, all were ideas on their options list.

The parish that wanted to become more friendly had a long list of possible options. One that struck their interest the most was a suggestion by one of the Catholic school teachers. She said that the school children pick a name of a fellow student to be a secret friend to for a month. During the month, wonderful things happen as the children outdo one another in doing something nice for their secret friend.

We are now at the fifth and final step in problem-solving. From the list of possible alternatives, the group picks the one idea that looks the *best* to them, the one that has the best chance of meeting the need, the one that gets people's juices going, the one they would like to work on for the coming six months to a year.

As the leaders looked over their list of possible options for improving parish friendliness, they hit upon the secret family idea. On a given Sunday all those who wanted to take part put into the collection basket not only their envelope but a card listing birthdays and anniversaries, along with their name, address and phone number. The next weekend, everyone who put in their name the previous weekend pulled out the name of their secret family. For the next three months, they did nice things for their secret family. At the end of three months everyone came together for a potluck in order to identify themselves and tell stories about their experience.

When the leaders introduced the idea, they were amazed by the response. Almost everyone who came to church put a card in the collection basket. Over the next few months, the parish was a much friendlier place. One teacher sent a pie to her secret family by way of an eighth-grade boy. After a few days, when he didn't say anything about what had happened, she discovered that the pie never reached its destination.

A second attempt, with a new deliverer, worked better. Another family called on the home of an elderly couple to sing happy birthday to the wife. They had bags over their heads so as not to be recognized. When the husband answered the door and explained that his wife was out, they sang happy birthday to him instead.

At the end of the three months, the participants came together for a celebration. Unfortunately it rained and everyone was forced into the parish hall that was too small for the crowd. The experience solved more than the need for improving community spirit. It uncovered another need as well, that there was not enough space for socializing in the parish.

## *Discernment*

The fifth level of decision-making is discernment. This is reserved for the weightier matters that affect the whole parish. These might include renovating the sanctuary, closing the school, building a new facility, changing the Mass schedule. Such issues involve the vested interests of a large percentage of the membership. Those affected by the decision need to be included in the decision-making process.

Discernment needs a focus. The leadership cannot go to the parishioners and ask them what they think about a particular issue. The leaders must focus the need and provide the people with a tentative solution. This focusing is accomplished by using the problem-solving method described in the fourth level of decision-making. One pastor wanted to ask his people about renovating the interior of the church. He assembled a committee and together they came up with a tentative plan. He went to the people and during each Mass on two consecutive weekends he walked around the church and described what the new plan included. He made clear to the people that nothing had been settled. It was still undecided. He provided each household with a packet of information about the plan, the reasons behind the renovation and the costs involved. Over the next two weeks the pastor asked parishioners to pray over the issue. He asked them to write down on the sheet in the back of their packets all the reasons *against* renovating the church. He invited them to pray over their insights, asking God to guide the parish through this decision. They were encouraged to talk about their ideas with their friends and neighbors.

After the two weeks were up, he once again talked at all the Masses. He now invited people to write down all the reasons *for* the renovation, even if they didn't think it was a good idea. At the end of the month, he asked people to look over their list of reasons for and against. If they were to make the decision, what would it be? He invited them to use the card in the pews which asked, "Do we renovate, yes or no? Give one reason for your answer." He then explained that all the cards would go to a discerning group. These were people made up of a few staff and council members, as well as a few well-trusted people in the community. He asked the parishioners to pray over the discerning group that stood before the assembly at each of the Masses. The pastor explained that the cards were not a vote but a way of letting the discernment group know the ideas and wisdom of the congregation.

When the discerners looked over the cards, they discovered that an overwhelming majority favored the renovation. It surprised the pastor to receive so much affirmation and support. He thought more people would have trouble with the change. The only concern voiced by some of the respondents was the plan to put the statue of St. Thomas outside in the entrance to the church. Once he assured them that it would be winterized and protected from damage, the people warmly accepted the decision of the discerning group and the parish proceeded with the renovation

The steps in the discernment process include:

1. Focus the need and tentative solution through a problem-solving-method.
2. Attempt to free people from vested interests by inviting them to pray that the parish might follow God's will and desire in this issue.
3. Give people all the information from which they can make an informed decision.
4. Start with asking people to list all the reasons *against* the proposed solution. Only then ask for the reasons *for*. This gets out the negative emotions and frees people to see the other side more clearly.
5. Explain that people are not voting on the question but are giving their wisdom to a discerning group. This matter will not be decided by a majority vote, in other words.
6. Realize that the people's results are likely to be split and many parishioners may not even take part. This is not an indication of disfavor. It often means that they are praying for a good result and trust the discerners to come up with a good decision.
7. Pay attention to the reasons people give for their response. This may point to a new alternative not thought of previously.
8. Have the discerners submit a tentative decision to the parish and see what reaction this creates. If a groundswell of discontent occurs, then the discernment process is not finished. We have never had this happen, however. Instead, people are usually happy with the results and offer their support and financial backing to the project.
9. Celebrate the result as an entire parish. The conclusion is not only a decision well made but a triumph of shared wisdom over individual preferences and vested interests. On one occasion, a woman who was against the proposed moving of a parish school had to admit when the final decision went against her wishes, "It really is

the best solution for the parish. I just happen to live closer to the old site and this will mean a little longer drive in picking up my children. As I look at it now, I'm very happy with the final result. I never thought I would say that."

The discernment process can also be used for subgroups in the parish. For example, one staff we worked with spent a whole day going through a discernment model just among themselves, trying to come up with reasons against or for hiring either a liturgy director or adult education minister. In the end they decided that no new position was necessary at that time. All that was needed was a rearrangement of jobs for the current staff.

These are the five levels of decision-making: nitty-gritty, voting, consensus, problem-solving and discernment. In the exercise we described earlier, in which we ask groups of three to come to a consensus as to which level would be the best for recent parish decisions, people discover that much depends on which decision-making group people had in mind. For example, in trying to decide what level to use in establishing a new staff position, if it is viewed from the council's vantage point, it is a nitty-gritty for the staff to decide. Others thought that perhaps the council should give a vote of confidence once the staff submitted a recommendation. Seen from a staff perspective, however, it should be handled either through consensus or problem-solving, once the needs of the staff and the parish are uncovered.

## C-D-I

The missing ingredient in applying the five levels of decision-making is what we call C-D-I. So important is this concept to creative decision-making that one parish staff had sweatshirts made up with these letters spelled across the front. C-D-I stands for Consult-Decide-Inform.

When any decision comes up, the distinction must be made between those who are the actual *deciders,* those who are being *consulted before* the decision is made and those who should be *informed after* it is decided but before the decision is implemented. In the level five discernment process described above, the parishioners need to know that they are being consulted. They are not the deciders. The discernment group of 5–10 people are the actual deciders. This frees the leadership from having to take a vote on deciding matters by the majority. The parishioners also have to be assured, however, that they are being consulted before any decision has been made. They are not merely being informed of an already-settled issue, in other words.

This is so simple a concept but one that is profound in its execution. If the pastor, staff, council and subgroups can distinguish between who are the deciders, who needs to be consulted beforehand and who needs to be informed afterwards, they will save themselves much grief and miscommunication.

Examples abound. A liturgy committee thought it would be a good idea to change the place of adoration following Holy Thursday's services in Holy Week. It was their decision to make. They did consult the pastor about it and he gave his okay. A brief announcement was made at Mass prior to the event. The result was not pretty. The space was far too small for all who showed up for adoration. It was too hot with all the lights and candles burning. Some of the old-timers were angry at not being "consulted" about the change.

The breakdown was on both ends. The liturgy committee didn't consult enough people beforehand. The pastor was not enough in touch with the logistics to know it would not work out. Other staff members, a few active parishioners, even the sacristan could have alerted the deciders about the problem, had they been consulted. They were, however, only informed afterwards. On the other end, there was not enough communication about the change and the reasons for the shift. The people were not given time to make adjustments and settle into this new approach.

We mentioned earlier the example of buying a van for senior citizens. Who are the deciders, the finance committee, the senior citizens themselves, the outreach commission, the pastor? When we brought this up to a group of leaders, many yelled out, "The pastor!" "Why?" we asked. "Should he be the only decider in the parish?" After some discussion the pastor was relegated to a consultant. The actual deciders were those whose job it was to see to the needs of the seniors. In this parish it was the Parish Life Commission. Those who needed to be consulted *beforehand* included the finance committee to see if there was money for it, the seniors to see if they would use it and the local government to see if there were any regulations related to the transportation of the elderly. Those who needed to be informed *after* the matter was decided included the council to get their support and to settle issues related to what other groups could use the van, other parish groups and activities as to the van's purpose and, of course, the parishioners as a whole so they could appreciate what was being done for the elderly in the parish. Whatever parish we work with, we can never stress enough the need to clarify the C-D-I of decision-making.

We are still in search of new ways for being parish in the next century. Whatever the outcome, it will have to address the three issues raised in this chapter.

1. What structure will it have and how will all the groups and ministries relate to each other? How will the structure vary according to the locale and makeup of the membership? 2. How will it manage itself, utilizing its physical resources and people power? 3. How will decisions be made so that people feel they are consulted before a matter is decided, that they are partners in the decision-making process when appropriate and that they are well-informed about present events and future directions in the parish?

## Questions for Review and Reflection

*Parish As A System*

Draw a picture of your parish structure. Draw it as it presently exists, not as the organizational chart "says" it is. Connect all the groups and ministries as each relates to the parish. Do you have a number of free-floating organizations and ministries? Who is responsible for them? Is there a staff person connected to the various ministries? Where does the council fit in? What does the diagram tell you about the way things happen in the parish?

*Managing Structures*

How do people get on the council? Do they have any experience with the structure before they become part of the council? What type of orientation takes place? Is there a common booklet that every council and committee member has that describes the "way we do things around here"? Does the parish do a better job at managing structures and people than it does managing politics and image? What areas need more work?

*Decision-Making*

Identify three recent parish decisions. Using the five levels of decision-making, which level would have been the best way to handle these decisions? How were they actually decided? Was it clear who were the deciders, who needed to be consulted beforehand and who informed afterwards?

# Prayer Ritual

*Music*

   "Choose Life" by Carey Landry (Phoenix: NALR, 1979)

*Reading*

   Ask two people to read the following poem, alternating stanzas. The group as a whole repeats the following phrase after every other stanza of the reading:

   *"I came that you might have life and have it more abundantly."* (John 10:10)


   "In Search of Freeing Structures"


   About the teasing and timing
   Of collaborative ministry,
   The image forlorn and focused;
   A circle is seen but not unclosed.

   There is some dialogue and disagreement
   To close it or not to close it,
   Reweaving and rebirthing
   Some yes and some no.

   Opposite and polarities
   The Church narrowed, neat, known.
   Painful it is
   Plain to see and hear.

   But so too compassion
   The cross and coming
   To create anew
   That we might have life.
   Room for the Spirit
   The spirit of each person.
   Affirmed and included in wisdom
   No one in the center, no one to close off.

   Asking not once but twice.
   Hearing and seeing not once but twice.
   Defining and drawing the structure
   Not once but many a time.

All are invited and gifted
Being there, partner-like
Announcing that we might have life.

The new place freeing
Letting go of the past
And creating tomorrow
Not once but many a time.

*Process*

Prepare beforehand five flash cards, each 8 ½ x 11 inches, that have the following words on them:

Card One:              DEFINITION                    In A Phrase
Card Two:              SUPPORT                         In A Word
Card Three: DISTRIBUTION OF AUTHORITY     In A Color
Card Four:            COMMUNICATION         In A Body Sculpture
Card Five:            DECISION-MAKING              In An Image

Divide the people into small groups of 4–6 each. Keep them in the same room but spread them around the room, giving each group room to maneuver. All should remain standing. Ask each group to think of a *staff* model and a *team* model of structure. Then flash the first card before the groups and ask them to come up with a definition of *staff* and a definition of *team,* but using only a phrase. Allow them one minute to caucus among themselves, and then call time and ask each group for their phrase defining staff and team. Do the same for the other four flash cards. Have the groups describe support on a staff and support on a team, using only a single word. The card that asks for a body sculpture means that the group as a whole must provide a common bodily figure or statue that describes how a staff and how a team communicates.

Once the exercise is completed, gather as a single group and talk about what happened to the participants in the process. What did they discover, in other words?

*Closing*

Repeat the scripture used at the beginning: "I came that you might have life and have it more abundantly." Conclude with the refrain from "Choose Life."

# CHAPTER SEVEN

# *Searching for Meaningful Liturgies*

AS WE CONTINUE OUR SEARCH FOR A NEW WAY OF BEING parish, one focus must be the weekend liturgies. This is the one place most Catholics experience church. For many it's the place they'll encounter God's Word in Scripture. This is the place they satisfy their obligation as Catholics of weekly Mass attendance. What will give these people meaning? What type of worshipping ritual will stay with them throughout the week and influence their daily choices and life direction, foster more loving relationships and challenge their business decisions?

Before ritual comes faith, something to believe in. This is the glue that holds the local church together. For a Christian it is faith in the Risen Christ. Those attending church believe in a reality beyond themselves, a mystery that shapes and gives meaning to our lives. This touches into the underlying spirituality described in Chapter Three. One expression of a spirituality which includes the personal, communal and social aspects is the celebration of Christ in the Eucharist. People need to spend time together listening to how God has dealt with our world throughout the ages and continues to interact with it at the present time.

Jesus is the focus of this history. He asked his followers to gather for a special meal of presence, a manifestation of his presence in the break-ing of the bread. This is called table-ministry: faith-filled people gathered together in Jesus' memory, in Jesus' presence, to offer a thanksgiving prayer to our Creator, Parent, Father/Mother, Source of Being, whatever metaphor of God speaks best to people. No matter the term, the reality is the same: people coming together to acknowledge God as the source of life and meaning, and acknowledging Jesus as present in a variety of modes, but especially in the consecrated bread and wine.

Who is going to gather the believing people together? A presider, someone who is able to draw out the best in people, draw out the Spirit. This must be a person the believers can accept as one who sets them free to worship God in their midst, one who can challenge them in both word and example to be a Gospel people.

The leader not only gathers the people together but creates a conducive environment and structure for the gathered people to hear and reflect on God's Word and action in the world. The leader not only guides people through a prayerful response to God's Word, but also leads them through the thanksgiving prayer and ritual actions of praise, petition, forgiveness and communion. These actions put the believers in contact with a long tradition of Eucharistic presence.

This is a great ideal. Unfortunately, many present weekend liturgical rituals are so structured that they lose significance. The core of liturgy is to provide a celebration of Christ's presence that stirs people's hearts rather than putting them to sleep. Because this isn't happening, large numbers of Catholics, especially the young, no longer attend Mass. Those who do come are lulled into a routine that is perfunctory and devoid of spark and enthusiasm. The involved and dedicated parishioners remain committed. They keep trying to find inspiration and meaning in the Mass. Even these highly-motivated ones sometimes lose heart in the deadly routine. How can the weekend liturgy once again become a source of nourishment to the parishioners, both old and young, the active and inactive alike?

## Anticipation

Part of the problem has nothing to do with the Mass itself. What happens before people come to church is the issue. Their lives are filled with rituals, ranging from sports events to television programs, from outings to gatherings of friends around a meal or card game, from celebrating birthdays and anniversaries to love-making. These are events people treasure and look forward to with relish. They provide enjoyment, relaxation, meaning and spark to their lives.

The pageantry associated with Super Bowl Sunday is one example. Watching the fireworks on the Fourth of July is another. People get ready for these events by baking special treats, making plans to gather together with friends. Plans are made months in advance. Both children and adults are filled with anticipation. These occasions are not nearly as important as what people bring to the events themselves. This is what heightens the enjoyment.

The same anticipation should apply to the celebration of the Eucharist. The Mass itself, however, cannot carry the burden of making it a meaningful experience. Much depends on what people bring to it from their own lives. If the people, whether individuals or families, have a sense of anticipation that something good will happen, there is a better chance something good will happen, no matter how routine and staid the liturgy might be. Dressing up for Mass, putting on one's Sunday best, celebrating the event with a meal afterwards, thinking ahead about the significance of the Mass, reflecting afterwards about its impact on the week, all these gestures help make the liturgy more meaningful. It enhances what happens during the event itself.

Those people who, either individually or with others, have a chance to read over and reflect on the readings will get so much more out of the Word of God than those who hear it for the first time at Mass. What people bring out of their own prayer and heightened awareness not only helps them find greater meaning, it helps all those around them as well. Even the celebrant is aided by their interest and active involvement. Looking out over a congregation of stoic faces does little to spark the celebrant's motivation. Seeing people who appear attentive and interested in what's happening, on the other hand, raises up the level of the celebrant's enthusiasm. We call this the ministry of the "pew-people." They have a part to play in making the liturgy "work." The burden of success does not all depend on the liturgical ministers, the lectors, choir, greeters, readers, servers, Eucharistic ministers, ushers or celebrant. Much depends on the people themselves and to what extent they become involved in the service.

## Different Masses for Different Folks

This being said, much still does depend on the leaders for a worthwhile, life-giving, nourishing Eucharistic celebration.

Those who do come to Mass prepared and ready to celebrate can still have their enthusiasm dashed as they encounter a boring, predictable routine. Nothing is there to pique their interest or challenge their everyday lives. In a word, it's boring.

What can be done? One place to start is to attack the problem of routine. Every Mass on the weekend follows the same pattern of: song - prayer - reading - song - reading - alleluia - reading - homily - collection -long prayer - Our Father - shake hands - communion - announcements -song - leave. Nothing new, nothing challenging, nothing inspiring.

During a class on parish planning, we were helping students develop goals for different aspects of parish life. The group working on the weekend Masses could not come up with an inspiring, energizing goal for the liturgy. Then one person's eyes lit up and said, "What if we had as a goal, when people come out of church they are saying to one another, 'Wow, I want to come back to that!'" This is the kind of spirit that should be present at all the weekend Masses.

Regardless of which Mass people attend, there are some common aspects that need to be stressed to help people from becoming bored. The first requirement is *variety*. This is what makes Christmas, Holy Week and Easter so special. It is out of the ordinary. Can the same attention to creativity and ingenuity be given to the weekend Masses throughout the year?

People also need to feel there is a Mass they can go to that fits their needs and desires. In most parishes there is not much variety from one week to the next, or even among Masses on the same weekend. People say they like to keep things the same. "Don't change anything. I like what I'm used to." Often this is an excuse for not wanting to get involved or be challenged. What can be done to change the routine?

For starters, each Mass on the weekend could have a unique flavor, targeting different interests and ages. This allows more flexibility in planning liturgies. If people complain about one liturgy, they have the option to go to another with a different style or focus.

Liturgical planning committees find variety difficult, however. It is easier to keep all Masses uniform and make up one liturgical program for the entire weekend. This is easier for the planners and priests, perhaps, but not helpful for the participants. Having only one format means settling for the least-common denominator. Creativity is replaced by conformity. The result is routine which, in turn, fosters boredom.

Perhaps it is asking too much of one committee to plan all the liturgies. Each Mass may need its own planning committee. The committees could be coordinated by a worship commission. This allows for more people to get involved in planning liturgies. The best way to reduce boredom is by getting people to take an active part. Planning is one way to do this. If each weekend Mass had its own focus or style, then the options for overcoming routine will vary according to the particular flavor of each Mass.

The target group for the Saturday evening Mass, for instance, might be the teenagers, young adults, singles and newly-married parishioners. Some of the planners for this liturgy will have to be teens and young adults themselves. The music will be contemporary, the style more relaxed and informal, the symbols and images suited to young people. The ushers, ministers, lectors and greeters are geared toward the under-30 crowd. The priest will also have to adjust his style and presentation to fit the mood of the Mass. This Mass belongs to the young and not to the priest, in other words. It speaks their language and addresses their concerns.

The first Mass on Sunday morning will be entirely different. There will be fewer songs and more time for quiet contemplation. Here the target group is "morning" people, both old and young. The mood is subdued, with an emphasis on transcendence and contemplation. The presider and ministers adjust their style to fit the needs and desires of this group. For one thing, it will be shorter in length, yet creative in how the style of worship can lift people's minds and hearts. People who attend this Mass know what to expect. They choose it not out of convenience but because it fits their needs and expectations.

Depending on the makeup of the parish, the second Mass on Sunday morning might focus on families with young children. This Mass would be more active so as to help keep interest alive among little ones. Those 5–10 years of age are invited to a special liturgy of the Word and reflection while the parents remain in church for their own experience of the Word. Babysitting is provided for those who wish, but children are not discouraged from being part of the Mass if parents so wish.

Much attention is paid to parenting and coping with the pressures of married life, especially when both spouses are working outside the home. The strains of single parenting are also emphasized.

It is no news to anyone that family life is going through a transition in America. This Mass is geared toward helping parents and children through this transition. The priest and planners for this Mass will have to be attentive to the pressures families are undergoing and provide support and help during this weekly liturgical gathering of families.

The next Mass on Sunday morning might be more "high church" in tone. Ritual is stressed at this Mass so that those who desire a more formalized style of worship can have their needs met. The music at this Mass might be led by a choir with musical instruments for accompaniment. Special vestments could be used, along with processions and special rituals during Mass. These might include incense, sprinkling with holy water, a procession from the altar to the ambo for the Gospel, dismissing the catechumens after the homily, a formal entry and exit rite. All this is done as a way of helping people experience the majestic and regal aspects of the Roman Rite. It can lift people's minds and hearts in a way no other ritual can.

The last Mass on Sunday morning or early afternoon might be geared toward the less active and more marginal members. Keeping this group from becoming bored with Mass is the greatest challenge of the weekend liturgical planners.

One thing that might help is to view this Mass as unique and not just the last of many similar Masses on the weekend. What should be the special focus of this Mass? Perhaps simplicity and directness might be keys to its success.

The theme for the Mass must be well-focused and directed to fit people's needs. Over a given month the themes might include a sense of belonging vs. loneliness, dealing with addiction, coping with dependency, surviving the rat race of life in the fast lane, the "Me-First" generation. The best cantors of the parish should be used for this Mass as a means of stirring people's interest and involvement.

Humor and concrete examples should be stressed in the homily. Above all else, don't wear people out. Be brief and direct, providing just one thought or focus for the coming week. A deadline for finishing the Mass is essential so that people feel encouraged to return the following week. Special handouts or bulletin inserts might help, such as the *Catholic Update* series from St. Anthony Press. This is the only experience of Church and the only opportunity for adult formation most of these people will have. It needs to be well focused and to the point. Greeters and hospitality following the Mass also help people feel good about being a member of the parish, or to feel welcomed if they are not members. No one way of conducting the worship service, in other words, will fit every target group on the weekend.

## Sight and Sound

Such a detail as the sound system can make a world of difference in the way a Mass is celebrated. Protestant churches can teach Catholic parishes a great deal about providing strong, clear and recognizable sound systems at worship. When someone is reading or speaking or singing, all those present must be able to hear every word or note as directed to them personally. The sound must be able to get inside and move people. Mediocre sound means apathy and boredom from the participants. No amount of money spent on a good sound system will go unrewarded in the way people respond to what's happening at the worship service. Some parishes even have a "control booth" where the mixing of sound levels is continually monitored and changed so as to produce the optimal effect and clearest sound.

Conducive space is another key to good liturgy. The place people come together affects the gathering. Millions of dollars are spent on providing sacred space for worship, but churches often miss the mark. Wood, stone and brick won't do it. Neither will banners, hangings, flowers or streamers. These help but they are not the essence. Warmth, comfortableness, a balance between sacredness and friendliness are what count the most. This is what creates the qualities of good worship space. People must be able to come into church and immediately feel "at home" with their God and with one another.

Think of people's homes you have visited. Some are lovely places to visit but they don't look lived in. Everything is too fragile, too beautiful, too perfect, too "right." Think of other homes that you have visited, places where you feel you could kick off your shoes, settle into a comfortable chair and talk about what really matters to you. This is not unlike our experience of church environments. Some seem cold and indifferent, while others feel warm and inviting. We don't need museum pieces for our worship space. Europe is filled with empty church museums. The new paradigm for parishes must help people feel at home, as a place where they belong, instead of feeling like strangers or merely visitors.

This implies that the space for worship must be flexible in order to cater to a wide variety of tastes and interests. It must be prayerful so people can find a quiet place to talk to their God. At the same time, it must be informal so that when the community gathers together to worship, they feel comfortable enough to share their stories of God working in their everyday lives. Some churches have achieved this balance in their worship space. Most still have a long way to go in providing an environment where people can feel it belongs to them, a place where real liturgy can happen. It touches them, no matter one's inclination or background or desires.

The language used during Mass. is also important for good worship. Attitudes of the participants differ. Some are attuned to the use of nonsexist, balanced language, even for speaking about God. Others are not. This issue needs sensitivity and understanding so as not to alienate those who seek inclusive language or those who don't.

We are amazed, however, as we visit different parishes each weekend, how few have made an effort to correct the use of male pronouns in prayer and songs at Mass. In one parish, we even discovered a change *back* to noninclusive pronouns from a new hymnal that had balanced language. The excuse was that people were more familiar with the traditional songs with the old words. Unfortunately, some attending Mass were so distracted by the wording of the songs that they could not concentrate on the Mass itself.

We have heard many excuses for not making the language at Mass inclusive for both men and women. "The people are not ready for this yet," is one. This usually means the leaders are not ready themselves to make an effort to correct the language. Even such a simple change in the Nicene Creed from "all men" to "all" is a rare phenomenon in Catholic parishes.

Changing prayers and songs is not as problematic as changing scripture and language related to God. In these cases more dialogue and planning is necessary. It can no longer be ignored, however. Parishes in the third millennium will have inclusive language, that is a given. We need to prepare people now for this change. The place to begin is with the celebrants and liturgical ministers themselves. The parishioners are not the stumbling block. It is the resistance of the leadership that needs to be addressed.

Exposure to liturgies with balanced language is perhaps the best path to new awareness. This means visiting churches that are conscious of the need for inclusive language. Pay attention to how sensitive the celebrant is to addressing both men and women in the prayers, scripture and Eucharistic canons. Even the Sign of the Cross may include a reference to God as more than Father. God is Parent, Mother, Provider, Creator. The list of synonyms is endless. The worship service itself is enhanced when both men and women are included and the understanding of God is broadened.

Once people catch on to the significance of these inclusive, expressive words at Mass, they will begin to translate this understanding into their daily lives and personal prayer.

Worship is a reflection of people's lives. Language is one of many symbols that is used at Mass. It needs special attention so that it speaks the reality of what is taking place, that God is Creator, Redeemer and Unifier.

The issue comes to a head when a congregation begins praying the Lord's Prayer. This comes from a long tradition with many memories of the "Our Father." In some people's lives it is not unlike the ordination of women. "If Jesus wanted women priests, he would not have had only men for apostles," the argument goes. Times are changing, however. Our vision expands. New insights of what we are called to be as God's People is dawning upon us. So it is with this special prayer of Jesus. It becomes a manifestation of who we are and who is our God. Parishes of the next century will find the right expression. For now we search for an appropriate way to address our God, either as "Loving God" or "Our Father/Mother," "Creator God" or "Our Parent." This is more than an attempt to appease the protestor. It's a way of discovering what we are to become as God's people and how to address the One we worship at Mass.

## Touch Hearts Through Example

The ability to touch hearts is another ingredient of good liturgy. No amount of planning or good techniques will accomplish this. Only good example will do it. Those leading worship, whether singers, ministers, ushers, readers or presider, all must *live* the message and not just act it out. People are drawn out of their boredom if they experience the Spirit alive in their leaders and ministers of worship.

That is why the planners and liturgical ministers need to develop their own prayer lives. They need to gather for communal prayer and reflection on the weekend readings. They must spend time talking to one another about their ministry, what they themselves gain from it and how it helps others worship. It is this modeling that people remember more than what the ministers do or say at Mass. We experienced a blind person who read the first reading at one of the Masses we attended. He used his fingers to read the text and spoke it directly to the congregation. At one point, he hesitated for a moment, then came out with "Nebacanezzor." It made people smile but it had a great impact on them as well. They could see that the person was not just reading the Word, even though it was in braille. It made a difference in his personal life as well. It was not just words, it had a meaning for him and for all who were listening.

Imagination and creativity are also essential ingredients to good liturgy. The story at the beginning of Chapter Two described a liturgy in which people had a chance to share with one another how the Gospel affected their everyday lives. This worked because the people were prepared. It didn't catch them by surprise. As they left Mass the previous weekend, they were each handed a sheet that included the first reading and the Gospel, along with two questions that helped focus their reflection. The Gospel was on Jesus healing the paralytic that was lowered through the roof. One set of questions was "When have you felt closed out from the presence and healing powers of Jesus? What did it feel like and how long did it take before a path was opened up for you?" Another set asked, "Have you ever felt like Jesus, all hemmed in by people making demands on you? In the midst of this feeling, has a person ever come into your life from an unknown source? How did you react?" By the time people come to Mass and hear this Gospel read at Mass, they are ready to talk. They don't need the priest to say anything other than "Go to it." Quieting the group down for the rest of the Mass will be the problem. What a nice difficulty. So often it is just the opposite, trying to get people interested in the readings or stiffed up at Mass.

This is but one of a myriad of creative ideas that could be used at Mass to touch people's minds and hearts. So many options lie open to help parishioners encounter their God and one another. If each Mass on the weekend were to target a different group and emphasize a different style of worship, then there would be more leeway for creative options that appeal to the Mass's unique clientele. Music, gestures, symbols, pageantry, praying, responding, interacting, all can be adapted and changed to suit the needs and desires of the people attending a particular Mass.

The leadership at one parish we worked with wanted to have a ministry fair as a means of showing off to the parishioners all the groups, organizations and ministries that were taking place in the parish. They wanted to have it at a time and place where people would most likely attend. Before or after the weekend Masses was the most logical choice because that was when most of the people came to church. They were reluctant to do it outdoors because it might rain and ruin all the booths and displays. The school gym was the only other alternative but it was some distance from the church building. Then a light bulb went off in the group. "Have Mass in the gym so people will have to come and see our displays." The pastor was hesitant. "What about the older people? They'll never go for that."

Eventually he was persuaded and the event took place. As it turned out, it did rain on that weekend. Despite repeated notices and announcements, cars kept pulling up to the church wondering where everyone was. A big sign on the church door read "Mass in the school gym this weekend!"

"What's wrong with the church, is it being repaired or something?" people kept asking. Some parishioners had never been in the gym and didn't even know where it was or what it looked like.

In they came, hesitant and apprehensive at first, a sentiment matched by the pastor's own trepidation. But as each liturgy unfolded, one with a new children's choir, another with the senior choir, a third with guitars and a flute, the people, especially the elderly, became more relaxed and "at home." They stayed after Mass for coffee and refreshments and to look over the exhibits. Some of the old-timers asked the pastor if this was going to be a regular feature from now on. "Why," the pastor asked, "don't you like the change?" "Oh, no," they exclaimed. "This is such a good idea, we should do it more often." The pastor's mouth dropped open in surprise at the people's positive comments.

## Leadership in Liturgy

This brings up the issue of leadership. The way the presider calls people to prayer, forgiveness, petition, thanksgiving, and communion can either inspire them or put them to sleep. The leader is the key to worship, in other words. The priest can kill the spirit of a gathered community just as easily as bring it to life. People are so hungry for a personal touch that it doesn't take much to change bored, apathetic listeners into active, involved participants in prayer and worship. All it takes are simple gestures such as a warm greeting at the beginning, stepping from behind the ambo to reflect on the Word for the homily, smiling while distributing communion, encouraging people's participation in the singing and prayers; all of these help people come out of their shells and join with others in the celebration of the Mass.

This does entail large measures of creativity, self-confidence and risk-taking but it can be done. As we have already said, for most parishioners, their only experience of church is the weekend Masses. Fewer Catholics, especially the younger adults, are coming to church in recent years because it has nothing to offer them. This is such a waste and is so unnecessary. Twenty years ago the altar was turned around so that the priest faced the people. This shift signified that priest and people celebrated the Eucharist together. It is time to turn the Mass itself around, not just the altar, so that the people feel more encouraged and inspired by the liturgical celebration. How best to do this? One way is to put more of the ownership and initiative into the hands of the parishioners.

This is happening in many parishes to varying degrees. We encountered a church where one liturgy each Sunday morning took place in the school gym. What follows is no fantasy. It happened one January in a suburban parish outside a midwestern city.

For 20 years, parishioners had been taking turns planning the Sunday gym Masses. They had done their work well. After a number of years, however, they felt stuck in a rut. The parishioners enjoyed the Mass and the feeling of community around coffee and donuts that followed, but so much more was possible. What options did they have for putting more life into this Sunday morning experience?

They decided to initiate a "Liturgy and Life, Faith and Future" project that would carry them through the weeks between New Year's and Ash Wednesday. They asked us to help facilitate the planning process. What resulted from this concerted effort surprised us all and gave us hope that the weekend liturgy could be a creative and life-giving event.

The process began with a meeting of the planners, celebrants and music ministers to brainstorm ideas for the six weeks of innovation. All agreed that they wanted to discover new ways of being Church. They wanted to try out new options and establish new traditions. How could they help people get more out of the 10:00 AM Sunday liturgy?

First, they sent out to all parishioners, not just those who regularly attended the 10:00 AM Mass, a letter that outlined the project and invited everyone to attend. The committee prepared handouts and take-home materials. These included questions that would help people reflect on the Sunday experience during the week following the Mass and would prepare them for the next week's liturgy.

The 6-week period of innovation began in mid-January. When people arrived for the first Mass they were greeted in the vestibule and invited to take off their coats and boots and put on a name tag. Everyone obliged because they were aware that this Mass would be somewhat different from previous liturgies. They had been well-prepared in advance, in other words.

As people walked into the gym they noticed that the wall behind the portable altar had a 15-foot long, 3-foot high sheet of paper attached to it. The Gospel touched on the apostles discovering where Jesus lived and being invited to follow him on the faith journey. As an expansion on this theme, a long line was drawn on the paper. As part of the homily, people were invited to share their memories of significant events and important people that contributed to the life of the gym Mass community. They had been prepared in advance to think up key moments in the community's history so there was no lack of input.

After 15 minutes of "remembering," the Mass continued with a new awareness of how much of the Mass is a "remembering" of God's gifts and works, especially as manifested in the life of Jesus. At the end of Mass, during coffee and donuts, people were invited to add more events they remembered to the history line. They were also given take-home sheets and encouraged to do the same exercise with their families and loved ones in their own homes.

As people returned for the second Sunday of "Liturgy and Life, Faith and Future," they talked about how much they had learned from last week's history session. Many had more to add from their reflections during the week. The focus of the second Sunday was the extension of the history line into the future. What would the community be like in 5–10 years? What options were possible?

The Gospel was from the first chapter of Mark about the call of Andrew and Simon, James and John. A guest speaker from the diocesan liturgical commission talked about dropping some of the nets that held us captive, even ones related to liturgy, and to follow Jesus in new and challenging ways. The following month's Masses would provide an experience of possible options.

For example, at the next Sunday's Mass, the people would be the homilists. All would have a chance to share with one another the meaning of the Gospel as it related to their lives. The take-home materials included the readings for the following Sunday, along with some questions to center their thoughts. People were not so sure what this would mean, but they were glad for the warning and interested enough to come back and see what would unfold.

As people entered the gym on the third Sunday, they noticed the seating arrangement had changed. The chairs were not all facing the altar. The altar was now at one end and the ambo at the other. Between the two were clusters of chairs facing each other.

Before the readings, the celebrant explained that during the homily, everyone would be asked to share with the person next to them one insight about what the Scriptures had to say about their coming week. Given this preparation, attention was high during the readings. After the Gospel, people spent 10 minutes reflecting in pairs what significance the readings had for them.

For example, the Gospel mentioned that Jesus' teaching had the "ring of authority, unlike the scribes." People talked about being a parent and "wooing" their children rather than scolding them. Others talked about feeling powerless in the face of world events. They also remembered the example of "little people" who had spoken with much authority, people such as Dorothy Day or Martin Luther King. The participants mentioned after Mass how much impact the readings had on them, much more than if someone had been "preaching" to them.

At the end of Mass, everyone was told that the next Sunday would emphasize small groups. They were welcome to sit with their family or friends, or try out a new group. The clusters would be from 6–8 people each.

When parishioners returned for the fourth Sunday, they were by now used to meeting in the vestibule and putting on name tags. As they entered the gym they saw that the chairs were arranged in small groups. While the musicians played "Gather Us In," people found a seat and introduced themselves to one another in the small gatherings. After all were settled, the celebrant explained that the first and third reading for the day would be read at the beginning. For a few minutes people would quietly reflect on the readings and then turn to others in their group to share reactions. He asked that each person be given a chance to talk about the meaning of the Scripture, even the children. At the end of this period, all would be invited to pick up their chairs and gather around the altar for the presentation of gifts and liturgy of the Eucharist.

The two readings were read for all to hear and then small group reflection and sharing followed. Because of the previous Sunday's experience, people felt comfortable reflecting in their group the significance of the Scriptures for their daily lives. Each group had a facilitator who guided the participants through the discussion.

At the end of the interaction, people gathered as a single community around the altar. Once again they sang, "Gather Us In," now with a new awareness of what a community gathering together looks like. The second reading for the day was read as a meditation after communion.

The take-home materials encouraged each family to use the blessing before meals as a dialogue, everyone giving thanks for a special gift received during the week. This was in preparation for the fifth Sunday's emphasis on the Mass as a banquet of thanksgiving. People were encouraged to bring to the next Mass something from the abundance they had received, perhaps food for the poor, or a flower, a candle, perhaps a drawing that could be used as a decoration at Mass.

The Mass for the fifth Sunday continued on the previous week's experience of sharing and was built around people's own life patterns. The parish was located in a suburban area. The planners used this as a model for liturgy.

When people arrived, not only did they take off their coats and put on a name tag, they also spent time in the vestibule talking with each other about their past week. People shared their stories, much as they would do at a dinner party. They then listened to the Gospel story as an example of the wider expression of salvation history. This was done while still in the vestibule or around the periphery of the gym.

After 20 minutes of storytelling, the celebrant invited everyone to come into the gym around the table, much as a host would invite guests into the dining room for supper. The altar was a long table with a white cloth over it, similar to a banquet table. People brought up wine and bread, flowers and candles, and placed them on the table. Other gifts of food, pictures and decorations were placed on the stage at one end of the gym for all to see.

The celebrant sat at the table, along with the ministers of communion, while everyone gathered close around in a circle. What followed was a moving experience, frequently mentioned in people's evaluations afterwards. The Eucharistic prayer, Lord's Prayer and greeting of peace were done as a gathering of friends celebrating Jesus' presence in their midst. People came up to the table for communion as they would for a meal in their own homes, but with much reverence and insight into the meaning of being fed and nourished by Jesus and one another.

After communion, people retired to where they had been when they first came in as if they were going back to the living room after supper. During coffee and donuts individuals were encouraged to sign up for small groups. The groups would meet either immediately after Mass or sometime during the week. The purpose of the group discussion was to discover what people thought of the five weeks of innovation, what questions or issues surfaced and what should be continued in future Masses.

The configuration for the sixth Sunday was back to the original format before the project began. The seating arrangement was the same but the people had changed. The reflection on the readings was short so as to allow more time at the end for reactions from the small groups as to what the experience meant to people and what issues it raised. Each group had a one-page summary of their reflections that went to the planning committee for evaluation. The committee submitted a final report to the gym Mass community during March about how people reacted to the experience and what should be continued in the future.

Some of the aspects people wanted to hang on to were the hospitality in the vestibule at the beginning of each Mass, the chance to rearrange the chairs occasionally so as to place the people at the center of the Eucharist, and the linking of liturgy to everyday experience as manifested by the dinner party focus. People realized this may not be a regular tradition but it did get them thinking about the meaning and relevance of liturgy in their daily lives. The small group discussions were also appreciated by those who participated.

A concern was raised as to how children fit into the liturgies. Babysitting was offered over the six weeks for those who wished. A few Masses included a special liturgy of the Word for the children in a room next to the gym. People liked this idea but also wanted an occasional role-play of the Word by children of different age groups. One tradition was established during the six weeks that continues to this day. After communion the presider sits down in the middle of the group and blesses the little children as the assembly sings a special blessing song.

The reports from many of the small groups included a special note of thanks and congratulations to all who were involved in the planning and execution of the "Liturgy and Life, Faith and Future" project. The planning group also wrote up an article for the whole parish which appeared as an insert in the bulletin. They wanted to be sure no one felt left out or that the gym liturgy was in any way separate from the parish community as a whole.

Not all that happened during the six weeks of innovation continued as a regular tradition. Something, however, happened to the people who took part. They began to experience what liturgy could be like if some thought and creativity were added to the celebration. Liturgy came alive for them. It was not something that they sat back and watched happen. They were part of it.

It did, however, make demands on the congregation. The people had to pay close attention because they were at times required to give their own insights and reflections. It was harder to hide behind a curtain of formality and indifference.

As we mentioned at the outset, this is not for everyone. It should at least be an option for those who wish to give it a try. All that is required are creative planners who are willing to dream about what could be and then do it. What might be lost in the process is dull liturgies and dead faces.

What does this suggest about a new way of being parish in the next century? First, that liturgy is a critical aspect of parish life. Catholics have a right to Eucharist. The pressure will keep mounting for the institutional Church to make changes in the requirement for ordination so that enough people will be ordained to meet the demand for Mass in the future.

Having enough priests, however, will not solve the problem of dull, routine liturgies. Even Masses presided over by women and married men could still become lifeless and boring once the novelty wears off. Discovering liturgical rituals that speak to people's needs, stir up their interest and involvement, challenge them to live lives that reflect Gospel values, that is the key to good liturgy. We can begin that process now. In fact, many places already have.

What is needed is to uncover people's desires and expectations. Target the liturgies to respond to a variety of interests and include people of varying inclinations in the planning of these liturgies. This effort at putting life into liturgies will succeed because we are not alone. Jesus and the Spirit continue to save us from ourselves and keep calling us to new life. All that is needed is to be open to God's graces flooding into our hearts, liturgies and parishes as a whole.

Mass is not the whole of parish life, however. Other aspects are also important. These include building community, faith formation, Christian service, stewardship and coordinating volunteers. It is to these other essentials of parish life that we now turn, always searching for a new way of being parish and trying to uncover new paradigms that will carry us into the next century.

## Questions for Review and Reflection

*Anticipation*

What do you expect when you attend Mass? Are your expectations realized? If not, what options do you have? Do you experience others coming to Mass with any expectations? Are they different from your own? In what ways?

*Environment*

In what ways does the worship space draw you in and help you relate to God and to others at Mass? What's missing? Is the gathering space before and after Mass conducive to forming community? Could any improvements be made?

*Planning*

How are the special needs of various age and interest groups addressed in the parish liturgies? Is there enough variety, something for everyone? In what ways is the issue of balanced language addressed or not addressed? How do the liturgies and homilies touch people's everyday lives and experience?

*Leadership*

Who leads the Mass? How much depends on the priests and how much on other ministers? What aspects of the weekend liturgies are the most creative? What aspects give you hope for the future?

## Prayer Ritual

*Music*

"We Remember" by Marty Haugen (Chicago: G.I.A. Publications, Inc. 1980)

*Process*

As a large group, one person reads the following phrases and the people respond.

In the presence of God whose Word has called the
universe into being,
All: We stand in awe.
In the presence of God whose arms have held children,
whose eyes have sparkled with laughter.
All: We stand in trust.
In the presence of God whose breath has stirred within us
and given us hearts open to love,
All: We stand in need.
In the presence of God who offers us countless symbols
for understanding, growth, and new life,
All: Be with us and hear us, we pray.

After the prayer, divide into small clusters around the room of from 6–10 people. In the middle of each group there should be a small table or stand on which is placed a bowl of water. Ask the people to stand around the table and listen while one person reads the passage on the Beatitudes. (Matthew 5:1–11) Ask another person to read the following reflection:

The scriptures speak of blessedness in a number of paradoxical statements. We experience blessedness in many unlikely ways and through unlikely persons. We are all blessed in unique and special ways. In order to symbolize our blessedness, we will alternate reading the following prayers and then bless each other with the water, each person blessing in turn the person to the left, using whatever words of blessing you wish.

Right: Blessed are You, Loving God. You are the wellspring and omega point. Your Spirit binds us together in respect, in dignity and in service.

Left: Blessed are you, Creator of all that is! In Your image we are made. In your likeness you fashion and form us.

Right: Your breath gives us life. Day by day You pour out Your love to us that we might see the beauty of all You have done.

Left: Blessed are you, Steadfast lover! You are ever faithful, Your promises endure through all generations. Though we wander far from You, Your ardent desire to be our God ever calls us back.

Right: Blessed are you, Source of all Compassion! You tremble as a mother giving birth. For when we, Your people, suffer in darkness, You bring forth light.

Left: Blessed are You, Gracious Giver of life. Your compassion wells up within us to be our strength, to be our hope, to be our glory.

One person now takes the bowl of water and blesses the person to his or her left, telling them, "You are blessed because . . ." Response: "Amen."

Return to the large group to share a greeting of peace and the final song.

*Closing*

Sing the refrain from the opening song, "We Remember."

# CHAPTER EIGHT

# *Small Faith Communities*

THE AMERICAN CATHOLIC PARISH IS DEVELOPING INTO
A mega-church. Because of the decline in the number of priests and the
increase in the number of Catholics, the ratio of parishioners to priest will
continue to grow. For the same reason, the number of Masses on the
weekend will drop and the size of the congregation will increase. As a
result, the danger of the parishioners getting lost in the crowd becomes
more of a problem.

Each person comes to church with personal needs and concerns, with
longings, struggles and triumphs. Each comes with a story to tell, in other
words. Who will listen to this story in a liturgical gathering so large and
impersonal?

Outlets must be found to allow the average Catholic to feel "at home"
in church, to be attended to, listened to and supported. Other avenues
must be found for people to exercise their baptismal calling to care for
one another and live out Gospel values in their personal and family lives.

Some find an outlet in ministries and parish organizations. They volunteer to sing in the choir, teach catechism, be a sponsor for Christian initiation, help out at a shelter. They join the Knights of Columbus, women's
club or singles' group.

These activities help but they touch only a small percentage of the
people. Even those who are active find that something is missing. They
don't have a chance to share much of their own faith journey. They long
for an opportunity to tell their story.

Enter Small Faith Communities. These are gatherings of from 6–15
people who meet on a regular basis, at least once a month. They are committed to being church on a small scale. Some of these small groups are
attached to a parish structure, others operate independently of a parish,
but they still consider themselves part of the Church.

When they meet, they tell their stories, share their experiences of God
working in their lives, reflect on Scripture, challenge each other to live out
their call to put the Gospels into action, participate in common rituals of

prayer and nourishment, and support one another in a life of Christian service. As a result they grow in deep relationship to one another and to their God.

## Macro-Church and Micro-Church

A distinction is made between the micro- and macro-church. The
micro-church is the small group which gathers because of a special faith
bond and Gospel reflection. In the New Testament, these groups were
called house church." Central and South Americans use the term "basic
Christian Communities" or *"Comunidades de Base."*

The macro-church is the parish, the diocese or religious community.
This includes the assembly of people at the weekend Masses or the peri-
odic gathering of parishes for a diocesan synod, or a religious community
gathered together for "community days." The macro-church is essential
for providing continuity and visibility, but it often comes up short in providing personal faith development or prophetic witness.

The micro-church, on the other hand, provides opportunities for companionship and familiarity, while at the same time maintaining a connection with the macro-church. Micro-church allows for a level of intimacy,
self-disclosure and faith-sharing not possible in the macro-church setting.
Macro-church, by its very size, must operate with rules of order, with recognized, usually ordained, leadership, with formal communications and
explicit teachings. Personal recounting and celebration of individual stories is rarely possible in the macro-church.

Until recently, theology was an exercise of the macro-church. We are
now in the midst of a new paradigm of personal storytelling that is taking
place in the micro-church. This storytelling stresses a theology of faith in
action. This method of "theologizing" stresses not so much speculation
and theory but application of Gospel values as manifested in concrete,
direct action.

The experience of faith-sharing and action-response must eventually
be integrated into the larger tradition of macro-church in order to provide
life to the larger church and future to the small faith community. For
example, the parents in a micro-church group experience decide to teach
religious values to their children through a storytelling method that
includes both old and young in the formation process. The parish
(macro-church) becomes interested in this approach and recommends that
all parents become involved in the sacramental preparation of their children, primarily through storytelling and personal sharing. Both macro-
and micro-church work together in searching for new ways of being
God's People. They need each other. They cannot exist without the gift
each brings to the full understanding of Church.

## Types of Small Groups

Many other forms of small group interaction exist alongside the Small Faith Community experience. The family is one. This is sometimes known as the "domestic church" or one cell of the macro-church.

Much of what makes up family living relates to the essentials of being church. A mother provides nourishment to her child, an action not unlike the nourishment available for those receiving communion. Unfortunately, this connection between the family and church is not often made. Marital partners minister to each other and to their children. They give thanks for the joys of living together and repeatedly ask forgiveness for their failings and shortcomings. Thanksgiving and reconciliation are two mainstays of what is essential to being church. Once again, this connection is not often apparent to families who attend church on the weekend.

Family life is filled with rituals. Saying prayers at meals or at bedtime, reading stories to the younger children, eating popcorn while watching a video movie on the weekend, trips to the zoo or to the family cabin, visits to parents after Sunday Mass are typical rituals. These can strengthen the rituals of the weekend liturgy if reflected upon and made relevant to family interaction. This, however, is not a common experience. Church and family reside in two separate spheres of existence.

The "domestic church" has difficulty establishing a foothold in family living amid the stress of both parents working outside the home, children in daycare or absorbed in school activities. Television, fast foods and shopping at the mall make life easier, but these also mesmerize the family and make interaction and reflection on family life more difficult.

The "domestic church" needs help, help that is not always forthcoming from the parish, or macro-church. Some other vehicle is needed to lend support and assistance to the family. Small faith communities could be that vehicle. There are, however, other options.

One is the "Twelve-Step Community." These are gatherings of people who come together for support, challenge and encouragement in order to overcome some area of addiction in their lives. They are in effect "places of faith" because they are modeled on the Twelve Steps of Alcoholics Anonymous as a means for gaining freedom over addictive behavior. Addiction is any form of compulsion in which we do something over and over again, thinking we will get different results. In the process we lose the freedom to stop the repetitive behavior which results in inner confusion and self-destruction. The gathering of Twelve-Step Communities challenges each member to clarify the difference between freedom and non-freedom.

Twelve-Step groups are not necessarily faith communities. Participants often remain anonymous. Their intervention and conversion flow from a supportive, caring, loving group of people. This experience of intervention continues through the personal movement of each individual within the twelve steps. Stories are told, they are heard, they are respected and they are understood because each person shares similar oppressions and limitations. In the process of sharing, community is established. Individuals do come to know themselves as gaining freedom and accepting themselves as they are. A centering happens wherein an "Absolute Being" is accepted and known. Individuals know themselves as "enough," thus letting go of the search for another substance or experience. This acceptance describes "a free place" and is celebrated within the Twelve-Step Community.

The focus of Twelve-Step groups is personal recovery. There is no expectation of forming a permanent group to be a faith community on a continual basis. They do provide the groundwork for small faith communities, however. The experience of personal sharing and a willingness to risk self-disclosure found in Twelve-Step groups can prepare people for more productive involvement in a small faith community.

The same is true for other experiences of small group interaction within and outside the parish structure. Group discussion sessions, such as Renew or Genesis II, adult formation programs, Christian Initiation programs, parish organizations and study groups all pave the way for involvement in small faith communities. These experiences break down the suspicion and resistance to small group interaction and give people a thirst for deeper personal sharing on a continual basis.

## Base Communities of Central and South America

Although local groups may open people up to small faith communities, the recent impetus towards micro-church comes from outside the United States. The lived experience of small faith communities has been transforming the church and society in Latin America for the last 25 years. These groups are called Base Communities or *Communidades de Base*. This long tradition has given expression to a new and more practical study of religion called Liberation Theology. Both in its written form and in the unwritten, oral tradition expressed in the base communities, the emphasis is on God in our daily lives as the One who supports, challenges and calls us to greater freedom and commitment.

The base community model starts with what is possible. The "folks" come when they can. Those who show up become the base community for that moment. They reflect on the Gospels. They break open the Word for personal and communal conversion and action. The participants believe they have not heard the gospel until they are willing to act on it. For this reason, base communities are dangerous groups. They reflect on and challenge the local situation, not the world beyond. They press for change in the process of mutual reflection and action response.

In many areas of Latin America, base communities exist parallel to the local parish. This is because the parish cannot function properly since it is often subject to persecution by government officials. In Honduras, for instance, from 1980–1987, worship happened in hiding. War and strife forced people into secret gatherings of small faith communities. Some communities found the environment so dangerous that they had to meet "on the road" while traveling from one place to another. Patricia Forster herself was part of such "traveling" experiences of Gospel reflection and action. They listened to and reflected on the Word and took action that was at once personal, communal and political.

In Venezuela, on the other hand, the base communities intersected with the local parish for "festival." "Festival" meant that the "folks" would come from their small barrios to the main church. The trip itself, because of the long distance, proclaimed the day as special. Where there was no persecution, people felt freer to come for parish celebrations. The intimate sharing still took place. within the base communities, however. The small communities shared differently because of differing needs from barrio to barrio. The base communities helped people act collectively, not just as individuals. They discovered that God hears their voices in community and this gave them hope.

Charismatic groups are also active in Latin America, but these emphasize personal healing received from God rather than concrete action and social change. They tend to exist within the hierarchical structure of the church to a greater extent than base communities. Their focus may lead to action but their emphasis is more on prayer and healing. The charismatic movement is also present in the United States and much good has come from the energy and enthusiasm they engender. Those who are more committed to this movement have formed Charismatic Households. These tend toward a more authoritarian structure which can lead to dependency by the members on a single leader. The trust is in the leaders more than in the people. In base communities, the trust is in the people rather than in the leaders.

## Mainstream vs Marginal

Mainstream communities operate within the boundaries of a mainstream church. This usually means within the context of the local parish.

This assures a certain fidelity to a tradition that maintains secure and stable relationships. Mainstream faith communities are developed as a part of pastoral planning and are initiated by the leadership. They come from the top down, in other words. The pastor, staff and lay leaders initiate and foster small faith communities within the context of parish life. They also need to give the communities enough room to grow and develop on their own. If parish leaders place too much structure on small faith communities, this will stymie their creativity and self-initiative. They will become institutionalized. This is an inherent danger of mainstream small faith communities.

Marginal small faith communities operate outside of parish structures and are more intentional in their makeup. People choose to gather together. They may reflect on the Scriptures and even share the Eucharist as a group. Those who make up these marginal communities often experience an acute need to make a difference in the world, to be engaged in the pressing social issues of our time and to call into question some of the traditions and practices of the institutional church. They may include persons of different faiths. The faith community becomes the primary place people experience church. The local parish is a secondary structure that may serve as an outlet for ministry, a place for educating children or a source for networking with other faith groups.

Many marginal faith communities believe that the celebration of the Eucharist is central to its genuine ecclesial status. When they gather, they gather to be Church. The breaking open of Word and the breaking of Bread are integral to their mutual understanding and celebration.

Mainstream faith communities, on the other hand, see the Sunday parish Eucharist as central. The role of small faith communities becomes a place for telling the story of one's life experience which, in turn, is integrated into the reflection on the Word and Catholic tradition at the weekend liturgies.

Leonardo Boff in his book, *Ecclesiogenesis* (Orbis, 1986), hopes for the coexistence of these two forms of small communities. Both have strengths. Both are needed. Any efforts to curtail or reabsorb these communities into the institutional church will deaden their ferment for renewal. The static, permanent institution, and the dynamic, critical small faith community must learn to coexist. The formal "institutional Church" needs to respect and value the marginal Christian community as a vital force for renewal, and rediscover in the process its own meaning and responsibility. For their part, the marginal small communities must come to understand their need for the institution as a means for maintaining their continuity, for preserving their oneness over fragmentation and disunity, and for networking and affirming their Catholic identity.

The mainstream community trusts its traditions. The past has proven trustworthy and this provides security and continuity. Renewal is couched in terms of "What can we do better?" "Where is improvement needed?"

The marginal community has a different perspective. It asks the question "Why?" For example, why are the ordained only male? Why are decisions made from above? Why is the institution so rigid? Why are structures so oppressive to the poor and marginalized? Much can be learned from each approach. Both have strengths and both have weaknesses. If the future of grassroots initiatives is to retain a nurturing and transforming power, creative mutual conversations must take place between the mainstream and the marginal communities.

Some religious congregations have used the small faith community model for their own membership. This is a different experience than sharing a meal or Mass together as a religious house. It is, instead, a conscious effort to form groups of from 4–8 religious who meet once or twice a month for mutual support, faith sharing and theological reflection. The members of the group may not all live in the same house.

In some ways this is an attempt at blending the marginal and mainstream approaches. Those leading the congregation encourage the formation of these small communities but the initiative comes from the grassroots.

The authors have participated in a number of such groups. The level of personal sharing was deeper than might be experienced at "house meetings" or "community gatherings." The groups were also open to a common action flowing out of their reflection that went beyond the personal ministries exercised by the participants. Examples included helping out at an overnight shelter for the homeless, participating in peace vigils or providing solidarity with those experiencing prejudice or oppression.

## Getting Started

Why is there such an emphasis on small faith communities in the United States at this time? We believe it is because people are looking for a way to be church that has meaning and value to them. Individualism is attractive. Doing our own thing looks inviting. But it's lonely and egocentric. People are looking for another option.

The country is in trouble. Violence, racial tension, crime, economic insecurity, broken families, disrespect for life, destruction of natural resources plague us and make us feel powerless and ineffective. Working on one's own will never alleviate these problems. People look around for others with whom to share their fears and concerns. They seek to establish links with those who share similar desires and who seek a better world.

The local parish does not often provide much help in overcoming a concentration on one's own small world, or a place to share difficulties and concerns for the future. Some other vehicle is needed. Many parishes are tapping into this desire and setting up small faith communities within the structure of the parish itself. Other parishes have not responded directly, but parishioners within the parish have formed groups on their own and sought recognition by the parish leadership. Still others have left the local parish behind and have established independent small faith communities that still remain committed to the Church as a whole. Depending on the situation, all are legitimate ways of operating.

How does one start a small faith community? There are two typical routes to follow, one from within the parish structure and one parallel to it. We will begin with the marginal group. Two books describe options for the formation of freestanding small faith communities. Both are personal journeys. One is by Richard Currier and Frances Gram and is called *Forming A Small Christian Community* (Twenty-third Publications, 1992). The other is *Good Things Happen* by Dick Westley (Twenty-third Publications, 1992).

The process is simple and direct. Suppose you are interested in starting a group. Begin by gathering information about small faith communities. Talk to people who belong to groups or seek out places that have had experience with small groups. A number of different formats exist. Some small faith communities are centered around Eucharist. These are usually larger gatherings of people who come together for the celebration of Mass. They may take place in a facility attached to a parish, such as a gym or meeting room, but they still consider themselves independent of the parish structure. Others take place in people's homes or rented space in a public school or hotel. The membership is fluid. Whoever shows up for Mass is part of the community for that day. There are often spin-off small groups that form as a result of the gathering for Eucharist. These smaller groupings come closer to a small faith community because they provide greater opportunities for personal story telling and dialogue.

Other small groups do not have Mass as a regular part of their interaction. They may share a meal together, but even this is not a necessity. The core of the small faith community is sharing personal stories, reflecting on Scripture or a common issue, and then deciding what actions or commitments flow from the discussion. One common method used by these groups is a process of theological reflection described later in this chapter.

To start a small faith community, one does not need permission from the Church or local parish leadership. All that is needed is desire and a plan. After reading about options and visiting some existing groups, sit down with a friend and talk about your dreams and desires. See what questions arise or insights the person might have about your idea. Next, pray about your desire to form a small faith community and pay attention to the movements and directions coming from within. You will discover from this prayer and dialogue how to get started and with whom.

The next step is to call together people you think might be interested in being part of the small community, usually from 6–10 individuals. Have an initial gathering to describe your idea and see how they react. The people do not have to know each other or have a common background. The only requirement is an openness to talk about their own experience in the context of the Gospels and a willingness to make a commitment to a regular meeting every three or four weeks. This is not a support group but a faith community. That means that people are open to not only sharing their concerns and feelings, but to taking action in areas of service and ministry to others. The group will go through the initial stages of orientation and identity as people grow in their comfortableness with each other and awareness of what the group is about. People will come and go, but a core group will become established and this will provide continuity.

In the beginning stages, a single leader may be necessary to provide the vision and format. Eventually, the group will gain more confidence and the leadership role will be assumed by a number of people, each with a different perspective and style for leading. The objective is to become a permanent gathering of Christians committed to *being* church on a small scale. The group does this by meeting regularly, reflecting on Scripture and current events, sharing their experience of God working in their lives, challenging each other to live out the call to put the Gospels into action and supporting each other in a life of service and ministry.

This is a large order for one person to establish on his or her own initiative. People find it easier to fit into an established group or ready-made plan. This is where the parish fits in. Local church can provide an invaluable service to its membership and the larger community by fostering the formation of small faith communities. This is the path followed by Arthur Baranowski in *Creating Small Faith Communities* (St. Anthony Messenger Press, 1988) and Thomas Kleissler, Margo LeBert and Mary McGinness in *Small Christian Communities* (Paulist Press, 1991). Both of these approaches work within existing parish structures. Fr. Baranowski, for instance, suggests starting with a small group experience of limited duration. This might be a Renew small group, a Genesis II program or a weekend renewal process. People are invited to sign up in groups of 8–12 for six or more weekly sessions. This is the initial phase in which people are introduced to sharing their faith and lived experience.

No demands are placed on participants for further commitment.

This first step opens up a window of opportunity in which people can experience what small faith communities are like. They are given an invitation to go deeper if they wish. Jesus' words to the first disciples, "Come and see," is the operative sentiment in this initial phase.

Step Two goes deeper. It asks people to commit themselves to regular periods of personal prayer, as well as to prayer in the group. This is a period of personal conversion in which people are willing to spend time each day in prayer and personal reflection. The prayer is reinforced in a further commitment to small group sharing on a regular basis.

This commitment, too, is for a limited time in order to see if people are ready and willing to journey deeper into a conversion and conversation with their God.

Step Three is the formation of the small Christian communities. These communities meet every third week under the direction of a pastoral facilitator. They meet to support and challenge each other to personal prayer, to reflect on the weekend Bible readings and to express their commitment in service to others.

Each community has a pastoral facilitator, a person carefully chosen by the parish staff to lead the meetings. The pastoral facilitators themselves meet on a regular basis in order to support each other in their unique ministry of leadership and to prepare the community meetings.

This is one approach for starting up a small faith community within a parish structure. Other methods have also proven successful. Fr. James Friedel, OSA, for instance, provides a resource to Catholic parishes using the Parish Mission structure. He calls his one-week Mission, "One Parish, Many Communities." In preparation for the week, the staff or pastoral council selects 9–12 people to serve as the Parish Mission Team that is the organizing core committee for the process. They begin meeting a number of months before the Mission takes place. The team chooses leaders for what will eventually be small faith communities in the parish. An initial mini-retreat is held for the team and group leaders.

When the Mission takes place, the people who attend divide into small groups during the Mission, each with a group facilitator. The themes for the four evenings of the week-long Mission are: "We Gather To Tell The Story of God's Love For Us," "We Gather To Celebrate The Gift Of God's Forgiveness," "We Gather As A Gifted Parish," "We Gather To Listen, To Be Fed, To Go Forth."

At the conclusion of the Mission, the participants are offered the opportunity to sign up to continue the process throughout the rest of the year in small groups. They are free to stay with the same one that was formed during the Mission, or to join a new group. Other parishioners who did not attend the Mission are also free to become part of a group. The makeup of the groups are not built around geographical location in the parish, interests, age or background. Usually the one factor determining who is in what group is the time of the meeting. Those who want to meet on Monday nights form one group, those on Saturday mornings or Sunday afternoons or Wednesdays at noon become other groups. Each has a trained leader and a sample format to follow. Some groups stay with the model suggested and find it helpful. Others soon strike out on their own and follow unique and creative designs. The intention is the same, to provide an opportunity for people to gather together in small groups to talk about what is important to them, what church, God and faith means to them, and what implications this has for their daily lives.

Whatever method is used in forming small faith communities within a parish structure, the leadership must realize that there are inherent risks involved in the attempt to form these groups. One risk is the extra time and effort it takes to train leaders and foster the formation of these groups amid the many other demands and cares associated with running a modern parish. All other ministries and programs remain in operation, from the weekend liturgies to the religious education programs, from parish organizations and fund-raisers to pastoral care and outreach. These responsibilities cannot be ignored while an effort is made to form small faith communities. Once the groups are in operation, they will provide a resource and help to parish ministries as they look for outlets and opportunities to put their faith into operation. That takes time, however, and time is one very rare commodity in pastoral ministry.

A second risk is more subtle. Small faith communities, once they have been in operation for a year or two, may be seen as divisive and subversive by parish leaders or by those not involved. They can appear countercultural because they are. Deep reflection on the Gospel message calls into question our consumer, waste-prone, short-sighted society. Because they cannot be easily controlled, these communities are a threat to those in control. Participants have been set free by their prayer, reflection and Gospel values.

Sooner or later, members of these groups will make demands on parish leaders. "Think of what the parish could be," they say. "If only people could catch on to the real meaning of being Christian!" To the leaders this translates into "We're not doing a good job here." That's risky. Often the leaders, and especially the pastor, are stuck in the middle between these "turned on" members of the small faith communities and the demands of the parish as a whole, or the diocese, or Rome, or canon law, or traditionally-minded parishioners. The theory and practice do not always match and this causes problems.

Although the risks are present, it appears that the Spirit is pushing people to give it a try, whether as part of a parish structure or striking out on their own. Whichever approach is used, there are some key issues that each small faith community must address.

## Key Issues

The first issue is one of leadership. Who will lead the meetings and give direction? For those groups operating within a parish structure, it is helpful to have one person who acts as the resource to the group and provides a link to the pastoral staff or core team. For communities that are independent of the local parish, there must still be one person or perhaps a lead couple that provide continuity and direction. The people leading each session may rotate so that those who wish or have the ability are given the opportunity to facilitate the gathering. A small faith community cannot long survive, however, without designated facilitators to prepare materials beforehand, provide direction during the sessions, handle conflicts, identify feelings and needs, and process what is happening among the members. The group itself may decide who these leaders will be but some form of facilitation and direction is necessary.

A second issue is providing a conducive environment for mutual sharing and self-disclosure. People must feel confident that what is said at the sessions is confidential and sacred to the group. Individuals will differ in their willingness and ability to tell personal stories or in their capacity to reflect on Scripture. Some will talk a great deal, others hardly at all. If one or other person is missing, the interaction will not be the same. It is, in effect, a different group. These are issues associated with any small group sharing but ones that must be addressed during the formative stages of the small faith community. Those who are more experienced in group interaction become a resource to those who are less familiar with group process. Each person has a unique insight and gift to offer, however. No one is superior to another, no matter one's background or experience.

A third issue is support versus action. One of the attractions of small faith communities is the opportunity they provide for intimate, close interaction and dialogue. It becomes a place to gain support and strength in life's trials and challenges. The emphasis is on belonging and interpersonal bonding. This, however, is not the only focus. If this is the group's only reason for coming together, then it is a support group and not a small faith community. An authentic faith community must also have a focus that lies outside the group.

As members reflect on their own stories in light of the Gospels, there is a natural progression to question values or priorities in their lives and in the surrounding culture. People begin to experience a link with the poor and suffering of the world. It is a grace that comes from the small faith community dynamic. This new consciousness is one sign that the group is maturing in its faith and in a fuller sense of *being* church on a small scale. The discussion begins to touch upon what each person is doing in his or her own life to live out the Gospel imperatives. Is more needed? Does the group as a whole need to address any issue or concern in the area or world at large?

Michael Cowan addressed this issue in an article that appeared in the August, 1992 issue of *Chicago Studies,* entitled "Seeking the Welfare of the City: The Public Life of Small Communities of Faith," (pp. 205–214). He wrote that "to be an authentic small faith community, both a sense of belonging similar to that found in family life, as well as a public commitment to change structures must be present within a faith context and Gospel orientation." (p. 214) He also warned that a public commitment to change structures can overwhelm a group and reduce it to frustration and non-action. What's needed, he contends, is to "imagine forms of solidarity for small communities that make it possible to be part of a larger whole: that is, to stand with others as a larger body." (p. 211) Not only must a community challenge its own members to put their reflections into action, it must also seek out other small faith communities, whether within a parish or outside that structure. It must then form a network of communities working together to confront injustices and, in this way, more effectively help the poor and needy. An authentic small community must link support and reflection with action. It must also link up with other groups to make its action more productive.

A fourth issue is personality conflicts and disputes that inevitably arise in the midst of the small group discussion. This is a group made up of human beings. It touches deep chords within people, ones that perhaps have not been dealt with previously and that have a great deal of emotion attached to them. As the members risk more in relating important aspects of their lives, they become vulnerable and are less able to defend against careless comments, misplaced humor or misconstrued reactions.

Great sensitivity and understanding are required of all, especially in moments of conflict and anger. Good leadership becomes essential as an anchor and confidence-builder during these turbulent moments. Group members must commit themselves to listen with an open mind rather than making judgments or offering unwarranted opinions. Listening comes from an attitude of acceptance. This acceptance comes from a desire to respect and support one another, no matter the differences of opinion or outlook. If a small faith community can survive these moments of emotion and disagreement, it can outlast many other setbacks and difficulties. It reveals a level of commitment that goes beyond the group itself, one that is centered in God in the midst of the people gathered together in Jesus' name.

Another issue that small faith communities need to face is the establishment of meaningful rituals as part of their life together. How do they greet each other at the beginning and say good-bye at the end? How often do they meet and what environment is used for interaction? These rituals provide the framework out of which the group operates. People become familiar with "the way we do things around here." A comfortableness and ease of interaction settles in as people find patterns for expressing their life together as a group.

As mentioned earlier, some groups include the celebration of Eucharist together. Others don't have a Mass but establish a ritual of prayer and thanksgiving in other forms. They might all bring special dishes and share a potluck supper together. The host couple might prepare snacks or a dessert. Special dinners become a tradition on various holidays of the year. All of these rituals provide nourishment on many levels for the small community.

Reflecting on Scripture can be ritualized so that people come to know what to expect and what to prepare for in advance. The way passages are read, the questions used to draw out applications, the form of interaction, either in pairs, or with similar age groups, or reflecting as a whole, all of these can become meaningful traditions for a community.

Reconciliation can also be ritualized in various ways. Private confession is not a frequent practice for Catholics these days, but seeking forgiveness from those one has harmed is common. A small faith community can help people seek forgiveness for failures within the group and among loved ones. It can find ways of helping people become more attentive to other cultures and lifestyles or in seeking forgiveness for personal prejudices and insensitivity. At one gathering of a small community, everyone put on each other's shoes and tried to walk around in ones that were too big or too small for the evening. It was a graphic awareness of what it was like trying out another identity for awhile.

Another small community used a ball of yarn. The members formed a circle and the leader held the end of the yarn and tossed the ball to someone else, asking forgiveness for some fault or omission, or asked help in responding to a person or group needing assistance. The ball kept being tossed from person to person until they were all linked together with a network of colored yarn. It represented for the group how our failings keep us held in bondage, but also how a common experience of failure and vulnerability can provide avenues for support and solidarity.

One ritual many small faith communities establish is the way in which they reflect upon their own experience and upon Scripture. It has many forms but contains a common thread. It is called the method of Theological Reflection.

## Theological Reflection

This method follows these five steps: 1) Tell the story, 2) Describe relevant details, 3) Reflect on the tradition, 4) Name the experience, 5) Discern the action.

The first step is to *tell the story.* When people come together as a small faith community, they come with a willingness to tell their story. The group begins with a brief period of rebonding. What has happened in people's lives since last they met? This is not the storytelling period but a communal ritual of regrouping.

Then comes the storytelling part of the session. An individual relates a personal experience. This experience flows out of a scripture passage or is centered around a common theme. One example of the Gospels providing a focus for the storytelling would be Jesus telling his followers, "Go now and sell your property and give the money away to the poor—you will have riches in Heaven. Then come and follow me!" (Mt. 19:20) The group might spend some quiet time reflecting on this passage and then someone would tell a story from his or her own experience that relates to this passage.

One of the women, for instance, tells of her experience when her eldest daughter left home for college. She knew her daughter had become almost a possession of hers. After some time she was able to see what a blessing her life had been while her daughter was at home but that she had become too possessive. Letting go of her daughter and communicating the depth of her loss to her daughter was a freeing experience. She had to put trust in her daughter and in the Lord's care for her.

Others in the group might also tell stories related to the Scripture, or they may decide to stay with this one story and continue the theological reflection focused on this one story. The next step is to spell out *the details of the story* so that everyone can "get into" the experience as much as possible. What was the daughter's reaction, for instance, or how did the deeper sharing with her daughter take place?

Step three is discovering *what the tradition of Scripture and Church bring to this story.* For instance, not only did Jesus tell the rich man to go

This leads to the fourth step of *naming the experience*. As people locate other Scripture references or aspects of their faith that relate to the story of the woman letting go of her daughter, a common theme or insight begins to emerge. In this case some named the experience "loss," or "stripped." Others called it "letting go" or "new freedom." The value of giving it a name is that the group begins to gain new insights and see new aspects in the experience. People's feelings and vulnerabilities are better understood and in the process healing takes place. Naming the experience can also produce new energy in the group. Others start making connections to their own situation. The story becomes universal. It no longer belongs to one person but to the entire group.

Naming the experience helps the group move to the next step of *discerning the action* or response that might flow from the experience. One action might be to pay more attention to other members of the group who must "let go" of children leaving home. Other members might find strength to leave "safe" environments and head out into the "unknown," as did the woman's daughter.

A group action might be to plan a ritual for leave-taking that could be used in the youth ministry of the parish as a help for teenagers and their parents when it's time for them to leave "the nest." The group might wish to go deeper and challenge one another to "let go" of superfluous baggage as they seek to bring the Good News to those around them. This might mean striving for a simpler lifestyle or "fasting" from extra, unnecessary possessions.

The progression of the theological reflection method is not rigid. Some group members may have had a scripture quotation on their minds all week and want to share it before relating a personal story. Other communities might spend an entire session telling personal stories and saving the scripture reflection for the next meeting. The essence of theological reflection is that the group is gathered together to let the Word of God affect their lives and to encourage one another to share experiences that benefit the entire group and provide avenues for Christian service and ministry.

## A New Way of Being Church

Not everyone will buy into the small faith community model. Only a minority will take the risk to share with others important aspects of their lives and commit themselves to Christian service and witnessing. At the same time, this experience, if it is to be offered as a viable option, must be presented at a time and in a manner that fits people's life patterns and overworked schedules. The weekend liturgy could be that time. With some forethought and planning it could provide people a chance to reflect on the Scripture and talk to others about its significance in their daily lives. As mentioned in previous chapters, this involves a shift from passively watching the priest "do his thing" to an active participation in the Mass. The liturgy becomes a summation of one's own experience of God over the past week and a challenge to live out Gospel values in the next. This is best done as a community experience, rather than one centered only on the presider and leaders of worship.

We will describe in Chapter Thirteen how this might take place in a parish setting. It's not the only way of being church but the formation of small faith communities is *one* option among many for bringing the Church of the next century to life.

## Questions for Review and Reflection

*Large vs. Small Church*

The parish is a large collection of people. Within the parish, however, are many smaller groups. How many of these smaller groupings do you belong to or participate in? How many small groups not connected with the parish do you belong to? How do these groups differ, either within or outside the parish? Family is one such group. In what ways is your family or those you live with similar to a small faith community?

*Getting Started*

Have you thought about starting a small faith community? What are the blocks that stand in the way? How does your parish help or hinder the formation of small faith communities? What steps could be taken in the parish to foster small faith communities? How could the key issues of effective leadership, conducive environment, community action, conflict management and meaningful rituals be addressed?

*Theological Reflection*

The theological reflection process follows five steps. In your experience of small groups, which of these steps gives you the most insight or excitement? Which ones are the most difficult and why? Are there any changes in the process that better fit your experience or desires?

## Prayer Ritual

*Music*

"We are many parts, We are all one body," by Marty Haugen. (Chicago: G.I.A., 1986)

*Reading*

Read aloud the story of the loaves and fishes. (Luke 9:10–15, Mark 6:30–44, Matthew 14:13–21)

*Process*

Divide into small groups of 4–6 people. Invite each person in the group to share a personal story that relates to the scripture story read at the beginning. Ask the group to reflect on these stories and "name" two aspects of the stories:

1. Where were there scarcities, shortages, needs?
2. Where were there abundances, plenty, surplus?

Discuss as a group the similarities between the scripture story and people's own experiences. Identify one action which would express the insights of the small group discussion. This action can vary from a simple gesture or symbol to a concrete plan that could be carried out at some time after the discussion. Prepare a brief summary of the group's discussion and insights for the large group.

Return to the large group to report on the small group experience.

*Closing*

Conclude with the last line of the scripture passage and the refrain from the opening song, "We are many parts."sell all his possessions in Matthew 19, he also told the apostles in Matthew 10 that, as they proclaim the Good News, "Don't take any gold or silver or even coppers to put in your purse; nor a knapsack for the journey, nor even a change of clothes, or sandals or a staff—the worker is worth your keep." (Mt. 10:13) People located other passages that spoke the same message of gaining freedom by letting go of possessions.

CHAPTER NINE

# Refounding Church—
# A Paradigm Shift

## Vincent Donovan, C.S.Sp.

Note: The following article originally appeared in the
August 1992 edition of *Chicago Studies* (Vol. 31,
Number 2). It came from a talk that Fr. Donovan gave at
the Institute of Pastoral Studies of Loyola University in
Chicago. The talk was part of a Symposium on Small
Faith Communities held in the summer of 1991. We
found it so insightful that we gained permission to reprint
it as part of our attempt to search for new paradigms.

NEWLY-ELECTED PAUL VI RUSHED INTO THE VACUUM CREATED
by the death of John XXIII. He had to address the Second Session of
Vatican II, which was scheduled to speak at length about the Church. He
pointed out that no word in any language can capture the full meaning of
the Church. The Church is a "mystery" requiring constant exploration and
discovery, and so we have the right to explore further and discover the
meaning of the Church for our time.

The Fathers of the Council produced several magnificent documents
about the Church, such as *Gaudium et Spes* and *Lumen Gentium*. But they
by no means thought they had said the last word on the subject. Instead
they spoke of opening the door to further exploration and discovery. But
I believe a mental block has frozen us in the midst of that discovery, a
mental block formed by the "one model," the one form of the Church that
we know. All the changes that have taken place since the Vatican Council
are changes on only one level—countless changes, all on the same level
around that one form of the Church.

The form of the Church with which we are familiar today was generated almost entirely in the time of the Industrial Revolution. Many
changes did arise at the time of the Council of Trent, but I would suggest
that the Council of Trent was not as influential in bringing us the form
of the Church we now know as was the Industrial Revolution. For all

practical purposes, with very few exceptions, we have no experience of any form of the Church, except that form which came into existence at that time. Even when we work with newly-created small Christian communities, we find ourselves haunted and mesmerized by the form the Church has taken in recent centuries. The Church has been galvanized by the methods, efficiency, power and success of the Industrial Revolution into a form so rigid as to allow no deviation from it, a form considered as sacred and unchanging and divine as its gospel and its Founder.

What I suggest is that we, in our different works, should not become involved in the reform of the Church, or the revival of the Church, which really leaves the 'retouched' Church on the same level as it was before. We must lift the entire process to a different level. What we must become involved in is the refounding of the Church of Jesus Christ for our age, just as St. Paul refounded it for his age, always according to the mind of Christ and the meaning of the gospel. What is required is a paradigm shift, which means that the successful methods of the past are the very methods that must be put aside and not used again. We must start again and from square one. Square one in this case is Christ—the mind of Christ and the meaning of the gospel.

## 1. Maximization

Maximization is a goal of the Industrial Revolution. Bigger is better. It should not be a goal of the Church. St. Paul talked a great deal about the Church, theologically and spiritually. He talked about it practically, as well. It is interesting and revealing to see how he talked about the Church practically. In the writings of Paul and in the Acts of the Apostles, we are familiar with the way he talked about the Church in this practical manner. St. Paul wrote letters to God's Beloved in Rome, to the Church of God in Corinth, to the Saints who were at Ephesus, to "you the people of Philippi," to the Saints in Colossae, to the Church in Thessalonica. At different times he sent various greetings to the deaconesses of the Church of Cenchreae, to the Church that met in the house of Gaius, to the Churches of Laodicea, to the Churches that met in the houses of Nymphas and Philemon. Finally, he mentions the Churches in Galatia, the Churches in Asia, and all the Churches that sent greetings to the Church in Rome. Paul believed in the one Church of Christ, as he believed in one Lord, one faith, one baptism. But for him, the reality of the Church, where his beloved Christians would experience the New Testament present in the Risen Christ, was the local Church, not some Super-Church.

When Paul spoke of the Church spread over a vast area, he spoke of it in the plural. He did not speak of the "Church" in Asia, or the "Church" in Galatia, or the "World Church," as we often call it. We do not really experience the World Church very often in our lives. We scarcely experience the "Diocesan Church." Daily and weekly in our lives the only Church we ever experience is the local Church. We will find that New Testament experience, that incredible love that once walked the earth, in a local Church or we will not experience it at all. We have come to recognize the reality and the importance of the *local* Church. This bigness concept, this maximization idea does not come from the Church. We cannot blame the Council of Trent for that. It mentioned nothing about maximization, about being the biggest parish in the diocese, or the largest diocese in the country with several dioceses vying back and forth as the population changes, along with the importance of the bishop occupying the See. The Council of Trent says nothing about St. Peter's being the biggest Church building in the world. Maximization is a necessary component of the success of the Industrial Revolution—the biggest companies in the country, in the world! For multinational organizations, bigger is certainly better.

## 2. Standardization

There is something else we take for granted from the Industrial Revolution: *standardization*. We say standardization is necessary, for instance, in our ministry, in our training of ministers, in our seminaries. We consider standardization and uniformity, in such a matter, as essential. A standardized priest is the ideal. If we have a shortage of priests, don't tamper with the standardization process. Simply step up our recruiting process, with more Madison Avenue techniques. If we have a problem with proper training for the Church of tomorrow, set up a more modern seminary by merging faculties from different diocesan and religious congregational backgrounds. We can blame the family for the lack of priests today and say the family no longer encourages vocations. The problem lies with the family, not the seminary. As far as the seminary is concerned, we can make it more relevant and up-to-date with personal counseling programs. All these changes, however, are at the same level. That is, they aim at reforming and renewing the Church. We must lift the process to another level, if we dare. What is not needed is a modern standardization of priests. We need a PARADIGM SHIFT.

The seminaries up to now have been standardized seminaries, priest factories, turning out identical products along the assembly line: standardized priests. It is astonishing how similar the products of these priest factories are, no matter where they come from: North America, South America, Europe, Africa, or Asia. Their vocabulary and thought processes are similar, as is their spirituality. On the factory assembly line, this standardization might insure that identical products are produced everywhere, with seminarians who are below or above the standard filtered out of the seminary. But it is possible that the standard itself might be defective. This was proven in Detroit by Ralph Nader about a certain standard product which he called "unsafe at any speed." The product itself was defective. I think there are elements in our Church life, having to do with the priesthood, which are standardized to the limit, but are defective. In the Church as we know it, they will continue to be passed on and accepted. One such element, one such "product" is authority.

## Authority in the Church

Authority in the Church is a very important subject. I would suggest that, as it is understood and practiced, it is defective. Making such a statement is not all that surprising or revolutionary. Jesus himself warned us about such a defect in the use of authority. He said, "Among the pagans those in authority make their authority felt, they lord it over those under them. But you must not let this happen with you. The one who is first among you must be the least of all, and the servant of all." (Mt. 20:25–28)

In my years in the Church, I have never seen authority carried out properly, not the way Jesus said it should be carried out. Jesus had a word for that defective kind of authority. He called it *pagan*. We could call it male authority. It is unilateral. This type of authority is considered the rightful possession of one person alone. Were that person to share authority, it would mean doling it out as one's possession. It is quantifiable and limited. The more you dole out, the less you have. An increase in someone else's power in the community means a decrease in the authority of the superior. It becomes a system of powerful people and powerless people. *As long as any people in a Christian community are powerless, that Christian community is defective.* It is crippled. It is paralyzed. That is pagan power. "With you it will not be this way." (Mt. 20:26)

Jesus used power in a unique way. He created a circle of healing. How did he use his power? He used his power to save people, to heal people, to enable people, to empower people. That is *not* the pagan notion of power. When we think of Jesus passing on his power to his disciples, we conceive of it in a "pagan" way, a "male" way. We say he could not have passed on *all* his power to his disciples, just some of it. So the disciples had less power than he had and we have even less than they did when it finally reaches us in the "trickle-down" theory of pagan power.

As a matter of fact, Jesus did not pass on to his disciples less power than he had. In Mt. 10:6f., Jesus is quoted as saying to them: "Preach the gospel of the kingdom, cure the sick, cleanse lepers, cast out devils, raise the dead." Jesus did not pass on less power than he possessed. He gave them the exact same power that he had.

I wonder if we would have the courage to do what Jesus did. The bishops of the United States several years ago put out a pastoral letter that was titled "To Teach As Jesus Did." It is time to write another pastoral letter called "To Empower as Jesus Empowered." I wonder if we have the courage to pass on the *full* power of the gospel to the people with whom we work. We always pass out just a parcel of it, the rest to be supplied later. That was the essential missionary method. In some cases, they intended to pass on the power a hundred years later, when the people would be ready. I think that today the small Christian communities are the place where this will happen, if it is to happen at all. It will never happen in the standardized Church, built on a parcelization of power which is essential to the functioning of the modem standardized Church. An alternative way of operating can happen only in small Christian communities. Here, finally, those haunting words of Jesus can come true: "With you it will not be this way"—this "pagan" use of power. This new form of power would be a paradigm shift. It is a refounding of the Church. The small faith community becomes a place where power can be relational, where the empowering becomes mutual, a circle of healing for all those involved, where one person is empowered by the others, with no one being impoverished in the process. Perhaps it could be called a feminine use of power.

## 3. Specialization

In industry, "specialization" is a necessary component of "standardization." Parts are assembled on an assembly line, and that is all that the people who are involved are interested in: the parts. Attention is paid to only one phase of an operation, not to the "whole" operation. It is work done by one part of a person, not the whole person. In the Church, it would be the emphasis on one aspect of Christianity for the Church to the exclusion of all other aspects—all of Christianity, for instance, under the aspect of "morality" alone, or "canon law" alone. So much damage has been done to the American Church by looking at Christianity and Church life under the one light of "canon law" alone. Dogmatic theology stands quite apart from the pastoral ministry of passing on the Gospel as a message of hope for a forlorn world. There is no connection between the two. The theology that many priests received can never be used in their pastoral preaching or ministry. It implies the restriction of knowledge to the specialist trained for it. There are "dogmatic" theologians, there are "moral" theologians, there are canon lawyers, there are Scripture scholars, there are spiritual directors. It is all this "specialization" which makes standardization possible, just as in industry.

The Pope, in his encyclical on the missions at the end of 1990 and the beginning of 1991, asked very intriguing questions. The *New York Times* said: "He asked very important questions, but he did not answer them. He left the answers to others." (*New York Times,* Wednesday, January 23, 1991, Marlene Simons, p. A2) We would say, "Oh, ask the theologians." I would say, "No, ask *more* than the theologians—ask the people!"

Father Gutierrez, the founder of "Liberation Theology," has always said that he did not invent Liberation Theology: the people of the basic Christian communities invented it. He only organized it. The people of God, the lay people, have been silent for centuries. NOW it is their time to speak.

## What Say You of Jesus the Christ?

In this matter of the question of Christ, the Pope asked, "How are we ever going to say that Christ is a universal Savior *vis-a-vis* the Hindus, the Buddhists, the Muslims and the rest of the world?" He does not answer that question. But we know something about that Christ, and I think the people in smaller communities know it, too. They just need a little help sometimes, and sometimes a little organization. We can begin with the thought that Jesus, the night before he died, said: "It is good for you that I go. Because if I don't go you won't receive the Paraclete. If I do, I'll send the Paraclete to you and the Paraclete will bring you to the complete truth." (Jn 16:7, 13) He was not talking to the theologians, he was talking to the apostles, the only Church existing then. He was talking to the People of God, to the complete truth about himself.

Every time a person laughs in joy, every time a person cries in sorrow, every time a person loves what is beautiful, takes responsibility, pulls away from selfishness, stands up for the truth, refuses to despair when everyone around is despairing, that is the manifestation of God in history, that is the mystery of Christ, that is Jesus becoming the Christ. We know it just as we know our own human lives. We in the temple, we keepers of the temple sometimes refused to grant that sacredness to the world outside. The lay people know well enough that it is a sacred arena. This time, this age, the Church is in the world as if finally we are beginning to see it. It is not a contradictory idea that I am suggesting to you.

Our world is more sacred than we have treated it. It is not a garbage dump. It is not a storage closet from which we can plunder resources. Our world is a sacred place. It is time now for the church to be evangelized by the world. I use those words "evangelized by the world" very deliberately. The full meaning of the gospel *will come from the world and ourselves in dialogue with the world.*

## 4. Centralization

It became absolutely necessary in the Industrial Revolution to have a central headquarters—one central headquarters, national or international, where all final decisions were to be made on policy and administrative matters. Centralization was not always necessary in the Catholic Church, only recently. Starting with the Gospel, Christ is depicted as passing on detailed and special powers to each of the apostles, not just to Peter. Paul describes all the apostles as having the special unique power of the Church. This sharing of power continued in the creation of Eastern rites in four major Patriarchies and several minor ones. Then, bishops were appointed by the people themselves. The period of the 12th to the 19th centuries was one of increasing centralization. We take this for granted. We think it is natural. We think it is essential to the Church. It did not come from the Gospel at all, it came from the Industrial Revolution: parishes strictly chained to a diocese and its chancery; the bishop of the diocese inextricably bound to Rome. By the end of the 19th century, the "centralization" was complete.

Small Christian communities stand for just the opposite. They stand against Standardization, Specialization, Maximization, Centralization, the code of the Industrial Revolution. The revolution in our time is the paradigm shift, the refounding of the Church, which must come from the local churches; it will never come from central headquarters.

These are the signs of the times: the closing of the churches in Detroit, Chicago, Pittsburgh and Cleveland. The solution to these problems are not financial remedies, with bankers in the driver's seat, with 10-year auditing, fundraising ideas to keep the parishes and their buildings viable. The signs of the times may be telling us that we spend too much of our time and our interest in buildings. Now it is time to look more and more to the people, to the "living" Church, not the building.

The Church is a Eucharistic community with a mission; and so we may be tempted to think we can solve our problems from that perspective. We'll just get some liturgists in, we'll get better music. But I think the people living or working in small Christian communities do not need a liturgist or a specialist. I do not think we can leave the meaning of sacraments to the liturgists and specialists. More and more, the meaning of the sacraments will be found outside the Sign, and outside the Church. We are used to doing it the other way around. We are saying that the

"Temple" is the Sacred Place, the Sacramental Signs are the sacred things. We are now beginning to see that it has to be the reverse. The greater meaning is outside the Sign and outside the Church.

Take, for instance, the Eucharist. We believe in the "real presence" of Christ in the Eucharist. This is a "sign" for the real presence of Christ in the world. Which is more important? Which is the greater meaning of the sign? Father Arrupé, former head of the Jesuits, gave the keynote address at the Eucharistic Congress in Philadelphia in which he set this theme for the whole Congress. He said, "Eucharist everywhere in the world will be incomplete as long as there is hunger anywhere in the world." (41st International Eucharistic Congress, Philadelphia: August 1–8, 1976)

I think that we are beginning to see that the deepest meaning of the sacraments of the Church is outside the Temple. It is as if Jesus, or God, were calling us and saying, as he said to Abraham and Sarah: "Come away from your land, your stock, your blood, your ancestors. You've made a small God of me. Come and follow me. Come, let us go and search for the High God." (Gn 12: 1–3) It is as if God were saying to us: "Come away from your Temple, from your altars, from your sanctuaries, come out into the midst of human life where people live and laugh and love and marry and toil and die." Out there you will find God. That is the final meaning of Christianity and the Gospel. Out there!

We need a paradigm shift. Can we say the unthinkable, that the heart of our ministry in our Christian communities today will not be the Mass, it will be where we live, where we value; it will be in the midst of the human lives of our people?

If something is not done on the outside, if hungry people are not fed and ordinary activities of human life like eating, sleeping, and playing are done in a forlorn atmosphere, then our Eucharistic sign will be an empty sign, an empty symbol with no meaning at all for the world. The greatest Eucharistic ministry will be performed, not with a lot of people clustered around an altar fighting about who is going to say the words of consecration or absolution, celibate or single, male or female. The greatest significance might well be the outside sign. The future of the Church might lie outside the Sign, outside the Temple. It has always been true that the Word of truth, the Word of prophesy, is spoken outside the Temple, not inside the Temple.

The small Christian base community might well be pointing us toward the Church of the future. In the true basic small Christian community, the ministerial priesthood will fall into place to function with nothing of the extreme and exclusive importance that was attached to it in the past. That is already happening in the existing basic Christian communities.

People who were formed before the Second Vatican Council in their values and their visions are "yesterday" people. People who were formed after the Council in their visions, their beliefs and faith are "tomorrow" people. It is impossible for yesterday to dialogue with tomorrow with nothing in between. There is only one way yesterday can dialogue with tomorrow: through "today" people, who stand in the arena of today and take the values of yesterday and enshrine them in forms that will speak to tomorrow. "Today" people will respond to a Christian message which is an open, developing and growing message. This message seeks to open people to the radically new which leads to unpredictable results. Our mission—for we are a Eucharistic community with a mission—will not be primarily to establish or to preserve the Church. It will be to participate in the development of the very reign of God.

## Questions for Review and Reflection

*Standards*

When Vincent Donovan speaks of living out of one standard form of church, what examples of parish life come to your mind that fits this one standard form? The concept of "Bigger is better" has affected all of our lives. How does it affect your parish and its life and operation?

*Authority*

Look at the present authority paradigm or model in your parish. Are there persons in the parish community who are powerless? How might they be empowered? Are there areas of "specialization" in your parish that get more attention while other areas are left untouched, are excluded or silenced?

*New Church*

Are there any indications in your parish or in your own experience that the deepest meaning of sacrament might be found "outside the temple"? What aspects of your parish are living in "yesterday's church"? What aspects are part of "today's church"? What is the difference between the two? In what ways might small Christian communities point us to the Church of the future? What would be gained? What would be lost?

## Prayer Ritual

*Music*

"We Walk by Faith and Not by Sight." by Marty Haugen (Chicago: G.I.A. Publications, Inc., 1984)

*Reading*

The revelation of a new heaven and a new earth found in Rev. 21:1–7.

*Process*

Ask the people to quietly reflect on the reading and to think of a symbol that best describes their own model or paradigm of church. After a few moments, ask people to describe the symbol and its meaning to the person next to them. Then, as a large group, share the symbols around the circle and what type of church they reveal.

After the discussion, the following reflection is read by four separate readers. It came from an article by Peter Hebblethwaite that appeared in the October 24, 1980, issue of the *National Catholic Reporter,* entitled "Synod Dreams of Cardinal Hume."

Reader 1:  I am a fortress. I am the church, strong and upstanding. Every approaching stranger I regard with fear. Those who guard me treat those who draw near to me as enemies to be repelled. From my fortress, voices of those outside cannot be heard.

Reader 2:  I am a pilgrim, a pilgrim through history and through life. I am the Church. I am hastening toward a vision, toward all truth. But I have not yet reached it. I limp along the road.

Reader 3:  There are signposts to show the way, or rather, they tell me that this or that road is not the right one. The road signs are often weather-beaten and new paint is needed. It takes time to get the work done. The wrong paint is sometimes being put on the signposts and I am afraid.

Reader 4:  1 am searching. This is so painful for me. My leaders, too, along the pilgrimage are often not always clear themselves. I must never fail to listen to the other pilgrims with me. All pilgrims need encouragement. I must speak gently, compassionately, co-agonize with them, lead them gradually and speak a language which enables all.

Ask the group to quietly reflect on the reading as it relates to their model or symbol of church.

*Closing*

As a large group, read aloud the following prayer, rotating sides. After each section everyone sings the refrain from David Haas' "Harvest of Justice" (G.I.A. Publications, Inc., 1985).

Right Side: We are the church, inside and outside. We envision our- selves evolving into a new paradigm. You are our source of new life and new vision.

Response: Refrain from "Harvest of Justice"

Left Side: We image a church which is inclusive, a church which goes beyond the standard, beyond maximization, beyond specialization and beyond one form. You are our courage and compassion.

Response: Refrain from "Harvest of Justice"

Riqht Side: We long for a new form of church which respects the needs of "yesterday" and "tomorrow." Grant us the wis- dom to live "today" in such a way that our future is re-created anew.

Response: Refrain from "Harvest of Justice"

Left Side: In all of our unknowns, we give you thanks for being the integrating God of our lives who is ever-present in all of creation, in the plants, animals, people, and in the prom- ises of hope and love.

Response: Refrain from "Harvest of Justice"

Conclude with a Greeting of Peace.

# CHAPTER TEN

# The Inner and Outer Mission

RELIGIOUS FORMATION IS A KEY INGREDIENT OF PARISH LIFE and operation. So is Christian service. This covers both service to the poor and needy and confrontation of unjust structures and situations. Formation and service are not separate entities but aspects of the same mission.

To be fully formed as a follower of Christ includes not only personal development but a sensitivity to the needs of others. Conversely, when an individual or group begins confronting an area of injustice or oppression, they undergo personal growth and transformation as well.

This interplay of personal development and Christian service reveals how closely connected are the inner and outer mission of a parish. Part of the inner mission is the religious formation and personal development of its own members. The outer mission is the impact of the local church on its surrounding neighborhood and in the world at large. These two missions are the same. They are two sides of the same coin. A parish is not Christian if only one aspect is operative.

Many techniques and approaches can be used for the religious formation of youth and adults in a parish. These may be effective in themselves but they are not authentic unless people are confronted by the need to extend their practice of faith beyond themselves, their families and inner circle of friends and associates, even beyond their church to the world at large. However it is done, whether through a parochial school or religious education classes, in homes or small groups or parish missions or adult education programs, an integral part of these attempts at formation must be Christian service, which includes such areas as social action, evangelization, reaching out to the poor, the lonely, and the oppressed.

As an example of how the inner and outer mission of a parish interact, consider the following version of the parable of the wedding banquet found in Matthew 22:1–14.

## A Modern Parable

The adult formation committee spent many months planning a celebration of new life for the Saturday before Pentecost. They wanted people to experience what it would be like to be a new follower of Jesus, just as those who heard the apostles speak as they came out of the upper room on that first Pentecost morning.

The committee had set up the day so that as people came to the celebration they would be presented with a new sweatshirt. These would be of varied colors, each with a New Testament name such as Parthian, Mede, Elamite, Phrygian, Pamphylian or Egyptian. The committee was able to get a good price on the sweatshirts. The entire day, including lunch, was only $20.00 per person.

The sweatshirts would determine which small group a person belonged to for the day. Each group would have an "apostle" for its leader. Once people learned which group they belonged to and had a chance to get acquainted, they would gather as a large group to hear the Scripture reading from the Acts of the Apostles about the first Pentecost. From then on, they were to be identified as one of the churches of the 1st century. Once they heard the Scripture reading, they were to go off to their own "country" (classroom) to hear, as if for the first time, stories about Jesus. They were then to talk about miracles (stories) that had happened to them or their loved ones and begin to construct "The Scriptures" from personal experiences of Jesus in their lives. At lunch time, all the "Christian Churches" would gather for a meal, bringing with them provisions located in each classroom, as if coming from each local church or country. This was to symbolize the early church experience of placing all one's possessions before the assembly to be used for the good of all.

In the afternoon, the focus would be on the early persecutions and what the cost of being an early Christian might be. Its session would begin with a description of "Household Churches" in the 1st century, as described in the Acts of the Apostles. Throughout the afternoon, messengers would visit the various churches and bring words of encouragement from such people as Paul, Barnabas, James, and Peter.

All the Christians would gather at 4:00 for a common Eucharistic celebration. Snacks would follow as people evaluated the experience.

The committee was so enthusiastic about the day that they could hardly wait for it to happen. They sent out personal invitations to all registered parishioners and supplemented this with posters, bulletin notices, and announcements at all the Masses.

One slight glitch was that Pentecost fell on Memorial Day weekend. The committee, however, was undaunted. They knew they had such a good program that people would choose to attend despite other plans they might have made for the weekend. The planners were not sure just how many to expect but they ordered sweatshirts and food for over a hundred people. They hoped they would have enough to go around.

That they did and then some. At 9:00 on Saturday morning, the time the program was to begin, the committee, facilitators (apostles), sweatshirts, food, readings and rooms were all set, but no one showed up. By 9:15 AM a few faithful parishioners appeared, 10 people in all. The committee started calling people as a personal invitation. It was to be such a wonderful day, they were sure people would respond. All they got were answering machines. The few they did reach were busy making plans for the weekend or had relatives and friends coming over. The planners were crushed.

At 9:45 AM they all huddled together, including the 10 people who had shown up, and tried to figure out what to do next. They could absorb the cost of the sweatshirts and food if they had to, but what about all the wonderful events that were planned? Must all of this go for naught? One of the facilitators remembered the Gospel story about the king who had a wedding feast and none of his invited guests showed up. What did he do? He went out to the byways and invited everyone he could find to come to the banquet. "Why not give it a try?" they decided. "Whom do you think we could find?"

It seemed like a crazy idea but it was worth a try. Armed with a load of sweatshirts, everyone present set out, 25 in all, to invite whomever they could find to this special day on the Early Church.

It took over an hour, but by 11:00 people started showing up wearing bright new sweatshirts and looking very bewildered. Some were from the local overnight shelter. They had just finished breakfast and were heading out for the day, wondering what it might entail. This was the last thing they expected. Others came from the supermarket, kids in toe. A daycare was quickly set up, individuals offering to babysit, one or two hours at a time. One "apostle" had gone to the health club nearby and found a few young adults who had nothing better to do. Another "apostle" hit the local McDonald's and Burger King and discovered a number of people who took the risk, lured by the promise of a free sweatshirt.

In all, over 40 people showed up, a motley group by all accounts, but enough to make the process work. The agenda was shifted and shortened. It got off to a good start by 11:30 AM.

After an initial orientation and Scripture reading, they got into their local "early church" for a short session and returned to the large group for lunch around 12:30 PM. All those with the same color sweatshirt ate together. They began to get into the swing of the day and loosened up some. All, that is, except one young, rather muscular fellow. He had left his sweatshirt in the classroom and kept to himself, looking very much out of place. One of the organizers went over to him and asked him what was the matter. He didn't have much to say. It wasn't that he was angry or upset, he just didn't catch the spirit of the day. She could see that no amount of support and encouragement would help. In the end she asked him to leave. His attitude would only dampen the high spirits of the others in the room. He left quietly, leaving the sweatshirt behind.

After lunch, the people went back in their own "countries" to share stories and talk about common experiences. This was the history-making period of their local "early church." They had no problem getting into the persecution phase or the experience of the catacombs. Many of the participants had similar events from their own lives. One person was gay, another a single parent. Others were homeless or on drugs. Their lives were filled with oppression and experiences of hiding from prejudices. The facilitators, rather than having to lead the discussion, kept their mouths shut, their eyes getting wider with each new story.

The participants loved the messengers who brought "Epistles" of support and instruction. Many were more in tune with the Scriptures than the messengers themselves. They had been using these words of solace for years.

When it was time for Mass, the priest and planners looked at each other and wondered whether to go ahead with the Mass as planned or have just a prayer service to sum up the day. One of the "apostles" asked, "What would Jesus do? What would the real apostles do? They would break bread together."

It was done informally, as it might have happened in the early church. All the people gathered by country in their multicolored sweatshirts.

At homily time, people were invited to share their insights. This they did with great variety and much feeling. When communion time came, not everyone received. Those who wished were not refused the opportunity, however. Jesus had become alive in the group during the day. Communion was the culmination of the gift of Christ himself to all those who attended, organizers and participants alike. The liturgy was followed with cheese and soft drinks while people talked about what the day had meant to them.

Most of the participants gave high praise for the day, and were grateful for being invited. The people dispersed at 5:00 PM, each with a fond invitation that they were welcome to come to church whenever they wished. "Wear the sweatshirt," they were urged, "so we'll be sure to recognize you."

After everyone was gone, the planners put up their feet to talk about the day. It didn't go as originally planned, that's for sure, but it did go well, very well. There were shaky moments. One was when the young children showed up. Another was the person who didn't know any English. Fortunately these challenges were met without much difficulty. The babysitters took turns so that it was not too taxing. A translator was uncovered who spent the day paired up with the Spanish-speaking person. One leader did remark that she felt sorry for the young fellow who didn't fit in. "That was his choice. You can't force a horse to drink," she concluded. As the organizers reflected on the day, they felt relaxed and joyful about how well it went. They received much more than they gave and would never forget this "special day" of being church.

This modern version of the wedding feast has many facets. The original plan of the adult formation committee was to give parishioners an experience of the early church firsthand. It was to be a day of growth and religious development.

As the day unfolded, much more happened. The emphasis shifted from forming "our own people" to reaching out to the marginal and unlikely "Christians" and giving them a chance to be formed and, in turn, "inform" the planners about essential aspects of Christianity. The tables had been turned.

This is one example of how the inner and outer mission of a parish are interconnected. To concentrate on one to the exclusion of the other is a misrepresentation of the message that Jesus keeps trying to get through to us in our everyday experience. The people we meet, the situations we encounter, the insights and movements we experience have a purpose. They call us to new depths of understanding of what our mission and ministry is in life. The local parish should help provide understanding into what these occasions mean and a framework and support structure for responding generously to moments of grace.

## Implications

What implications does this story have for the future of religious formation and Christian service in a Catholic parish? The first insight is that God plays no favorites. Or if God does, it is the people we least expect, the ones who are hidden from our view unless we look very closely.

The parishioners who were invited "to the feast" had better things to do. Only 10 showed up. This is not a judgment on the others who didn't come. They are not bad people. They just got left out of a wonderful opportunity to be further formed in their faith. They will experience other occasions for growth and will once again have a chance to say yes or no. Grace is an invitation that is freely offered, not forced upon us.

The people who were formed through the experience were, first of all, the leaders and planners themselves. When they decided not to give up and cancel the day but to seek out other alternatives, their formation began. Their preconceptions and expectations were altered and readjusted as they opened up the program to new people from different lifestyles and backgrounds.

The committee, in other words, was not exempt from the formation process. There are no "haves" or "have-nots" needing formation in a parish. Even the most involved and well-educated, staff and lay leaders alike, are prime targets for God's ongoing formation process.

## *Personal Invitation*

A second implication from the story is that no judgments should be made about whom to invite to the "banquet." Personal invitation is the key. Announcements and notices in the bulletin will not do the trick. Reaching out personally is the most effective tool. Whom to contact is the question. God plays no favorites.

In one of the parishes we worked with, as the participants filed into the room, the pastor turned to us and said, "Oh, oh, we're in trouble." We asked why. "Because," he said, "there are two people in the parish with the same name. The people who made the calls phoned the wrong one. You'll see what I mean." Sure enough, as we were quieting down for prayer, the unexpected guest said, "Can I say something?" We responded, "No, not now. That will come later." That's all it took, a gentle but forceful response about the parameters of interaction. He settled down and responded well to our meeting. He came from a fundamentalist perspective and quoted Scripture whenever possible, but he was not disruptive or domineering. In fact, he gave the other participants a new perspective. When the day was over, the pastor was amazed at the outcome. He himself was opened up to a new reality, and was challenged to feel more positive toward the parishioners.

Sometimes it is helpful to think of the least likely candidates for a specific program or event. Take a risk in inviting them to participate or get them to help plan the function. This has been one key to the success of the Christian Initiation process. The least likely candidates became the shining examples of faith and commitment to others, sponsors and neophytes alike.

The success of the "early church experience" in our modern parable was the result of reaching out to the least likely candidates, the marginals, alienated and unchurched. This is one example of how the inner and outer vision of church are interconnected and linked together. How much of what is offered in parish formation programs is directed to the "saved"? It's like singing to the choir. It's a closed system.

Christian formation in the parishes of the next century will have to bridge the gap between the in-groups and the ones who could benefit the most from faith development, that is, the outsiders. It was the "outsiders'" experience that proved so valuable to the early church experiment. It put flesh on it and gave it a ring of reality. These "outsiders" spoke with authority, in other words.

## *Freedom to Choose*

A third implication from our story is that people are free to accept or reject God's invitation of grace and new life. The young man who came to the gathering but refused to participate is one example. God keeps giving the gift of new life. It is not a one-time-only offer. We are given new opportunities again and again. One rejection is not the end of grace-giving.

Nevertheless, the experience of one person having the chance for something good and rejecting it is a common occurrence. This is not the fault of the planners or leaders. People can be offered an opportunity but they must be allowed the freedom to say, "Thanks, but no thanks."

Those responsible for formation and Christian service must keep this in mind so as not to become discouraged. Their role is to offer the invitation, not to force or manipulate people against their will. Even worse, they are not to make people feel guilty for not participating. Whoever shows up are the ones who are "chosen" to be the "community of faith" for that event. Work within realistic limits is the key.

## *Abundance in the Midst of Scarcity*

A fourth lesson the parable revealed is that there is an abundance of formation and service opportunities waiting to be tapped, given the willingness to look beyond the scarcities and search for the occasions of growth those scarcities create. No one showed up for what the planners knew was a great and exciting event. They were not willing to accept defeat. People were scarce. Go out and look for new people. They let the Lord guide them into the marketplace, the byways and backwaters of urban life.

A suburban parish opens up a food kitchen, wondering if anyone will show up. "We don't see any poor around here but they must be somewhere," the planners contend. Show up they do and in record numbers, the elderly, the unemployed, the dependent mothers. The planners are awakened to a need they only guessed at. They were "formed" by the experience.

A small-town parish links up with a poor parish in Mexico. They send money at first. Pictures arrive from the sister parish. Parishioners start studying the Mexican culture and begin taking Spanish classes. Within a few years a parish work crew spends a month in Mexico, helping build a drainage and sewer system for their fellow Mexican parishioners. They return home never to be the same. In the words of the Jesuit Volunteer Corps, they were "ruined for life."

A city parish opens a shelter despite criticism from some parishioner's that this will "bring in the riffraff to the parish." Some of the people who volunteered to stay overnight or cook breakfast in the morning don't go to church. They like helping out and doing something practical for the homeless. As one of the workers mentioned, "Mass is not my bag." This prompted a discussion among the workers one morning after breakfast was served. A person who did attend church talked about the nourishment of the Eucharist, how feeding the hungry was a way of extending the Body of Christ to others. The meal they just served was, in a sense, a liturgy that flowed from the Eucharist. It got the person who didn't go to Mass thinking that he might try coming once in a while. This is an example of the outer mission, Christian service, fostering the inner mission, personal spiritual growth.

The opportunities for extending the dual mission of parish life are plentiful, just waiting to be noticed. What it takes is a leadership open to new ways of being church, to new avenues for doing religious education.

## Partnership

A fifth implication from the wedding feast is that formation and outreach happen best when it is done among equals. Jesus kept telling his followers not to "Lord it over others." The adult formation committee was humbled when people didn't show up for the day. They went out and invited new people in. But they did not look down on these newcomers. They accepted them with open arms and treated them as partners on the journey of faith. It was this willingness to be one with all who arrived that opened up the leaders to learning so much from the experience.

When each "early church" was gathered in classrooms, every person was a companion, a fellow traveler, an equal member of the church. This is the magic that Jesus worked among his followers, that he was one with their lives and sorrows, hurts and pains. We can do no less if we are to fulfill the inner and outer mission of the parish.

There is no privileged class, no group or individual that has a comer on formation or Christian service. We learn from each other, we serve one another and others as equals. We are all partners in the faith.

This sounds so obvious that we often forget that the image portrayed by the parish is often quite the opposite. We live in an age of trained professionals with ministerial credentials. There is a right and wrong way to educate or provide service. All of this is true, but what can be lost in the process is an openness to be "trained" by those with the least formal education. Each has a gift to share. Some are called to provide guidance and leadership, others come with riches in lived experience and insight. The environment must be one of partnership and shared wisdom if the formation and service is to be Christ-centered and grace-gifted.

## Symbols More Than Words

Finally, the use of symbols was a key ingredient to the "early church" experiment. The sweatshirts provided the calling card to the newly-invited participants. The shirts also gave people an identity and formed them into groups. It was a visible manifestation of what the day was all about, one that could be easily understood and that tapped into their lived experience.

Good symbols are essential to getting across the mission of a parish. They touch people's hearts and give flesh and meaning to the theory. Some of the traditional symbols have lost their impact. New and fresh ones need to be discovered, ones that communicate the power of the Gospel message.

We worked with a parish team and support staff that had a difficult time communicating with each other. As a way of symbolizing the present level of interaction, we had the group of 15 stand in a circle. One person held a ball of yarn. She tied one end to her wrist and tossed the ball to one other person she had communicated with over the last two weeks. That person held the yarn and tossed the ball to another, giving a concrete occasion of when he had talked to that person. The process continued until the ball of yam was used up. What resulted was an interlocking web of communication among members of the group. The people were surprised at how much communication was taking place, some of it quite deep. We asked that the web of yarn be placed on the floor in front of the group so they could see the "map" of interaction over the last two weeks. This symbol set a tone for the rest of the day and allowed them to grow in their appreciation and respect for each other. This same exercise was mentioned in Chapter Eight to help a small faith community express forgiveness. Here it is used to symbolize the communication network among staff members. One exercise manifesting different realities.

Sweatshirts, a ball of yarn, candles, car keys, telephones, hats, shoes, rings, the list of options is endless. Formation and service is best done with symbols that touch people's hearts and speak to a reality that is difficult to express directly. One good symbol can take the place of hours of theory and explanation.

## Shifts for the Future

What does this tell us about the way formation and Christian service will happen in a parish of the next millennium? For one thing, it will be varied. Some parishes will have schools and others will not. Hopefully the criteria for having a school will be linked to both the inner and outer mission.

Does the school help form people for Christian service? Does it provide for the education of the marginals and forgotten people or is it a haven for the rich and privileged? As more and more Catholic schools tend to be regionalized, serving a cluster of parishes, are they still linked into the mission of the parishes? Or are they cut adrift, becoming in effect private schools with little connection to local church? Interconnecting the inner and outer mission of church will help serve as a framework and challenge to the parochial school system of the next century.

## Parents As Educators

Too often parents send their children to a Catholic school or religious education program to make up for what is lacking in the home. They expect the religious formation to be taken care of by the institution instead of considering it as supporting and augmenting a growth in faith that takes place within the home.

A teacher in one of the parishes we worked with did an experiment. Over the course of the school year she visited all the parents of her students. The parish was located in a racially-mixed area. Many of the families who sent children to the parish school were not Catholic.

She discovered a significant difference between the parents of Catholic children and the non-Catholics. The Catholic parents said they sent their children to the school to give them a Catholic education, one that included high academics and Catholic formation.

Those who were not Catholic, on the other hand, said they sent their children to the parish school not only because it provided a better education than the public schools but also because it supported the same morals and religious values they were trying to instill in their children at home.

The difference between the two groups was subtle but significant. The Catholics were looking to the Catholic school to fill up what they felt was lacking at home. They did not feel equipped to give their children the religious formation that the school provided.

The parents who were not Catholic saw it another way. They felt responsible for the religious development of their children. They were the primary religious educators. The school was a support to their own efforts at forming their children into followers of Christ.

This is where the inner and outer mission of a parish blend together. We do a disservice to our parishioners, both young and old, if the parish becomes a closed system, a safe haven for its own members. It must see itself as a support and challenge to its people.

## Bridging Gaps

Too often a chasm exists between the church and people's everyday lives. Religious education is relegated to a few hours a week in a formal setting rather than seeing it as a lifelong experience of discovery and insight into God's call and our response.

The "classrooms" for religious formation in the new century will include a wide variety of settings and experiences. These will include small faith communities, family discussions, telephone chains, computer networks, recovery groups, faxed messages, videos, cable television, work camps, soup kitchens, shelters, prayer groups, urban plunges. These are some of the vehicles that will be used to get across what our religion is all about. It is not a reality to be protected and kept apart from the world. It is to be shared and used for the good of all.

It is the outer mission of church, the reaching out to the lonely, the needy and the oppressed that will nourish and transform the inner mission of personal and communal formation. It is the outer mission that will keep the formation programs relevant and grounded in reality. It is the outer mission that will touch hearts and convert the self-righteous and self-satisfied into apostolic followers of Christ. It is the linking of the inner and outer mission, in other words, that will save the Church in the third millennium.

## The Wedding Feast Revisited

What if the modern version of the wedding feast used earlier in this chapter were not an accident or the result of the invited guests not showing up? What if the formation program was planned that way?

Suppose the adult education committee decided to seek out the marginal people from the start. They asked everyone who came to church to locate one person within their family or among their friends who had stopped attending or never had attended church.

The parishioners were asked to bring this person with them to a Sunday afternoon potluck in the gym. "Bring a dish and a friend" was the slogan. The theme was "Christ in many places with many faces." The religious educators were not the committee members or even the church-going parishioners. The religious educators for this event were the invited guests, that is, the ones who were unchurched. They had just as much experience and insights into how Christ operates in the world as the active parishioners.

In groups of four, each person told a story about an unusual moment of grace, an occasion when God entered into their lives, a time when the seed fell on good ground. They then identified common aspects of the stories and wrote a headline on newsprint representing the foursome. These were put up around the room for all to see. "Alive and Well Amid The Chaos," read one. "Engines Restarted, Avoids Crash," was another. "Church Granted Absolution by Women," was a third.

The afternoon was simple. They told their stories, read their headlines, shared a common meal and were invited to come again if they so wished. The message was clear, whether they came to church or not. They had all experienced God working in their midst. They all had a lesson to give and to receive from one another. The lesson is the same-love God and love one another, no matter one's color, background or way of life.

We learn from each other—the inner mission—and we put our insights into action—the outer mission. The parish provides the framework and occasion for this simple message to take root in our hearts and be carried into the world around us.

Consider the following example of how the inner and outer mission might be related in raising people's consciousness about their call to minister in their everyday lives.

## Formation for Everyday Ministry

The place to start is the weekend liturgies. This is the place where the majority of parishioners can be reached. Once a month, one of the weekend liturgies would be devoted to a different occupation. Health care, sales, civil service, homemaking, consulting and data processing might be six to start with.

Suppose the first weekend of the series spotlights health care. The Scripture readings might be centered around the theme of healing and care for the sick. Any of the cures of Jesus would be appropriate, or his parables about healing, such as the one describing the Good Samaritan.

At the beginning of the liturgy, the commentator would explain the focus for the Mass and would ask those who are involved in the health care profession to stand so they could be recognized.

After the readings, the homily might be presented by the priest or deacon, along with someone involved in the health care profession, applying scripture to his or her occupation. The petitions would focus on the needs and ministries of those in the health care profession. The Masses, however, are only the first step toward people discovering how their jobs and occupations might serve as an outlet for their everyday ministry.

The most important step toward this new awareness is giving people the opportunity to talk about aspects of their daily routine that might be considered ministry. This step is best done in small groups. The question is how to form these groups. The period following Mass can be a critical moment for raising this awareness of one's everyday ministry and for offering people the opportunity to talk about their experience.

Those who identified themselves as being involved in health care are invited for coffee and doughnuts after Mass. During this time they, along with their spouses, are invited to participate in a six-week-long support group experience. Groups made up of 6–10 people to provide for better sharing. The meetings are limited to six weeks so that people do not feel they are signing their lives away.

Each health care group is led by a "gift-evoker." These are health care professionals contacted earlier to help the participants reflect on their work as ministry.

The spouses of those in health care professions can also give insights into how the person's work relates to their home and family lives as a ministry.

Don't be surprised if at the first invitation there might only be enough people for a single group. It takes time to build up a tradition of reflection groups related to one's everyday ministry. The role of staff members and parish leaders is to provide the occasion and opportunity for these groups to form and to monitor their progress.

As people begin to discover how their work could be a ministry, they begin to reflect on what God is asking of them. They experience a call to a deeper understanding of grace, prayer, service, and ministry. They start to look around for guidance. Spiritual counseling must be available as this need arises. This is where the staff comes in.

Members of the parish staff, whether priest, religious educator, or pastoral associate, must provide opportunities for people to talk about ways of transforming their jobs into ministry. "What is God calling me to do?" "Where can I find the strength to follow the call?" These are questions that need to be talked out with someone who will listen and offer feedback.

As the concept of empowering people to practice everyday ministry takes hold in a parish, it begins to change the way a parish operates. Its liturgies, for instance, begin to stress symbols and rituals that more closely reflect people's daily lives and occupations. The use of the symbols and artifacts of daily life, as well as special rituals, such as commissioning of different professionals, or asking people in service professions to come forward to share their experiences, can emphasize the connection between ministry and daily living.

The weekend liturgies, in other words, become intimately linked with the daily lives of the people. The gap between Mass and "the rest of life" begins to close. Religion is no longer relegated to an isolated compartment of people's lives, but instead enters into their deliberations and decisions throughout the week.

As this new approach takes hold, adult education programs change as well. Groups of people in similar jobs and occupations gather to reflect on their personal experience. They discover how the Scriptures amplify these experiences. A number of farmers, for instance, sits down one evening to discuss the difficulties of maintaining a family farm. They also talk over their concerns about caring for the soil and providing for hungry people, especially in Third World countries. After spending time talking about personal experiences, they reflect on the stories of Jesus, such as the one about the farmer who tore down his silos and built new ones to make room for all his surplus grain and then dies before being able to enjoy a life of leisure. That is the type of adult development and theologizing that people can relate to because it touches their life experiences.

Another example might be a group of senior citizens who come together to talk about keeping house, along with the difficulties of shopping, cleaning, and maintaining their property. Their ministry might be to help each other get to church, balance the checkbook, or do the shopping. Their Scripture reflection centers on the widow who lost a coin (or earring or keys or Social Security check) and scoured the house to find it. When she found it, she called up all her friends and had a party.

This linking of liturgy, education, and parish life to everyday experience can turn a parish into a vehicle for lay ministry training and personal conversion. One other essential aspect of encouraging everyday ministry is to recognize and reward those who catch on to what this means and who begin to practice it in their everyday lives. Acknowledging these people also provides models to the entire parish community of people who practice ministry in their daily lives. Their example gives others support and strength to do the same themselves.

## Ingredients for Everyday Ministry

To make this effort at empowering people for their everyday ministry effective, certain ingredients must be present:

1. Providing the occasion for people in similar types of occupations and lines of work to gather together in small groups to discuss the joys, difficulties, pressures and tensions of their work and to see what aspects of their jobs could be ministerial and what aspects are not.
2. These groups must be facilitated by "gift-evokers" who can draw out the gifts, talents, and inner movements of people so that they can experience what possibilities exist for being ministers on their jobs or in their daily lives.
3. As people grow in the realization of the call to be ministers, they must be given opportunities to talk to a counselor or spiritual guide about what this call might mean for them.
4. The weekend liturgies must reflect this emphasis on closing the gap between religion and daily living by use of symbols and rituals that relate to people's everyday lived experience.
5. Adult education models must emphasize concrete personal experience as a way of discovering what it means to be a Christian in today's world.
6. Role models must be found and acknowledged so that others can see that everyday ministry is possible for the ordinary person, that it is not reserved for only a few special people.

The parish, then, becomes a place in which people become aware of the call to everyday ministry (outer mission) and the place where they gain support and encouragement to exercise this ministry (inner mission). Volunteers who work in the parish as leaders or organizers of programs and activities are there for the primary purpose of helping the entire congregation live out this call to be full-time ministers in their personal lives. The focus of the parish, in other words, is in the marketplace, as it attempts to bridge the gap between the church and the world, between religious practice and daily living. This is part of the essence of being parish and an essential ingredient of lay ministry.

# Questions for Review and Reflection

*One Mission*

When have you experienced the religious formation of the parishioners linked to the outreach ministry of the parish? How common is this experience? How have the two aspects influenced one another? Could the story of the modern "Wedding Feast" happen in your parish? Where would the people from the "highways and byways" come from? What would be their impression of the parish? Would they be accepted and feel "at home"?

*Implications*

Identify an experience in your own life in which an unexpected event or chance encounter helped form your faith. How did you react? Did it include a personal invitation from someone? What kind of freedom or non-freedom did you experience? Did you discover any abundance in the midst of scarcities? What symbols or rituals come to mind that were part of the experience or that you use to keep the moment fresh in your mind? Did it help bridge any gaps between yourself and others that you don't usually associate with or encounter?

*Everyday Ministry*

In the work that occupies most of your time, are there aspects that you would consider a ministry more than a job? Can you identify the difference between the two? Do you experience others around you who are ministers?

# Prayer Ritual

*Music*

"Spirit Blowing Through Creation," by Marty Haugen. (Chicago: G.I.A. Publications, 1987)

*Prayer*

Leader: Come to our aid, Spirit of Transformation.

All: Spirit who moves among us, transform the face of the earth. Turn our hearts to the needs of the poor.

Leader: Come to us, Spirit of Compassion.

All: Spirit of love, open us to understanding and support.

Leader: Stay with us, Spirit of the Living One.

All: Rouse us from our slumber and bring forth a new awareness of greater life for all.

Leader: Conceive in us, Creative Spirit,

All:     A confident faith, an expectant hope and a lasting love for all your people.

*Reading*

Read aloud the account of Wisdom in our lives. (Wisdom 6:12–21)

*Process*

Give each person two index cards, each card having the same number written on it. Everyone should have a different number. Ask people to take off one shoe, put one card in the shoe and then throw it into the center of the group. Everyone then chooses a number from out of a hat and locates the shoe with that number. Ask people to put on this shoe and walk around the room for a few minutes and then return to the group to talk about the experience.

*Closing*

Read aloud the following prayer, each person reading a different line.

- We give you thanks, Spirit of Wisdom, for you speak to us in ways that often surprise us.
- You uncover truths that we have kept hidden from ourselves.
- You support us in tasks we fear to undertake alone.
- We give thanks for your invitation to the banquet.
- We give thanks for your call to growth and fullness of life.
- We give thanks for walking in other people's shoes.
- You comfort and encourage us in our struggle to minister and to be faithful.
- Inspire us.
- Encourage us.
- Fill us with enthusiasm for the mission of your church.
- We ask you to form us inside and outside.
- Give us a confident faith,
- An expectant hope,
- A lasting love
- For all your people.

Conclude with the refrain from "You Are The Presence" by David Haas (Chicago: G.I.A. Publications, 1987)

# CHAPTER ELEVEN

# *Money and Involvement*

MONEY IS NOT THE ESSENCE OF PARISH LIFE. IT IS HARD TO run one without any, however. Even Jesus sent Peter off in search of a coin in the mouth of a fish in order to pay the taxes. Looking for a new way to be parish includes looking for a new way of encouraging people to contribute to the life of the parish community, not only their time, talent and energy but their financial resources as well.

At the present time, only about a quarter to a third of the parish membership contribute to its upkeep through regular contributions. The majority, in other words, are only occasional givers, if they donate at all.

A Gallup poll conducted in 1990 showed that on the average Catholics give only 1.3% of their household income to all charities, 1% going to the church. By comparison, Protestants give 2.4% and Jews, 3.8%. Members of all other religions including Muslims, Mormons, Hindus and Buddhists and Eastern Orthodox, give 2.7% of their household incomes. *(National Catholic Reporter,* Nov. 9, 1990) Catholics, in other words, give the lowest percentage. Why is this?

A few years ago, Andrew Greeley and Bishop McManus teamed up to write a book on the reasons people do not give more. *(Catholic Contributions,* Thomas More Press, 1987.)

In the book they listed the reasons why Catholics are holding back their contributions. Primary among them was anger at the officials of the Church because of the content and authority of their teaching regarding sexual morality, "because of their lack of participation in the fiscal process, and because they do not understand the costs of running a modern, full-service parish . . " (p. 87)

These are some of the reasons, but not all. The phenomenon is far too complex for a simple explanation. Much depends on a person's level of involvement in the Church and parish. The 1990 Gallup Poll quoted earlier found that those who attended weekly religious services contributed more money than those who did not attend services, no matter what religious affiliation a person might have.

173

The breakdown of how many Catholics attend weekly Mass then becomes important. About 72% of all baptized Catholics are registered in a given parish. The rest identify themselves as Catholics, but have not taken the initiative or had the interest to sign up as members of a parish. The reasons are varied. Some were members when young, but once they moved out of their childhood home never bothered to link up with a parish.

Others married a spouse who was not Catholic, either as a first or second marriage, and did not have a common Catholic tradition in the home. The support structure for belonging to a Catholic parish was missing, so they never made the effort. Others, a much smaller group, got angry at the Church or local parish leadership and made a conscious choice to drop their membership.

Most of the nonregistered Catholics rarely, if ever, attend church, perhaps only on special occasions such as Christmas, Easter, weddings, funerals. Because the most common way of contributing to the church is at the collection during Mass, these people do not give to the church in the same proportion as those who belong to a parish.

Of the remaining 72% of Catholics who are registered in a parish, 25% of them do not attend Mass on a weekly basis. These people will have envelopes, but because they are not regular Mass-goers, they do not have a chance to drop their envelope in the collection basket. The impetus to contribute is missing.

This leaves 47% of the baptized Catholics in a given area who attend Mass on a weekly basis. Do these people contribute? No. The burden of supporting the church and the parish operation falls on those who not only come regularly to the weekend Masses, but who also attend other events in the parish, belong to parish groups or participate in parish ministries and programs. This group is half of the Mass-goers, that is, 24%. These are the people who give their time and money to the parish and other charitable causes. They give far more than 1.3% of their household income. They are closer to the Jewish average of 3.8%.

If we consider only registered parishioners and drop off the 28% who do not belong to any parish, then this 24% percent who are strong givers become a third of the parish membership. This is hardly enough support to keep the operation afloat.

Why the reluctance? Why the reticence among Catholics to contribute to their church? As mentioned earlier, the reasons are mixed and varied. Our work with parishes has uncovered 19 reasons, and this, of course, is not a complete list.

These reasons come from written comments to our surveys, from conversations with leaders and parishioners, as well as from personal observation. Each reason plays a part depending on the person's background, level of involvement in the parish and at-home religious support structures. At the conclusion we will share our reflections as to which reasons may have the greater impact.

## 19 REASONS FOR NON-GIVING

### The Church Is Rich:

Many people don't really believe that the Church or parish needs the money. It is such a large institution; it can survive without their contribution. They look around and see that the parish and Church is pretty well off, thank you. Their own money, at least very much of it, is not needed. There is no crisis here. The Church has survived for centuries. It has all of those treasures in Rome it could sell off, if necessary. The diocese has nice buildings, the rectory looks substantial. It doesn't need my money.

### At Odds with Teachings:

The Church, especially the celibate clergy, doesn't have a clue as to what it means to be married and raise a family. All it does is tell us what not to do. People translate what they experience as an unrealistic stance on birth control, divorce or abortion into noninvolvement and little financial support. Only 12% of Catholic parishioners consider birth control to be wrong, 15% feel divorce and remarriage is wrong, 58% feel abortion is wrong. This disjunction between official Church teachings and people's lived experience causes alienation. The alienation is reflected in nonattendance at Mass and as a result, little or no contribution is made to the parish or institutional Church.

### Catholics on the Fringe:

As mentioned earlier, many Catholics have slowly lost the habit of attending church. It was not so much a conscious choice as an eroding of the will to attend. Home patterns start the trend. While growing up, the parents were not frequent Mass-goers. Even if they were, once a person left home for college or career, lifestyles changed. Mass attendance got pushed to the background. More and more Catholics are not marrying Catholics so that church attendance is not part of one's tradition. Even the advent of children, usually the cause of a re-awakening of religious practice, is not enough to prompt Mass attendance. As the person becomes more and more marginal, any obligation to contribute financially to the Church is lost.

## *Not Asked:*

Hard as it may seem to some pastors and parish leaders, one reason people do not contribute more to the Church is because they have not been asked directly. Some of the comments to our survey say that "All I ever hear from the pulpit is pleas for money." This, of course, is a skewed response based on what captures people's attention. But even the occasional pleas for contributions are not always done well. We heard pastors tell us that they never ask for money. "I don't want people to have a poor experience of liturgy or a watered-down message from the readings." We have also experienced well-planned and well-focused requests for tithing or increases in contributions that have reaped amazing results. People just were not asked, were not made aware of how little they had increased their contributions over the years, how they were not holding up their share of the responsibility for being a member of the parish. They were not asked, in other words.

## *Poor Fiscal Management:*

Catholics are not dumb. They can see if their money is being put to good use. One reason that they are reluctant to give more is because they are afraid that their hard-earned money will be squandered. Most Catholic parishioners, of course, have no idea how their money is being spent, but they are good guessers. They look at the school that has 90 students and takes 50% of the parish budget. They are asked to contribute to a new rectory and wonder if it has to be so elaborate. They don't understand why there have to be so many new staff positions, or why we need new song books, or a $50,000 organ. "Why are we dipping into our savings to keep the parish afloat? Where is all the money going?" they complain.

We are not saying that these are not legitimate expenses, and reasons can be given for any and all of them, and many others besides. But one reason people are reluctant to contribute more is because of a perception they have that the money is not going to good use, especially to areas that fit *their* interests, whether it is school, sports, music, religious education, socializing, peace and justice, etc.

## *No Tradition of Giving:*

The lack of a tradition for contributing to the Church and parish goes back to childhood. The old, pre-Vatican II days of Catholic upbringing had built into it a tradition of giving. These included envelopes for each child in the family, ransoming pagan babies—$5 to the missions and you could name your own baby—special homeroom competitions for giving to the missions and special causes. These traditions—for good or ill—are no longer part of Catholic family life. Children are not accustomed to giving to the same extent as in days gone by. The special seasons of Lent and Advent—traditional periods for collections in the home and school—do not have the same impact or intensity. As a result, Catholics are not accustomed to contributing to the Church when they grow older. When the collection basket comes around, they put in whatever they have in their pockets. They do not consider the parish or Church as a legitimate place for planned giving. They do not set aside, on a regular basis, a set amount for the Church. It is not part of their tradition. They are not in the custom of giving to the Church. Catholics give whatever is left over, which is not usually that much, according to the recent Gallup Poll, about $9.90 per week per household. It is more of a hit-and-miss experience, and unfortunately, mostly miss.

## *In a Rut:*

One reason Catholics do not give more to their church is because they are not used to giving a percentage of their income. They are used to giving a set amount, $1 or $5 or $10 a weekend. They have been consistently giving that same amount for years, despite a continual and by now substantial increase in their income as compared with what they earned when they began giving this set amount. Obviously, from time to time, they will increase their dollar amount, but it is not related to a percentage increase in income. As a result, their contribution does not keep up with their own salaries or promotions, let alone the offsetting impact of inflation. The Church, therefore, receives a much smaller percentage of the person's income now than it did five, ten or fifteen years ago, although the dollar amount may be more.

## *School Tuition:*

Although the number of families with children attending a Catholic school has dropped in recent years, it still is a factor in contribution patterns. In the past, charging tuition for the parish school was the exception. The school was free, or nearly so. It was supported by the contributed services of the "good Sisters" and donations to the parish by the parishioners. That is no longer the case.

Catholic schools are becoming regional institutions, private endeavors supported by tuition and subsidies from the local parishes. The people with children in that regional school give less to the parish because they are contributing to the private education of their children. Many see this as satisfying, at least in part, their commitment to the financial upkeep of the parish and thus put less into the collection basket.

## No Concrete Focus:

Sometimes the lack of giving is a lack of focus. We have often heard from parish leaders that people will give to a building, parish center, organ, Christmas fund, mission appeal, but not to the general operating fund. If the issue or need is concrete, visible and practical, if people see some return for their money, then they will give far more than to the regular weekly collection.

Perhaps leaders are not always concrete in helping people focus attention on visible needs. Parishes that keep issues and needs before their people have better luck raising contribution levels. This is especially true for social issues, such as linking up with a parish south of the border or a mission appeal. Seldom is the carryover made to regular giving, however. People need to know what happens to their money.

## Bored With Mass/Church:

People support what they find attractive, exciting and meaningful. They spend large percentages of their income on entertainment, sports and recreation; very little on Church. Part of the reason is because they find Mass dull and unexciting. It has no spark, no meaning. It does not translate into people's everyday experience. When we ask people what is the primary reason they attend Mass on the weekend, 40% say it is out of a sense of obligation. Twenty percent come primarily out of convenience, or because a family member or friend attends. The more active parishioners say they come because of the feeling of community. Not so those who are not involved. Only 10% of the less-involved members come to Mass because of the music, the homily or the sense of community.

Many people come to Mass, in other words, out of guilt. They feel they have to come. Once they get there, it does not hold their interest. When it comes time for the collection, they give the minimal amount. They do not feel inspired to give. After all, what is the Church giving them in return? It doesn't touch their needs, spark their interest, hold their attention. As a result, it doesn't deserve their contribution.

## Church Is Too Big:

Protestant churches, as a whole, have much smaller congregations than Catholic parishes. Individual members are known by name, recognized when present at worship services, missed when absent. Not so Catholics. The weekend Masses are large gatherings of people who do not know each other. Individuals are lost in the crowd. Recent efforts at greeting people as they come in, introductions at the start of Mass, providing coffee and donuts afterwards have helped create an atmosphere of warmth and hospitality, but individuals are still just that, individuals. They feel lost. The greeting of peace doesn't help much. It has become for many a perfunctory gesture devoid of meaning, almost an interruption to Mass, rather than an integral part of community-building. We ask people on our surveys to react to the statement, "The priests are interested in me personally." Less than 40% agree with the statement. The parish is just too big and impersonal. This affects contribution levels. If a person feels alone, unimportant, part of a crowd, the impetus to contribute to the "crowd" is much less than if the person feels a part of the worshipping community. That is why contributions are so much higher among the more active parishioners. They feel part of the parish community. Their presence makes a difference. Not so for the majority of the Mass-goers.

## *Vague Initiation Rites:*

People who join Protestant churches, at one time or other in their lives, must make a conscious choice to be a member of that congregation. They are "confirmed" in their membership. Along with the choice goes duties and obligations, one of which is contributing to the church's well-being.

This is not the case with Catholics. Membership is far less explicit. Most Catholics are baptized at birth and grow into their Catholic identity. There is no moment when they are required to make a formal, conscious choice of "belonging" to the Church, let alone live up to established duties and responsibilities. Instead, they are to develop from childhood a tradition of church attendance and adherence to Catholic doctrine and teachings. It is a good theory and, given a strong family religious background, it works quite well. This, however, is not the experience for the majority of Catholics. The Sacrament of Confirmation should be the moment of accepting the responsibilities of being an adult Catholic. It happens at a young age. For many, what is supposed to be a formal commitment to the faith does not carry over into adulthood. Nor are those confirmed challenged to fulfill their financial obligation to the Church. As a result, they never get into the habit of giving to the extent that Protestants do who have a more explicit initiation rite.

## *Outdated Theology:*

One reason Catholics give less is because they are out of sync with what's happening in the post-Vatican II Church. Their theological education came to a standstill after Catholic grammar or high school or religious education classes. They have no experience of what Church is about these days. All they see is more and more staff being hired. For what? "Why can't the pastor take care of what has to be done, along with a core of volunteers?" they contend. "It worked in the past. Why do we need a liturgy coordinator and music minister, a primary *and* adult religious education director, a youth minister, *two* pastoral care people, a parish administrator, a principal and a social outreach/human concerns minister? That's not the Church I remember. When I was young the priests and Sisters took care of everything and we had a great parish! Why all this new staff, these new directions?"

Little do people realize that those good Sisters were slave labor and that those days are gone, along with the Sisters. Current theology stresses the obligation of all baptized Catholics to assume their role—their vocation—as lay ministers in the Church and everyday life. This is still a new concept for most Catholics. It has little or no impact on their behavior. A result, their contributions do not increase.

### Poor Leadership:

Our work with parishes across the country has shown that people will contribute more to the parish, both money and time, if the leadership (read pastor) manifests a participative, inclusive style. The "good old days" of the pastor ruling his parish do not go over well in today's Church. People are turned off by an authoritarian, commanding, dictatorial style of leadership. They are also put off by a *laissez-faire,* noncommitted, hermit style of pastoring. Modern-day Catholics have learned to "vote with their pocketbook." They become angry with unilateral decisions that affect their worship space, or children's education, or pet project about which they were not consulted.

Poor leadership affects giving patterns for active as well as inactive parishioners. This is most apparent when a parish has been experiencing rebirth and renewal because of a facilitating, inclusive leadership style. The pastor is then changed and the new leader is not able or willing to continue this participative approach. People react, first with anger and then with apathy. A typical reaction is, "Why bother? He has all the power. Let him run the show. But I'll not contribute as I have in the past. It's for naught." Giving patterns, in other words, become an indictment of poor leadership or an affirmation of good leadership in the parish.

Leadership in the Church beyond the parish can also have an effect. Catholics give smaller percentages of their income if they feel participation in diocesan policy and practice is blocked, if pastoral authority is arbitrary and without accountability. This is especially evident if the reorganization of a diocese, which includes the closing or combining of parishes, is done without the input and feedback of the people affected by the changes. They give up on Church and stop participating on all levels, contributions being one of them.

## *Poor Communication:*

People have no idea what it takes to run a parish these days. They have no knowledge of the costs involved, the time and personnel it takes to keep parish programs and ministries alive. As a result, they have not increased their contributions to keep pace with rising parish costs. For example, fuel prices increase. The gas pumps show it. Airplane prices reveal immediate adjustments, but the parish gets no boost to its income. Why? Because people are not kept informed of increasing costs. They are not told—poor communication—about needs and expenses.

We have suggested to some of the parishes we work with to hold a parish fair before and after the weekend Masses. Every group, project, ministry and organization have booths that explain what they contribute to the life of the parish. It often comes as a shock to parishioners to see all the various works and ministries going on in the parish. They had no inclination about all that made up their parish. This consciousness-raising translates immediately into more volunteers and increased contributions. Communication!

We also suggest an insert into the bulletin each month for each pastoral employee so that parishioners see who is doing what in the parish. Most people see only the priests and are unaware of what other staff members do or even who they are. This visibility translates into more awareness and higher contributions. Communication!

One parish even hired a full-time staff person just for communication and publicity. Contributions went up immediately. There is, in other words, a direct connection between good communication and contributions. The reverse is also true. Poor communication, lower giving.

## *Consumer Needs:*

Catholics are in the mainstream of society. Except for Hispanics and some recent arrivals from the Far East and Eastern Europe, the inferiority complex Catholics experienced because of their ethnic origins is over. "We've made it!" What the mainstream is all about is consumerism. We have to maintain the lifestyle to which we are accustomed, including cars, homes, travel, clothes, technology, the works. This quickly depletes the budget. Little is left over for giving to the Church. It is far down on people's spending priority lists. Rather than carving out a percentage of one's income for Church and charity, they get what is left over, not just from the necessities of tuition, day care, mortgage, but what is left over from the extras—a more expensive car, a boat or lavish Christmas gifts. The Church, in other words, comes after the cake and frosting. It gets the crumbs.

## *Never Enough:*

There is never enough money to go around. No matter how much is coming in from two or three salaries, there is never enough. People are leery about having enough saved for college tuition for the children, health care, retirement. With the uncertainty of America's rising debt and world unrest, people are cautious about where they spend their money. Once again, the Church gets the short end of the stick. The Reagan/Bush years of "trickle-down economics" did not produce any sizeable increases in contributions, especially among Catholics. Now with a tightening of the economic outlook, financial resources will become even more scarce as people start saving for an uncertain future. Those who are contributing to the parish have the same experience as those who don't. There is never enough for them as well. The difference is that those who do contribute put the Church near the top of their list of spending priorities rather than towards the bottom. It is a minority of the parishioners who do this, however.

## *I Deserve What I Worked For:*

Along with consumerism and never feeling there will be enough available for their needs, Catholics also fit into the dominate individualism of American culture. This myth about who we are as Americans stresses self-sufficiency, going it alone, not needing anyone else, doing our own thing. When it comes to money, the party line is, "I worked hard to make this money. I have a right to use it any way I wish. Me and my family come first. The Church has little right to my hard-earned cash."

This attitude translates into a giving pattern that is filled with suspicion and reticence to contribute money that may not protect one's own interests. So people keep the money to themselves.

Americans, for the most part, have grown complacent with their money. The hard days of the Depression are a distant memory. Contribution levels among Catholics were twice as high during the 1930s, 1940s and 1950s as a percentage of income than they are today. People were forced to depend on one another more. Community spirit counteracted the individualism myth. In recent years, more and more Catholics have achieved wealth and the pursuit of happiness. The Church was not part of their social climb. The Church, then, has no claim to the rewards of higher status and increased income levels. People keep it for their own needs instead. "It's my money, after all!" they exclaim.

## *Not Aware of God's Gifts:*

One way to increase parish contributions is to make people aware that whatever wealth or well-being we have comes from a loving God. We have an obligation, therefore, to give back to God a portion of what we have accumulated as an acknowledgment of the source of our gifts. It is an appreciation for how much we depend on God for our very existence. This is an ancient tradition found in prehistoric and native cultures, pouring out a libation as a way of giving thanks to the gods.

In our technological age where we control our environment (for better or worse) and feel less and less in need of an outside Force or Creator, this aspect of appreciation and acknowledgment is lost. Many Catholics do not make the connection between the gifts and benefits they have received and their obligation to give back to God, through charitable works and contributions, a portion of those gifts and benefits. Their faith is weak, their giving limited.

## TAKING POSITIVE STEPS

### *Keep It Personal*

Tithing programs have increased contribution levels significantly in recent years, but it still touches only about a third of the parishioners, those who have a faith grounded in good works, who make the connection between God's good work in them and their responsibility to give back a proportion of their income to God through church and charitable causes.

The first step in overcoming low contribution levels is to make face-to-face, phone-to-phone personal invitations. People need a direct contact. A general appeal from the pulpit or a note in the bulletin won't do it. Calling up someone and asking them to bring some of those wonderful chocolate bars she makes to the next bake sale will assure her presence. Contacting a family in the parish and asking them to bring up the gifts at Mass will make them feel special. Even if they refuse, they feel special for being asked. This can't be done at the last minute just before the priest heads down the aisle. It has to be done in advance, giving people a chance to alter their plans and get ready for their new assignment. A core of volunteers should be assigned for the one task of calling up or visiting individual parishioners and asking their opinion and feedback on a parish project, requesting their presence at a parish function or enlisting their support for a special event. That personal contact will soon translate into an increase in contributions.

## Shared Leadership

Inclusive, facilitating, participative pastoral leadership is also essential to a higher parish income. We have discovered this to be the most effective style of leadership for increasing parishioner involvement. Telling people what is good for them carries very little weight these days. Even selling them a bill of goods doesn't work. Once they discover they have been enticed into doing something they didn't want to, they feel manipulated and cheated. This happens in many subtle ways. Someone, out of the goodness of his or her heart, agrees to drive an elderly person to church. The next thing the person knows, he or she has been signed up to do it every Sunday for a year. Another person shows up for a townhall meeting and ends up being coerced into leading one of the small groups. This is not what we would describe as facilitating leadership.

Parishioners resent being "used" by the staff and parish leaders. They don't like being treated as children who have to be told what to do. On the other hand, if they experience an atmosphere of partnership where everyone has a part to play based upon one's gifts and talents, they tend not only to give of their time and energy, they give financially as well.

## Make Demands

A third way of increasing both the level of parish involvement and the level of financial contributions is to ask for a specific commitment from people. Don't be embarrassed about making demands on people. In the past, we demanded no meat on Friday all year long, no food or drink after midnight for those going to communion and every woman had to wear a hat in church. These requirements are gone. At the time, however, people complied. It was a part of what it meant to be a Catholic.

What demands do we place on our parish members today? Taking into account unique situations and special needs, people do respond when explicit demands are made so long as these demands are of limited duration, are within reason and are well-explained. For example, a pastor might announce, "During this Lent we request that every adult member come to at least one parish function outside of Mass. You have many opportunities and the sign-up sheets are in the pews. Choose one and drop it in the collection basket. You won't regret it." The positive response might be surprising. Many times, all people need is a nudge in the right direction. Remember that those who are involved in parish functions outside of Mass give more in the collection.

Being explicit about what is expected from each parishioner in their financial giving patterns, young and old alike, is more successful in raising funds than a general call to increase one's offertory donation.

Members of the finance committee might get up at the weekend Masses and state, "If your yearly household income before taxes is $30,000, then a suggested weekly contribution would be from $15 to $20. If your family income is $50,000, then your offering would be $25 to $30 a week. This is only 2–3% of your income. Surely God deserves this much from us. Suppose the income of husband and wife together comes to $75,000; a 3% contribution to the parish would be $43 a week or $188 a month. This applies to children and teenagers as well. If your weekly allowance is $10, then your share to God would be about 30¢ each weekend."

Making contribution levels concrete and spelling out expectations help people judge how they measure up to an explicit norm. This applies to all ages. As mentioned earlier, many children never get in the habit of contributing from their own income and, therefore, fail to learn the lesson for later life.

## Enjoying One's Involvement

Another way for increasing contribution levels is to give people a lift when they come to parish activities and functions. Becoming involved should be fun. People should feel supported and experience personal growth when they volunteer for a ministry. This is so essential to active involvement. It has to produce at least as much interest as watching sports on television and it has to have at least as much fulfillment as working out at the health club.

Church should not be a chore or a burden. People were attracted to Jesus because he promised them life and fulfillment, healing and growth. The parish, as an extension of Jesus' Church on the local level, should do the same. Having a chance to choose a secret family to be good to for three months is one way of having fun as a member of the parish. For those who like music, being turned on by singing in four-part harmony as a choir member is a great joy. Watching children come alive from the stories told to them at religious education classes is part of the rewards of teaching. That is what parish is all about, people coming together to praise God and serve others because they want to. It gives them a boost for being part of it all. With this mentality they can't help but share their financial resources as well.

## Keeping People Aware

Seeing a return for one's investment of time and money also contributes to higher financial giving. People must feel that their money and their involvement make a difference. They are not taken for granted, in other words. For the majority of parishioners, their experience of parish is as an unknown quantity. They come to Mass, go through the motions and leave without anyone knowing their name, asking their opinion or discovering their needs and inclinations. They put their contribution into the basket and that is the last they see for their efforts.

If, however, the situation is turned around and every member of the parish is made to feel at home and part of the parish, their interest and involvement will increase dramatically. How can this be done in a community of 2,000 people with only one priest and a few paid staff members? It is accomplished by giving it much thought and careful attention.

In the more successful parishes, every penny donated is accounted for. Frequent and easy-to-read reports are fed back to the parishioners about how their money is being spent for the good of the parish and the care of those in need. If there is a shortfall, the people are told. They are given the feeling that it is their problem, not just the pastor's, the council's or the finance committee's. If contributions are up, people are given a pat on the back. They are shown what a difference this makes in the running of the parish.

Some missionary appeal speakers are masters at raising people's awareness about the needs of the world. They tell stories of concrete situations and how much difference a few dollars can make. They also congratulate people on their generosity, telling them how important their contributions are. Parish leaders could learn much from this approach.

## Sharing in Decisions

Allowing people to share in the important decisions of the parish and its ministries is another way to increase involvement and financial assistance. We have already discussed the various levels of decision-making in Chapter Six. Spreading out the decision-making process to include as many people as possible helps them feel they are contributing more than just money to the parish. They are giving what is best of themselves, their knowledge, insights and experience. This does not imply that everyone is a decider. They do, however, have the right to be consulted before a conclusion is reached if they are going to be affected by the decision.

For example, the pastor is going on a six-month sabbatical. A retired priest will fill in during the interim. He is only able to preside at two Masses on the weekend. That leaves two Masses with no priest. What to do? Should two Masses be dropped altogether, and if so, which ones? Should the Masses alternate so as to keep the original schedule, but on one weekend there will be Mass at 7:30 and 11:30 on Sunday morning, and then Saturday at 5:30 PM and Sunday at 9:00 AM the next weekend? Perhaps all the times should be kept but have a Communion Service in place of two Masses on the weekend. Parishioners have a right to voice their opinions. After stating all the options, for instance, the people could indicate which plan best fits their schedules and desires. The council or worship commission may make the final decision but the people know that their opinions are heard and respected. If the atmosphere of asking people's opinion and taking into account their wisdom is fostered through the parish's ministries and activities, then parishioners will respond, not only with their ideas but with their contributions as well.

Contributing to the Church is a complex issue. To turn Catholic giving patterns around in the years ahead will take great imagination, concerted effort and insight into varying causes for the lower-than average contribution levels. Parish leaders will have to explore new options and alternatives in order to renew people's interest and involvement. It can be done, however. Many parishes that have addressed the reasons for nongiving have found a generous response from their people.

The Spirit leads in wonderfully mysterious ways. Perhaps lower contribution levels is one of many crises that is forcing Church and parish leaders to improve parish life and ministry., This may not be the best of motives, but may prove to be a blessing in the long run for all concerned, givers and receivers alike.

## Questions for Reflection and Review

*Contributions*

What percentage of the registered parishioners do you feel give their fair share to the support of the parish? What percentage give nothing at all? Is this information available to the membership? Would it make any difference? How has your own level of contributing changed in recent years and for what reasons?

*Reasons For Not Giving*

Of the 19 reasons listed for nongiving, which ones apply especially to your parish? Which two of the reasons listed would be worth emphasizing in order to change giving patterns? Does the parish publish a financial report? If so, is it easily understood and does it raise any interest? Does the budget reflect the priorities of the parish? Do homilies reflect a need for less consumerism and a better distribution of goods?

*Positive Steps*

Inclusive, participative, facilitating leadership helps raise parish income. How would you rate your parish leadership, on a scale from 1–10, as to how inclusive and facilitating it is? Which areas of parish leadership are better than others and how do people respond to the different styles? How are parishioners kept aware of parish needs and personally asked to contribute their fair share? In what ways do they have a say in how money is spent?

# Prayer Ritual

*Music*

" Praise God in His Dwelling" by Jan Vermulst. (Schiller Park, IL: World Library Publications, 1964)

*Prayer*

Read aloud the following prayer, everyone reading the first two lines, and then alternating sides for the following sections.

> All: IN THANKSGIVING FOR THE RESOURCES OF THE EARTH, FOR LIFE, ABUNDANCE AND HAPPI-NESS . . .

For the exchange of goods which belong to all of creation. For the exchange of air and water, the exchange of money and labor, the exchange of giving and receiving, we pour out our thanks to You, our God.

We praise you for plants growing in earth and water, for life inhabiting lakes and seas, for life creeping in soils and land, for creatures living in wetlands, for life flying above and around us, for beasts dwelling in woods and fields.

We give thanks for sun and moon and stars, for rain and dew and winds, for winter cold and summer heat.

How many and wonderful are your works, Our God! In wisdom you have made them all!

Because of your creativity, we have experienced good liturgies, shared wisdom, facilitating leadership and community support.

But we confess as creatures privileged with the care and keeping of your creation, we have abused your creation through arrogance, ignorance, consumerism and individualism.

We confess risking permanent damage to your handiwork. We confess impoverishing creation's ability to bring You praise. We confess we have not shared the abundance of Your daily sustenance. We have been selfish and insensitive.

We confess that Your handiwork provides the context of our living. It is our home, it is our realm in which we live our lives. Your dream is in our midst and coming to its fullness.

We confess that we are unaware of how deeply we have deprived the community, the earth and ourselves of Your vision by not empowering, not sharing, not reaching out beyond ourselves. We have abused creation and ourselves.

Oh Lord, we ask forgiveness and we ask for the vision needed to begin again as a global community. May we share what we have with generosity, giving praise to You who are our source of life.

*Closing*

"Canticle of the Sun" by Marty Haugen (Chicago: G.I.A. Publications, 1980)

# CHAPTER TWELVE

# *Parish Volunteers*

THE BACKBONE OF EVERY PARISH IS ITS VOLUNTEERS. THIS was the case in the pre–Vatican II Church. It is true today and will remain so in the Church of the future. What will be different in the years ahead is who will be their boss.

In the past, the parish belonged to the pastor. He established volunteers to assist him in the running of the parish. It was his parish. He was the boss. Volunteers worked for him. In most places this is no longer the situation.

At the present time, with the explosion of new ministries and the drop in the number of priests and religious Sisters, staffs have grown from one or two persons to, in some cases, 10–20 people. These are not volunteers. They are paid, professional pastoral ministers. Their role is to coordinate an area of ministry or activity in the parish. They enlist volunteers to lead and help out in these ministries. People volunteer to teach in the religious education programs that come under the jurisdiction of the Director of Religious Education. Lectors, communion ministers, musicians, sacristans and servers volunteer to enhance the weekend worship service. These people are the responsibility of the liturgy director.

The pastoral associate directs a cadre of volunteers who visit the sick in hospitals and nursing homes, staff the food pantry and take care of people in need. The parish administrator keeps track of the money-counters, the bulletin and newsletter editors, the maintenance helpers and the stewardship committee.

In subtle ways, the volunteers who in the past worked for the pastor now work for one of the pastoral staff members. Parishes are developing coordinating committees and commissions that give direction to various areas of ministry. The people who belong to these leadership groups are themselves volunteers. Staff members, on the other hand, are on the scene on a daily basis and have contact with the ministries under their care. As a result, the staff person ends up being the boss. This is not because anyone chooses to be the boss, it is just the way the system works best.

Will this continue to be the predominant model in the third millennium? Perhaps, but another option does suggest itself. Suppose in the future the shortage of clergy is not an issue. Changes made in Church law allow for a more inclusive priesthood. People respond to the change. Parishes are smaller because there are now enough priests to staff them. There is less need for larger staffs and more people take on the responsibility for helping out in the parish. The parish itself is well-structured so that each area of ministry is given direction by a coordinating group that has experience in the ministry of leadership. Many more parishioners have been trained in pastoral ministry so that, in effect, the volunteers are responsible to each other. The volunteers themselves are the "bosses" working for each other and for the good of the parish and its mission.

To prepare for this greater responsibility and sense of ownership, a number of steps need to be taken now to not only prepare for the future, but help the present coordination and direction of volunteers.

## ESSENTIAL ELEMENTS

### People First

The first essential element in dealing with parish volunteers is to think about the clients. These are the people for whom the volunteers are providing a ministry or service. Parishioners who come to Mass are the clients of the lector, the choir, the greeters, the ushers and communion ministers. The children who come to religious education are the clients of the teachers, aides and organizers. The homeless, hungry and unemployed are the clients of the Christian Service volunteers.

These clients need to be protected. They must be helped and not hindered through the ministry provided by the volunteers. The reputation of the parish is greatly affected by how these clients are treated and cared for.

If the music at Mass turns the people off, they will stop singing, stop giving, stop coming. If the children or adults are bored by religious education offerings, they will stay at home. If the people seeking assistance from the parish are not cared for, the word will get around and the image of the parish suffers. Volunteers have much to do with the positive or negative impression people have of the parish as a whole.

It is difficult to confront volunteers when they are doing a poor job. It is hard to fire a volunteer, in other words. Many other people suffer if appropriate action is not taken, however. The people suffer, the morale among other volunteers drops and the volunteer suffers as well.

The first essential element for managing volunteers, then, is to keep the needs of the parish first, not the feelings of the volunteers. The best way to do this is to spend a great deal of thought, energy and preparation in putting the right person in a job that fits the person's talents, inclinations and desires.

The key to a successful volunteer program is coordination. When parishes come to us asking, "How do we get more people involved?" we ask them, "Do you have a recruitment committee or coordinator of volunteers?" "No, we never thought of it," is their usual reply.

This is the first step. Form a small group whose only job is the recruitment and placement of volunteers. One woman in a class we taught had been a member of such a committee for five years. She helped start the group and over the five years saw the parish increase its number of volunteers fourfold. She had done such a good job that she was hired as a full-time staff person in charge of volunteers.

Her task and the task of her committee was to seek out people who were not involved and funnel them to ministries and projects that needed help. In a typical parish, from 12–20% of the membership volunteers to help out. Once a volunteer committee with a staff resource person is established, this percentage will double.

In most parishes, each area of ministry is responsible for enlisting volunteers. The more active parishioners are recruited for a number of ministries. When a gifted and generous newcomer is discovered, groups compete for that person's involvement. Once given a job, a volunteer can be stuck in it for years with little hope of "retirement." One parish we worked with inaugurated a special "volunteer of the year" award. They had to suspend the practice after two years. What they discovered was that once a person got the plaque, they were never heard from again. It gave people permission to "escape," as one person described her involvement.

A volunteer/recruitment committee provides an alternative to the competition for volunteers and the feeling of being stuck in a job for too long.

The task of the committee is to find fresh, new recruits to replenish the ranks and replace the "old-timers." This provides a limited term of commitment from those already involved.

## Job Descriptions

An important task of the volunteer/recruitment committee is to establish a standard form for describing the tasks that need help from of time required, how many meetings a person would have to attend and what type of skills or training is required. Figure 2 (on following page) is an example of what this form might look like.

The committee distributes this form to every ministry and program in the parish. If the parish is organized into areas of ministry as described in Chapter Six, then each commission discovers which areas need volunteers and has each one fill out a job description form. The volunteer committee collects all these forms and begins the recruitment process.

---

# Figure 2
# Job Description Card

Area of Ministry: _____

Name of the Job: _____

Job Description: _____
_____

Location of Job: _____

Day of Week/Time of Day: _____

Hours Per Month: _____

Skills Required: _____

Amount of Training Needed: _____

Meetings Required to Attend: _____

Person in Charge: _____

If Interested, Contact: _____

Phone: _____

Type of Job: (The X indicates primary focus of the job.)

WORKING ALONE_____        WORKING IN GROUP_____

LEADING OTHERS_____       FOLLOWING OTHERS_____

MUCH PREPARATION_____     LITTLE PREPARATION_____

DEFINED TASK_____         UNDEFINED TASK_____

REQUIRED SKILLS NEEDED_____ NO SKILLS NEEDED_____

---

## Recruitment

Once the job descriptions are in, the next step is finding people to fill the jobs. Recruitment has many levels. The first is a general call for volunteers once a year. This could be done in conjunction with a Ministry Fair. All the organizations and ministries have a booth that displays their activity. During the weekend Masses, forms are distributed to every adult, 16 years or older. The form includes all the activities of the parish and highlights those areas that need the most help. The number of hours per month required of the volunteers in each activity is also listed.

Parishioners have a week to fill out the form. In the meantime, they can visit the ministry booths between Masses and ask questions of those involved in parish activities. On the following weekend, everyone is encouraged to drop the form in the collection basket or they can mail it to the parish office during the week.

The volunteer committee collects all of the forms and makes a note of who volunteered for what activity or ministry. They divide the forms into two groups. One group includes the tasks that take little expertise and training. Examples would include gift-bearers, office helpers, money-counters or festival workers. The names of those who volunteered for these tasks are funneled to the appropriate commission or area of ministry. The groups are given a deadline by which time the new volunteers are to be contacted. After that deadline, the volunteer committee sends out a letter to everyone who volunteered, asking whether or not they had been contacted by a member of the parish. If not, they are to call the volunteer committee immediately. We have heard all too often that people volunteered, for an activity and were never contacted. The volunteer committee makes sure this does not happen in their parish. It is up to the coordinators of each activity and ministry to contact and train the new people, making sure the new volunteers know what is expected of them and whether the task fits their desires and schedules.

The second group of forms comes from people who volunteered for areas that require more care in matching the right person to the right task. In these cases, a telephone or face-to-face interview is necessary. Suppose someone volunteered to take communion to the sick. This requires an awareness of how to minister to the homebound, when to visit, what to say, how long to stay, how to listen. Not everyone is suited for this task. The primary emphasis is the person visited, not the needs or inclinations of the volunteer. Focus on the client is the rule of thumb.

One of the committee members contacts the new volunteer and, using the job description form, tries to help the person discover whether or not this would be a good choice for parish involvement.

## Matching People to Task

Marlene Wilson in *How to Mobilize Church Volunteers* (Mpls: Augsburg Press, 1983) mentioned three types of people who volunteer for church activities. One group is oriented toward achievement. These people want to see results. They are impatient with long meetings and socializing. They volunteered to solve a problem, accomplish a task, experience success. What they need is a challenge. They love to be given what seems like an impossible job and to sink their teeth into it until it is completed. The areas in which they excel include organizing a new fundraiser, fixing a roof that has always leaked, planning a parish anniversary, setting up a new parish computer system or revamping the welcoming committee. Once they know what has to be done, they get to it with little need for supervision or directions. The drawback is that they may not spend much time interacting with others. Small talk is not their strong suit. Bringing communion to a sick person week after week may not be the best job for an achievement-type volunteer. That is why a personal interview is important.

As the committee member talks to the person who volunteered for this job and explains what is required, it might become clear that the person is not suitable for the ministry. All is not lost, however. If this happens, the interviewer has other jobs ready so that if the original task is not a good match, another is suggested that better fits the person's inclinations and preferences. This is why personal contact is so important for the more responsible jobs.

Marlene Wilson describes a second type of volunteer who would be perfectly suited to this ministry. This is the affiliation type. The person volunteers because he or she is looking for people with whom to interact. Socializing and establishing relationships are more important than getting a task accomplished. Such a person would be a likely candidate for bringing communion to the sick. The desire to nurture, relate and listen are just the skills needed. In fact, even this amount of interaction may not be enough. The person might also enjoy gatherings with other home visitors in order to swap stories and share experiences. Long meetings with opportunities to socialize and enjoy companionship is part of what it means to be an affiliation-type of volunteer. On the other hand, such a person would not be suited for jobs that require organization and achievement. Care must also be taken that the individual responds to clientele needs, and not just to one's own. The task of the Volunteer Committee member is to be sure that people get matched up with a job that fits their inclinations and capabilities.

Consider a third type of volunteer. This person seeks to influence others rather than solve a problem or foster relationships. This kind of volunteer is more outspoken and has strong opinions on issues. Such people need an outlet for their ideas and a vehicle to express their concerns. They seek visibility and impact. These people can provide a great service to the parish if well placed. What these volunteers do best is put the parish on the map, make it known, show off what it is doing, put spark in a group. If there is an issue that needs attention, these persons can raise awarenesses and rally the troops to address the problem. Such people are also good at public relations and getting the message out to a wider audience.

If the volunteer committee member discovers such an inclination in the person who wants to visit the homebound, he or she might suggest another ministry more suited to influencing people. Examples might include publicity, writing articles, social justice issues, even a leadership position. Care must be taken so that a person who seeks to influence others does this for the benefit of the parish and not to satisfy one's own ends.

We experienced a woman in a parish we worked with who volunteered for everything. If a call went out for help, she was there. She tended to be overbearing and domineering. When the appeal was made for greeters at Mass, she volunteered. Unfortunately, she was just the type who should not be welcoming people into Mass. People tried to find another way into church so as to avoid her somewhat forceful greeting. Eventually, the pastor had to sit down with her and ask her to let go of this area of involvement. It was putting undue strain on the other greeters, as well as on the Mass-goers.

To soften the blow, he suggested focusing on another ministry, one that fit her talents better. He asked if she would help out at the nursery during Mass, especially setting up activities that would keep the children occupied. She thought about it and said she could do it once a month. She had children of her own and would bring in ideas for others to use when she was not there herself.

Had this parish a volunteer/recruitment committee, the original placement process would have discovered the person's abilities at the outset and not offered her the greeter's job. Nor would the pastor have had to get involved in confronting the misplacement. This would have been handled by the committee or the coordinator of the greeting ministry.

Often a combination of talents is needed to assure success. Some ministries need both an affiliation person for bonding and an achievement person for organization. That is why a team effort is the best approach. Not one but two people pair up to handle a task, each with an unique insight and mode of operating.

The pairing of volunteers also allows for better training and support. If one person has been successful teaching eighth-grade religious classes, let the new recruit team-teach for a year to learn the ropes. If door-to-door visitors are needed to do a census, send them out in pairs, just as Jesus did with his disciples. The two can complement one another, especially if they have different approaches: one an influencer, another an achiever or an affiliator.

## Other Options for Recruiting

So far the task of the volunteer committee has been a general call for volunteers, as well as interviewing people for the more responsible tasks and matching them up with appropriate areas of ministry. They then funnel these people to those coordinating various ministries for training and placement. The volunteers themselves feel valued and honored to be given this much attention and care. They are flattered to be asked their desires and matched to a job they will find enjoyable and fulfilling.

The next task for the committee is to seek out those who haven't volunteered to see if they would be willing to help out as well. Very often people don't sign up because they don't feel as qualified as those presently now involved in parish ministries. They need a personal invitation to become active.

This is done in two ways. The first step is a volunteer bulletin board in the vestibule of the Church. This contains cards with projects and programs that need volunteers. Each task has a card similar to the job description form mentioned earlier. It contains a contact person to call if people are interested. Parishes that have used this ongoing recruitment board have discovered that it is best to display the board only occasionally, so as to keep interest high. If it is there all the time, no one takes notice. If it is there once a month, it has more impact.

The bulletin board is not personal enough, however. The volunteer committee has the names of those who volunteered at the annual Ministry Fair. The committee eliminates these people and seeks out all those who didn't volunteer. The committee members choose a quota for the month. Suppose they each agree to contact five new people. During the course of the month, they call people at random and ask them if they are interested in helping out in an activity. The committee has at hand all the jobs that need volunteers. The response rate is surprisingly high if people have a variety of options and know there is a limited period of commitment. Many indicate they have seen the recruitment board but never took the time or effort to make a call. This invitation was all they needed. About a quarter of the people will agree to give it a try. These are new people who are not involved in any parish ministry. It is these new volunteers who make the work of the committees so valuable in the parish.

Newcomers to the parish are also prime targets for recruitment. The request for involvement comes after the welcoming committee has made an initial contact with the new people and has helped them feel at home. The volunteer committee follows up on this welcome and invites them to become active in the parish based on their previous experience, inclinations and time commitments. Some of the most gifted and experienced volunteers come from other parishes in other towns and cities. They were active there and might be willing to share their ideas in this new environment, if given the proper invitation and encouragement.

## Motivation

Volunteers need to feel good about the time and talent they contribute to the parish. Good placement is the first step in this direction. If someone has taken the time to sit down with them and listen to their desires and inclinations, they feel affirmed and are happy.

Placement is not enough, however. Once they are involved in their new ministry they need a sense of achievement. They must feel that what they are doing is accomplishing some good in the parish. This sense of achievement will be different for different types of volunteers.

The achievement-type person will feel satisfied if the project is successful. That is enough. Not many other rewards are necessary, other than the acclaim and acknowledgment that the problem or issue was solved.

The affiliation-type person, on the other hand, needs people around to feel a sense of community. Friendship and bonding is this person's reward. If the volunteer is getting to know more people and can more easily interact, then it is a worthwhile endeavor.

The influence-type person looks for another area of satisfaction. Recognition is this person's reward. He or she will feel a sense of achievement if the parish becomes known for helping the homeless, if the liturgy has more spark or if the children get turned on by the religious education classes. "It is time to give this place a shot in the arm and I'm here to help do that," is what excites the influence person.

An example of how the three groups of volunteers differ is evident in how each might respond to a five-year volunteer pin. The achievement type will throw it in a drawer and say, "I don't need any service pin; I know I did a good job and that's enough."

The affiliation type will accept it with some embarrassment, not wanting to draw attention for doing what, in his or her words, "anybody would do. I'm glad they recognized my contribution but the friends I've gained in the process is reward enough."

The influence type will exclaim, "It's about time they recognize people for their achievements around here. I'm only one of many but it is nice to be given credit for all the hard work. I'll wear this pin with pride so people will know what a great parish this is."

A second motivation for volunteers is challenge. Even the routine work must have something new to keep people interested. Reading at Mass may be the same each week, but if the lectors have an in-service every three months and are given a chance to listen to and critique each other, then it becomes a new and challenging ministry. Keeping standards high and encouraging people to reach those standards keep people coming back for more.

So does increasing people's level of responsibility. The longer people are in a ministry, the more opportunity they should have to be a leader in that area, if their talents and desires so dictate. One volunteer in a parish we were involved with was part of the Christian Initiation of Adults program (R.C.I.A.). He was not aware of new developments and kept referring to the sessions as "convert classes." He did have much desire and energy and was willing to learn more. Those in charge of the RCIA decided to send him out-of-state for two weeks of workshops. He came home a new person. He saw for the first time what the new approach was all about. He wanted to use his new insights in the program so the committee put him in charge of the sponsors. They also asked him to teach one of the sessions to the candidates. He was thrilled and did an outstanding job, so much so that he is now, a few years later, the new director of the program. Increasing his level of responsibility greatly increased his motivation and effectiveness.

Another way to motivate people is to provide opportunities for personal growth and development. Volunteers discover that they gain much more than they give. They may help out at the weekend Masses, teach a class, visit the homebound or count the money, but in the process they gain new insights into what it means to be a Christian and a member of the parish community.

The experiences people have in parish ministry should foster spiritual growth and provide insights that they could not gain on their own. They might come in touch with current developments in theology, church issues, or world affairs which they would have missed if they had not volunteered. They might come in contact with other parishioners and people outside the parish that expand their own horizons and categories. It should be an enriching experience, in other words. This is what volunteers should be feeling whenever they offer their time and energy to the parish and its activities.

## Evaluation

The final step in coordinating volunteers is to evaluate people's success as volunteers and the success of their ministry. These two may differ.

A volunteer may not feel satisfied but the work he or she is doing is excellent. Suppose a person edits the newsletter in the parish. The end product is hailed as a great communication vehicle. The editor is discouraged, however, because too much work lands on her shoulders. The reporters are not keeping to deadlines and groups are not sending in photos.

On the other hand, the volunteer may experience high enjoyment but the ministry is suffering. Consider the welcoming committee that is filled with affiliation-type people. They have a great time meeting together, enjoying each other's cookies and treats, but the newcomers are not being contacted.

To protect both the volunteer and the ministry, a tradition of evaluation is essential to a well-coordinated volunteer program. The volunteer committee is the group that helps establish this tradition in the parish.

For example, everyone who volunteers for any ministry is given a chance to review his or her commitment after six months. If it is not working out, another job is offered as an alternative, no questions asked. Those coordinating areas of ministry also have the option of reassigning new recruits after six months. People know this when they sign up. There is a six-month grace period for every position in the parish.

A second tradition is tenure. Every commitment has a limited period of involvement. Each year at the Gathering of Ministries (see Chapter Six), parishioners have a chance to rethink their involvement in the parish. If a person wants to concentrate on liturgy this year, he lets go of administration. If another wants to try teaching, she lets go of helping the elderly. Making choices such as these keep people from becoming overextended and creates vacuums that allow new people to become involved.

Whether or not a person does change an area of commitment, his or her involvement in one ministry is limited to these years. This keeps groups from building kingdoms unto themselves. One woman has been an officer of the Altar and Rosary Society for 15 years. The same choir has been singing together for over 10 years. A lector has been reading once a month for the last eight years. We don't doubt they are good at what they do, but putting limits on involvement spreads out the tasks among all the parishioners and opens up new avenues for involvement.

Another evaluation tool is an exit interview. This is especially helpful if people change ministries on a regular basis. Whenever a person leaves a job, the coordinator or the committee in charge asks the person to fill out a short evaluation sheet. Some of the questions asked might be: What did you find most and least satisfying about the job? What training did you receive and how helpful was it? What was missing? What would have helped you do a better job? What was a highlight for you in the job? What does the person coming after you need to know?

This kind of information is invaluable to new people coming into a ministry. Too often, the same mistakes are repeated again and again because no one took the time or made the effort to ask those doing the job what they thought or experienced. A tradition of asking people's insights will much improve the level of volunteer ministry in the parish.

So will peer ministry. People already involved train new people before they take their leave. The best trainers are often the ones "in the field." This is on-the-job evaluation as the experienced minister and the neophyte work out the best approach together.

## New Paradigms

The parish of the future will rely, perhaps even more than today, on volunteers. Much more attention will be devoted to the coordination and care of volunteers. Only a few parishes now have a volunteer/recruitment committee. Even less have a volunteer coordinator on staff. What is becoming common, however, is a restructuring of parishes around areas of ministry. This will help foster the coordination of volunteers and provide the attention this area of parish life deserves.

As people become more familiar with the call to ministry and better trained to answer this call, they will be more willing to volunteer to help out, both within and outside the parish community. The rising popularity of Small Faith Communities will also spark a rise in volunteer ministry. More people reflecting on scripture and seeking ways of carrying this reflection into action will prompt more parish involvement. The growing shortage of clergy and religious will continue to put pressure on church leaders to rely more heavily on volunteers to fill the void. All of these movements point to an increase in volunteers. How well they are matched to meaningful tasks, given support and direction that produces enjoyment and high motivation, are affirmed and evaluated so that both the volunteers and clients are well-served will be the challenge of the parish in the next century.

## Questions for Review and Reflection

*The Clients*

Think of an experience in which you volunteered for a task. Was the emphasis on the people being served or on the volunteer? What care is taken in the parish to match the right volunteers with the right ministry so that the parishioners are served well? Name one experience of good matching and one of bad matching.

*Recruitment*

Does your parish have a staff person or a committee whose primary task is the recruitment and care for volunteers? It so, how is it working? If not, could this happen in the near future? Describe the present forms of recruitment used in your parish. Is more emphasis or better coordination needed? Do people complain about volunteering for a task and never getting contacted? Do people feel worn out in their jobs, with no relief, rewards or tenure?

*Motivation*

People volunteer for different reasons, whether out of affiliation, affirmation or influence needs. Which fits you the best and how have you changed, depending on your interests and the job at hand? Name areas in the parish that would benefit from each of these three types of volunteers and ones that would suffer. How much attention is given to motivating volunteers and to a limited time of commitment?

## Prayer Ritual

*Reading*

Read aloud St. Paul's emphasis on being coworkers with God. (I Cor. 3:5–16)

*Process*

Introduction: Our prayer today is an invitation to extend our boundaries, to empower. We have listened to St. Paul tell the Corinthians that we are called to be partners with God, to be coworkers with the Lord and with one another. We are interdependent. We have been given the opportunity to have shared ownership. I invite you to read the following sentences in rotation, one person after another. After the reading we will form groups of threes to share insights into both the scripture reading and the story.

*Coyote Takes Water from the Frog People*

Coyote was out hunting and he found a dead deer. One of the deer's rib bones looked just like a big dentalia shell, and Coyote picked it up and took it with him. He went to see the frog people. The frog people had all the water. When anyone wanted any water to drink or cook with or to wash, they had to go and get it from the frog people.

Coyote came up. "Hey, frog people, I have a big dentalia shell. I want a big drink of water — I want to drink for a long time."

" Give us that shell," said the frog people, "and you can drink all you want."

Coyote gave them the shell and began drinking. The water was behind a large dam where Coyote drank.

"I'm going to keep my head down for a long time." Finally one of the frog people said, "Hey, Coyote, you sure are drinking a lot of water there. What are you doing that for?"

Coyote brought his head up out of the water. "I'm thirsty."

"Oh."

After a while one of the frog people said, "Coyote, you sure are drinking a lot. Maybe you better give us another shell."

"Just let me finish this drink," said Coyote, putting his head back under water.

The frog people wondered how a person could drink so much water. They didn't like this. They thought Coyote might be doing something.

Coyote was digging out under the dam all the time he had his head under water. When he was finished, he stood up and said, "That was a good drink. That was just what I needed."

Then the dam collapsed, and the water went out into the valley and made the creeks and rivers and waterfalls.

The frog people were very angry. "You have taken all the water, Coyote!"

"It is not right that one people have all the water. Now it is where everyone can have it."

Coyote did that. Now anyone can go down to the river and get a drink of water or some water to cook with, or just swim around.

—Giving Birth to Thunder, Sleeping with His Daughter, copyright 1977 by Barry Holstun Lopez. Reprinted with permission of Andrews & McMeel. All rights reserved.

In groups of threes, share any insights or reflections related to being coworkers with the Lord, volunteer ministry and the "Coyote" story. After 15 minutes return to the large group to share common themes or ideas.

*Closing*

"Peace Prayer" by John Foley, SJ (Portland, OR: New Dawn Music, 1976)

# CHAPTER THIRTEEN

# Parish for the Third Millennium

WE ARE NOW IN A NEW ERA. THE TURNING OF THE MILLENNIUM hour glass has happened. Now what? Is it business as usual, everything as it was in the last century? Hardly. The world is changing and so is the Church, and especially the local parish. In the first edition of this book we asked the reader to stand in a new place and in a new year. Look at what you hope will be happening at that future date and then what are the events that would have to happen to get your desired outcome accomplished. We called it "future history" and the date we chose was 2004. What, at the time of the first writing, seemed like a century away is now here. Now it is time to look even further ahead to what might be and to continue the journey into a new reality. What are the issues that will be facing the American Catholic parish as we step into this new era? What changes are likely, or even necessary?

Two thousand years before Christ, Abram and Sarah were asked to leave the security of their own homeland and venture into the unknown. Jesus did the same to a small group of followers two thousand years ago. The significance of these two great transitions should not be lost as we ponder this unique moment in history. We are on the edge of a new era. It deserves our attention as we try to peer into what lies ahead. What do we see?

Our scope is modest. We will extend our gaze into the future at a time only ten years from the present. What will be happening at that time? No doubt instant communication will be the hallmark of the age. Telephones, computers, networks and high-definition television will continue to shape our lives. We will be in global contact with everyone and information will come tumbling into our lives from all directions. Whether we will be relating with one another in meaningful ways is quite another matter.

Consumerism and a market-driven society will keep pushing products and services upon us, making us feel deficient, unworthy and "behind the times" if we don't have the latest, the fanciest, the most efficient, the most satisfying "gadget" or "service" they are selling. Whether all this "stuff" will bring us happiness is questionable, but the onslaught will continue.

With the pressure "to buy, buy, buy" comes a further deepening divide between those who are able to buy and those who are not, between those who have and those who do not, between those who experience success and those who do not. In the midst of this milieu sits the parish of the new generation. Ten years from now what should it look like, how should it be reacting to this surrounding culture, what changes will be needed or desirable? What issues will face the parish of the future?

## Priesthood and Eucharist

The first issue facing the parish in the near future is whether there will even be a local parish at all. The danger is that the shortage of ordained priests and the corresponding scarcity of Eucharist and the sacraments will lead to a collapse of the small parish. The pressure to make the Eucharist available to all will create a new configuration of mega-churches that offer only a few Masses which are attended by large congregations. Priesthood, in other words, is the first issue that will have to be addressed within the next ten years.

In the first edition of *Transforming the Parish* we described a process in which the shortage of clergy approached critical proportions by the end of the twentieth century. Priests were getting burned out, were retiring early or were dying at a young age because of the strain. Only a few new recruits were joining the ranks of priesthood. On top of that, the needs of the people were not being served. We described a scenario in which a small group of American bishops, seeing the situation going unaddressed, wrote a secret position paper for the conference of bishops. It demanded a papal hearing on the subject.

In a very short time the secret was out. Priests and people alike rejoiced at the initiative and a ground swell ensued. The momentum could not be stopped, the Spirit no longer denied. What began as a statement of concern from a few bishops led, in a short time, to the pope's own door. After much soul-searching and consultation, he agreed to call a special Ecumenical Council to explore new options for the priesthood and the requirements for ordination.

Our predictions were too optimistic. We thought that this issue would come to a head and that people would demand a change. This has not happened. Instead, bishops, priests and people continue to adapt to the growing shortage, taking stop-gap measures to stem the tide. But the problem will not go away. New vocations are in no way filling up the vacuum created by those who have left, died or retired.

Can such a substantial change in the requirements for priesthood take place in the next ten years? From our limited perspective, it must if the

Catholic Church is to remain a People of God gathered around the Table of the Lord. The tragedy is that in the effort to provide Eucharist to the widest population possible the system of local worshipping faith communities will be destroyed. The combining and closing of parishes in some situations does make sense, especially if churches were built in close proximity because of previous ethnic migrations. On the other hand, if a parish of 200, 500 or 1000 families is asked to combine with another one of even greater size, then the possibility of feeling "at home" and in close personal contact with one another, along with the rich traditions associated with each parish, will be lost forever. This is a great tragedy.

Why have the requirements for priesthood taken so long to change? The Church has had a married clergy for over half its history, and there exist married priests in the Roman Rite at this present time through Episcopal attrition. Is it a fear of change, a question of control over placements, a concern for the extra costs involved, an uneasiness with marriage itself? Or could it be instead that what has been developing over the last number of years is an act of God? Is this the Spirit's way of purifying the concept of priesthood? Could the Holy Spirit be offering us a chance to see that a simple change in the requirements of ordination is not enough? What is needed, instead, is a new system of priesthood that is more mutual, inclusive and collaborative. Some local parishes are learning a new way of operating. These are ones in which administrators who are not priests are pastoring congregations. Parishioners do not place these women and men on pedestals, call them by titles or sit back and expect to be provided with priestly services. Instead, the people pitch in and together with the pastoral administrator are creating a new way of being church that is a partnership between administrator and people. When Eucharist is celebrated, the sacramental minister (priest) and the administrator (pastor) preside side by side, and the people join them in a mutual celebration of the liturgy.

Is ten years too soon to see this change in the priestly system to become a reality? We certainly hope not. Time is running out. If the change does not happen soon, many parish communities will be destroyed, priests will get worn out and leave, potential candidates for priesthood who are not celibate males will be left unutilized, Catholics will have their rights denied.

A change in who can be ordained will not solve all the problems of the future parish but it will have many positive effects and implications. We can only begin to imagine what new avenues and insights this new system could bring to the exploration of married love and family issues. It will help all priests find a balance between being available to the people and having time for one's personal interests and pursuits. Raising a family brings into focus the essential values in life and helps maintain the balance. New topics for preaching and new insights into counseling are enhanced if the priest can draw upon personal experiences that are similar to those of the people they serve.

What will bring about this change to a new, inclusive priesthood? New models are being tried that indicate how much can be gained by a pastoring style that comes from a variety of life styles and personal experiences. Will the change come from above or below, from the bishops or the people, from outside the structures or from within? We do not know, but change it must. The risk of not changing is losing what is an essential aspect of the Church, people gathering around the Table of the Lord to celebrate Eucharist as a community of believers.

We have this vision that somewhere in the world, some unknown person is being called into a "burning bush" experience. Just as Moses was asked to "come closer," take off his shoes because he was standing on Holy Ground, and given the mandate to free his people from oppression, so too, somewhere, somehow, we believe this same experience is taking place now. Moses, of course, resisted the call but then he obeyed. He and his brother Aaron went to the seat of power in Egypt and demanded freedom from bondage. Could not this same event be in its infancy now? The question, of course, is whether we will be willing to say "yes" to the invitation to be part of the journey to a new land, to change this system and way of operating. The security and comfort of Egypt makes it difficult to let go and move into the desert. We may lose our treasures and cherished way of being Church – our first born – in the process. The next ten years may be a time for wandering in search of the new land of a renewed priesthood.

## The New Focus for Parish

Opening up the requirements for priesthood is not the only change that will be necessary for parishes over the next ten years. Young adults are not coming to church as they once did. The percentage of those attending weekly Masses has continued to fall in recent years. It could happen that we solve the priesthood shortage in another way. People will no longer come and as a result the churches are empty. How can the image of local church become more inviting and attractive to people, especially to the youth, the inactive and those on the fringe?

We suggest that over the next ten years the focus of the parish be shifted from "in here" to "out there." Instead of concentrating on inviting people back to church, go out to those on the fringe and address their issues and concerns. Put yourself in their shoes, live in their world, understand their needs, frustrations and fears.

The implication of this shift is a change in emphasis and expectations. No longer does regular attendance at Mass or parish functions mean as much as offering events that are meaningful and relate to people's everyday experiences. This appears to be the Jesus model of pastoral ministry revealed in the Gospels. He was with the outcasts and marginal people and was criticized because of it. His followers were not of the mainstream. What would a Catholic parish look like if it tried to do the same?

The first step would be to locate those "fringe people." That is not a difficult task. Begin with the registration lists. Many of those whose names are on the census files are inactive or nominal members of the parish. Connect with these people by phone, e-mail, personal visits, web sites. Have no other agenda other than to listen to their stories. These people will lead you to others even farther out on the periphery. Resist the temptation to invite them back to church. Just listen. Help them live lives that have meaning and purpose. In the listening you may discover a deep spiritual longing despite a lack of religious affiliation and identity. Help them reflect on their life experiences, call them to refocus and go deeper. Help them celebrate the high and low moments of their lives. The setting for this sharing may be one-on-one over the phone, through a personal visit, in small groups or by a computer connection. It may be far from the parish buildings.

One way of relating to those on the fringe is to stress events rather than regular attendance. That is what midnight Mass, Easter Sunday, Ash Wednesday and Mother's Day are for many people. It is the only time they see the inside of a church. Build on these and offer more like them, both within and outside the parish buildings. Sponsor special happenings, such as prayer services, outings, social justice efforts, work projects, socials and sports, appeal to youth and young adults, as well as to those of all ages. These events should include preparation and cooperative planning for the participants beforehand and group reflection afterward. These are the moments people remember years afterwards as positive experiences of being church. They test people's endurance, stretch their imaginations, demand involvement, challenge narrow, provincial outlooks. They also provide occasions to celebrate successes, experience solidarity with others and acknowledge a mystery at work in their lives.

We recently visited a parish that had a monthly Taize Prayer Service. Everyone was invited, no matter one's religious affiliation or spiritual inclination. The church was packed with people. They sat in the sanctuary, filled the choir loft, crowded into the aisles. The service was simple, mostly songs with few words and uncomplicated melodies. There was no sermon or collection, only singing and silence. Towards the end, people brought up lighted candles and placed them in containers filled with sand around the altar. By the end of the service, which lasted just an hour, the candles were burned down and spilling onto the sand. After it was over, people stood around the dying candles in quiet, prayerful conversation with one another. It was a profound experience of church, an "event" to remember.

The shift in focus to "out there" may take ten years to accomplish but it is worth planning now how to get to this new place and taking the first steps in this direction. It will mean changing the roles and positions of staff members so the "professionals" are freed to connect and attend to the marginal members. Staff members will need time to think up "events" that will appeal to a wide spectrum of interests and desires and then get the word out to the marginal and hesitant people. It will also mean challenging and redirecting the focus of the parishioners who do come regularly to church so that they themselves become the connectors and listeners to the alienated, the shy and the "too-busy-to-attend" people.

In keeping with this "out there" thinking, the staff would be charged to bring the parish *to the people,* not the people to the parish. How can the parish help the marginals achieve their spiritual goals, discover God's operation in their personal lives, affirm their many acts of everyday ministry? What if a staff were structured not around areas of ministry like education, youth, outreach, liturgy and administration, but around groups of people in the parish, such as working mothers, students, professionals, retired, marginal and inactive Catholics? The parish, in this model, would provide the framework, resources and encouragement for spiritual development, family growth, ministry in the workplace, integrity in moral decision-making. Staff members might visit work sites of parishioners and experience firsthand what issues and circumstances people face in trying to be ministers on the job. Such connections would be an endorsement by the parish of the value of people's work.

Taking the parish to the people will mean a change in how parish finances are spent, allowing for more open-ended, non-discretionary budgeting to be made available for new and unknown initiatives. Creative allocations will need to be made in order to connect with the voiceless and hidden members of the parish and with others who are uncovered when the parish reaches out beyond its normal boundaries. No longer will the emphasis be on regular attendance, rules and regulations, set and defined programs, a quantified series of classes or presentations. The new emphasis will be on meaningful events and open learning that is connected to people's own stories and relationships, on dialogue that adapts to changing situations and is open to a wide variety of options.

It is a "parish outside the walls" we are advocating, one that has a fluid membership and an adaptable structure. This model is being experienced in the business world with home-based work stations, flexible hours and interaction at a distance. This same fluid structure is possible for parishes over the next ten years. All that is needed is to "think outside the box" of the current parish structure and organization. The problem is not how to do this. People will supply the ideas once they are encouraged to explore options and are given seed money to put their ideas into operation. The parish could offer not only funding but also meeting space and staff resources for creative initiatives.

The current experience of small communities of faith could lead the way towards this future of a new locus for the parish. Unfortunately, many small communities quickly become closed groups that delight in their own interaction but are resistant to new members, new ministries and activities beyond their circle. These small communities need to be challenged with a new focus and purpose for their existence. The parish leadership needs to call these groups to be Gospel-oriented communities, encouraging them to reach out beyond themselves and risk the unfamiliar.

Establish traditions of tenure for small communities. After three years suggest they divide in half and form two new groups. Open the groups up to a diverse membership of different ages, ethnic identities and backgrounds. The parish will need to provide direction and support during the transition of these small communities into new groupings.

The continuous rise of a multi-cultural Catholic membership increases the urgency for taking the parish to those on the fringe. The advantaged parishioners, those with education and financial resources, will find a place to worship and a church community that fits their needs. They are used to picking and choosing what fits their desires and of having their expectations met. Recent immigrants, the poor and disenfranchised, the uneducated and unskilled, the elderly and disadvantaged don't have the ability to reach out for what fits their needs, either in the culture or in the Church. They have to be sought out and given a sense of self-worth. They need to be listened to and realize that they are heard. They must be included as part of God's People and affirmed in their own spiritual journey and insights.

How this will all happen, we cannot say. That it must happen we have no doubt. The alternative is to become a religion for the "saved" that is closed to the very people who can provide new life and direction to the Church. It is the people on the fringe who will tell us how to become a new Church in the twenty-first century.

## Reconciling Leadership

In ten years, with a new, inclusive priesthood and an emphasis on going out to the people on the fringe, the parish will have a good chance of becoming a Church modeled on the Gospels, one that reflects the mission and ministry of Jesus. One additional ingredient, however, is needed. The country and world at large has experienced many divisions and altercations. Some individuals and groups try to do each other harm. The same feuding and narrowness is found in the Church as well. What is needed in the coming years is a new type of leadership, both on the local level and in the Universal Church, one that is inclusive, reconciling and accepting of various factions and world views. Pope John XXIII had that charism and humanity was better for it. The world is in dire need of just such a charism in these early years of this new century.

The overriding sentiment is dialogue, interaction and sharing of differences. No longer can there be "us" and "them" in the parish of the future, whether among the parish membership or in relationship to other denominations and religions. It is the same God we all serve. Divisions only weaken the reign of God and make a lie of our profession of faith and professed values.

Our dream is that the parish of ten years hence be known for bridging the gaps and breaking down the walls that separate one group from another. The neighborhood community is full of people praying to the same God in different languages, gestures, methods and images. If local clusters of churches and places of worship can come together to confront common issues and problems, then "catholic" will take on a new meaning. The Church will begin to signify in its actions what the word catholic means, that is, universal. Each local parish will learn to accept a wide range of groups and interests, both within its own structure and in the surrounding area.

It might start slowly and in small pockets across the country. The staff and leaders in one parish might start concentrating on healing divisions among their own members and reaching out with reconciling gestures to churches and religious groups in the vicinity. They might begin by acknowledging areas where the parish and the larger Church have made mistakes, have acted in a derogatory fashion and, despite what Jesus said, have "lorded it over others." This admission of guilt could open the doors to new dialogue and understanding, paving the way for common prayer and worship, as well as joint activities and common service projects.

Such actions would give other parishes the courage to follow suit. Soon there could be large gatherings of "reconciling leaders" who speak of their own failures and limitations, as well as those of their churches.

This gives rise to a new spirituality of admitting failures and taking responsibility for one's own faults and limitations. Soon Catholic parishes are in the forefront of a new movement toward greater unity and mutual sharing, ranging from sharing resources to common work projects. This, in turn, could begin to change the image of Americans to those in other countries, from being a harsh and self-righteous people to a gentler, more caring society. Impossible? Perhaps, but never underestimate the power of an idea and of a few people who are willing to see the idea come to life and bear fruit. That is what happened in the early Church, 2000 years ago. There is no reason it could not happen again as we move into a new age.

The Spirit of Jesus is still alive in the Church and in the world. His Spirit will find a way to preach the Good News to those hungry for real spiritual substance. His Spirit will continue to gather people together and teach them the essentials of real gospel living. His Spirit will set people free, healing their hurts that hold them captive. His Spirit will continue to call people to prayer and worship, to deep loving and gentle kindness, to witnessing to the truth that sets people free, to standing up for the rights and needs of others. This will continue to happen in the years to come. The question is whether the Church and the local parish will face the challenge or will it be taken over by others. The choice is in our hands. Be Church and bring about the Reign of God, or get out of the way and let others answer the call to mission and ministry.

## Questions for Reflection and Review

*Future History*

Situate yourself ten years in the future. What decisions would you like the Church to have made by that time?

*Priesthood and Eucharist*

Think of your own parish. What difference would it make if priesthood was opened up to those experiencing the call and who were qualified to serve as priests? What would be lost and what would be gained? What would have to happen to keep parishes open although no more priests are available? What could ordinary parish ministers and parishioners do that might accelerate the shift toward a more inclusive priesthood?

*The "Out There" Focus*

What efforts are now going on in your parish to connect with the people on the fringe? Name as many other ways you can think of that would help change the focus of the parish from "in here" to "out there." How could small communities of faith help form a bridge between what goes on in church and what goes on in people's everyday lives? What changes would be needed in the way small communities are formed and operate that would make them more appealing and accessible to inactive and alienated individuals? In what ways could those who regularly attend church become the connectors and contacts with those who do not come to church?

### Reconciling Leadership

In your own parish, in what ways does it connect with churches and religious groups in the area? What more could be done to bridge the gulf between those of other faiths and beliefs? What would a reconciling leadership look like in your own parish? How would the pastor, staff and pastoral council operate that is different from what now goes on? What faults and failings need to be acknowledged and how could asking for forgiveness further dialogue with both the parish membership and those in the surrounding area? In what concrete ways could the ministry of the parish imitate the ministry of Jesus?

## Prayer Ritual

*Prayer*

### O GOD OF VISION (Alternate Sides)

O God of Vision, far greater than all human decisions,
Gather us now in your presence, refreshing, redeeming.
Show us those decisions that make the third millennium
Life in your breath-taking view
Good beyond our limitations.

Pour out your Spirit on all.
May our diversity here be a means of praising you,
Women and men, young and old
Open to a new tomorrow
Filled with unknowns.

Break the sun's rays into color.
Storm clouds, though real and near, are not enough.
A rainbow, arched in the sky,
Beauty and promise on high,
Giving us hope to respond.

Gratefully we enter the year 2000.
By your invitation
Come, let us answer the call,
Giving ourselves to life.

*Reading*

Read aloud the section from the prophet Habakkuk related to vision that comes slowly but does not deceive. (Habakkuk 2:1–4)

*Litany of Faith and Vision*

| | |
|---|---|
| All: | What is the vision? |
| Leader: | An image of the God of Abraham and Sarah who led the people into a new land. |
| All: | What else is the vision? |
| Leader: | An image of Esther and Sojourner Truth who took risks on behalf of others. |
| All: | Is there more? |
| Leader: | An image of priesthood expanded to include married, women, nonordained. |
| All: | Surely there is more? |
| Leader: | That image of small faith communities, leadership, and net-working which gives equal ownership and participation to all. |
| All: | Imagine a world where there are no more hierarchies and competition, only widening circles of personhood, a world where parishes do not have to close because the people "raise up their own leadership" and the Church blesses it. |
| Leader: | Envision a city where there is plenty for all-space, wine, community, life, freedom, ownership. |
| All: | Imagine a world that prefers peace to war, producing to consuming, empowering to controlling, sharing to possessing. |
| Leader: | Imagine a vision of you listening to me and me listening to you, and where we are both listening to God and we are growing. |
| All: | We are a people who have a vision for the year 2000. We are a people with a homeland. Here. Now. It is sacred and we respect it. It is our future. |

*Final Prayer: (Together)*

O God of Blessings, integrate our desires and our actions, our visions and our energies. Grant us the wisdom and knowledge to be creative in seeing what has been given in mystery and majesty. We sing our love, shout our joys, build our hopes, exclaim our thanks, and give ourselves in praise of you forever!

Amen.

*Closing*

"Let The People Say" by Tim Manion. (Phoenix: NALR, 1984)

# CHAPTER FOURTEEN

# *Ten Imperatives for Getting There*

"The Spirit came into them; they came alive
and stood upright..."(Ez 37:10)

We have been searching for paradigms that will bring new life to parishes. One way will not do it. Many options are needed, ones that speak to different backgrounds, interests, locations, clienteles and situations. What we have attempted to do is provide signposts and pointers that might suggest new ways for being parish. Some are happening now. Others are as yet untried. All are attempts to offer parishes stamina, courage and insight to stand upright. What we will attempt in this final chapter is to give suggestions for moving parishes toward new life. These are techniques and processes we have experienced ourselves as we worked with Catholic parishes in our ministry as pastoral consultants.

## THE TEN IMPERATIVES
1. Ask the Folks
2. Focus the Information
3. Gain Success with Short-Range Projects
4. Keep the Pastor Involved
5. Keep the Creative Juices Flowing
6. Organize for Continuity
7. Share the Load
8. Expand the Boundaries
9. Tap into the Spirit
10. Make Constant Adjustments

## *Ask the Folks*
The first step in getting there is knowing the present situation. This means gathering information. Whenever we begin working with a parish, we start with a survey of attitudes from among members, lay leaders and parishioners. This prepares the way for uncovering needs and desires. It allows the leadership an opportunity to construct a list of priorities based

217

not on their own impressions or inclinations but on concrete data. This is one important way of bringing a parish to life: consult the people. It seems so obvious. It is rarely done well. The people know what is wrong with a parish and they will tell the leadership if given the opportunity and the assurance that their ideas will be listened to, respected and acted upon.

Surveying is not the only way to uncover attitudes, however. Many options exist, depending on the size of the group. To tap into a large congregation, calling a few people will provide a great deal of information. Fifty names picked at random is enough to provide opinions on specific issues or approaches in the parish. Asking 10 people to react to a homily will provide much for the presenter to think about. Tear-off sections in the newsletter or bulletin give people a chance to express their opinions, as do home visits or specially-arranged focus sessions.

Suppose a parish is concerned about why the young adults are not more active in parish functions. The parish computer is able to identify every parishioner between the ages of 18 and 30. From that list, a young adults' committee picks 20 names at random and gives them a call. "Would the young adult be willing to come to a pizza party and gabfest next Tuesday night, all expenses paid?" they ask. If someone can't make it, they add a new name and continue until 20 people agree to attend. Only 15 might show up but that's enough for a focus session. The attempt, through probing questions and guided discussion, is to uncover reasons for nonattendance. Because the people were chosen at random, their ideas represent a cross-section of that age group in the parish. The focus group might even go a step further and suggest concrete activities that will attract young adults to church events. In the space of a single evening, enough information can be generated to keep a committee active for months. The same process can be used for any age, ethnic or special interest group in the parish. The first imperative for becoming an alive parish, in other words, is ASK THE FOLKS.

## *Focusing*

The second imperative is FOCUS THE INFORMATION. Once the leadership is serious about listening and responding to the parishioners, it quickly discovers that there is much more information flooding in than it knows what to do with. There has to be some way of sorting through the ideas and discovering which are the more pressing issues and which can wait until next year or the year after.

A process we have found successful is what we call "the prioritizing exercise." Once we have surveyed parishioners, we send a report of results to the pastor, staff and parish leaders.1 We ask them to read it thoroughly, making notes about findings that surprised them, didn't surprise them, and needs they felt surfaced in the report.

We then gather the leadership together for a day of prioritizing. We let people indicate areas of surprise and no surprise first. A result that surprised one person may be a "no surprise" for another. This preliminary exercise serves to refresh people's memories of the report materials. People also discover that everyone read the report from his or her own perspective and experience.

The next step is the most important. We divide the group of 25 to 30 people into small clusters of 6 to 8 people each. Everyone is given six index cards and is told to write down six needs, one per card. They are to complete the statement, "One need that surfaced as a result of the survey is . . ." We make clear that they are to identify needs and not solutions. An example of a need might be improving the congregational singing at the weekend Masses. Solutions to this need would be hiring a music director or getting better song leaders or choosing more familiar songs. The solutions come later. All we are looking for now are the needs.

Once everyone has filled out the six cards, each with a parish need, the facilitator asks one person to read a card. This need is listed on a large piece of newsprint. The next person then reads a need and this, too, is listed. The leader goes around the group six times so that everyone's cards are listed briefly on the newsprint. If two needs are similar, the initial item is checked with the addition of a word or two as a way of respecting everyone's ideas and insights.

Once the list of needs is completed, members of the small groups mill around the room or rooms looking at the lists of needs made up by the other small groups. They make notations on the back of their index cards if they discover a need that was not on their own list but was good enough for taking back to their group. After 10–15 minutes, the small groups reassemble and new items gleaned from other lists are added to their own. This process utilizes the best ideas from all the participants.

Once this list is complete, each person in the small group is given four more index cards. He or she is to identify the top four needs on the list and then write one need on each of the four cards. Once the four needs are noted, each person is asked to arrange the cards in order of priority. On a new piece of newsprint, the facilitator goes around the group and lists all the first choices of needs. As each need gets listed, it is given four points to show that it was the person's first choice and thus got the most points. The second time around each need gets three points. For the third round each need gets two points and on the last round, one point. Many needs will be similar and therefore might receive a number of points from the groups. The need for better congregational singing, for instance, might receive two "4's," a "3," four "2's" and no "1's." The total score for this need would be 19.

The newsprints from each small group are gathered together in order to provide a combined list of needs in order of priority. The final list of priorities might be as follows:

| *Ranking* | *Points* |
|---|---|
| 1. Need to get more parishioners involved in activities, especially the men: | 35 |
| 2. Need to reach out to the inactive and marginal members of the parish, especially those 18 to 30: | 31 |
| 3. Need to improve the homilies and make them more relevant to people's lives: | 25 |
| 4. Need to improve congregational singing at the weekend Masses: | 19 |
| 5. Need to get the teenagers more involved in activities, especially in ministries and leadership: | 12 |
| 6. Need to be more friendly and reach out to newcomers: | 9 |
| 7. Need to raise awareness among parishioners about social concerns and the needs of the poor: | 8 |
| 8. Need to provide opportunities for people to talk about personal and family issues, especially those related to moral questions and conflicts: | 5 |

This list is a way of focusing the information that came from the survey report so that issues can now be addressed. It provides an agenda for the coming year and beyond. Based upon the consensus of the leadership, these are the issues that need to be worked on. Many other needs, of course, surfaced during the process. These eight, however, are the ones deemed most important at this time. Take care of these needs and the parish will make great progress.

This is only one of many methods that could be used for focusing the information. Whatever approach is attempted, this aspect must remain. Don't try to tackle the whole parish or all its needs all at once. Decide which are more important and work on those few. Let the rest go for the time being.

## Gaining Success

Imperative Three is *GAIN SUCCESS WITH SHORT-RANGE PROJECTS*. Nothing gives people a lift more than to see something succeed.

They are amazed when they witness results based on their opinions. They had a complaint or an idea. They wrote it down on a survey and three months later it gets taken care of. This stirs enthusiasm.

With the priority list in hand, the next step in gaining success is to choose one item from the list and concentrate on that one to start with. Suppose welcoming newcomers is chosen by the leaders as the first priority to work on. The parish is in a growth area. The survey showed that 33% of the parishioners have joined the parish in the last four years. Using the problem-solving method of decision-making described in Chapter Six, they think of the ideal. What it would look like if newcomers really were made to feel welcome? It would be a friendlier place, people would feel at home, have a sense of belonging. New talents would be uncovered. There would be a fresh pool of talent to relieve the faithful few doing all the work. The church would be too small to handle the crowds. Collections would be up; the list goes on and on.

The description of what the ideal would look like is followed by a list of what is now being done for newcomers. This, however, turned out to be a short exercise. Not much was happening other than a notice in the bulletin and a sign in the back of church that newcomers should make an appointment at the church office to fill out a registration card. This was hardly a welcoming gesture, a way of reaching out in earnest to strangers.

The leaders started brainstorming new ideas. These were approaches that could be put into practice within the next four to six months. Some items included a newcomers committee, a packet of materials about parish events, a newcomers' Sunday, a phone call and personal visit to new people, making a video about the parish that could be loaned out to newcomers. There was no end to the possibilities.

Once all the suggestions were listed on newsprint, the leaders had to choose one that was most promising, the one that would prove most successful, the one people liked the most and wanted to see happen.

After some discussion, they finally settled on a newcomers' sponsor program. A special effort would be made to locate new people moving into the area through the local Welcome Wagon branch of the Chamber of Commerce. Attempts would also be made at all Masses on the first weekend of each month to have newcomers identify themselves to ushers or to the liturgical ministers. Newcomers would also be encouraged to fill out a card in the pews and deposit it in the collection basket.

At the same time, a request would go to the whole parish, through the bulletin, newsletter, announcements and requests made to parish organizations that the parish is looking for sponsors. People would be given a packet of materials and the name of a newcomer. For one month, they would be responsible for showing the new people around the parish, staying with them to answer questions, establishing support and showing them the ropes, making them feel at home. After the month, they would be finished. If they wanted a new assignment later on, that was up to them.

It took a few months to make up the information packets and set up the recruitment process for sponsors. It surprised the planners how many people volunteered to be sponsors. If it only took a month and the timing was up to them, they would be happy to respond. The task was simple, well-defined, had some interaction and sense of pride attached to it and most important, it had an endpoint.

The second thing that impressed the planners was how little the long-time parishioners knew about the parish. People who volunteered for the task said they would be glad to be a sponsor but they too needed to be informed about what the parish had to offer. Many had a narrow concept of what the parish was all about. They attended only one Mass and were part of only one or two activities. The rest was a mystery. The planners had to add a new aspect to the project, an orientation meeting for the sponsors. "A sponsoring of the sponsors," they called it. It turned out to be a fun event, just walking through the buildings, studying the structure, discovering what groups met when and where and for what task. The result of this experience was to open up the project not only to newcomers but to all parishioners, no matter when they had become members. It proved to be a boost to the spirit of the parish, groups of two to ten people wandering through the place discovering what made it tick. The whole project became a great success and it made the planners, sponsors, and parishioners feel proud of being associated with the parish.

## Pastor As Key

This attempt to welcome newcomers was a response to only one priority, that is, creating a more friendly environment. A similar approach could be used with all the others on the list. One way of doing this is to funnel the priorities to different commissions or committees for implementation.

This brings us to the next imperative for "getting there." Very little happens if the pastor does not like or gives little attention to a project or decision. The best model is when the pastor, staff, pastoral council and key leaders work together in providing a common direction for the parish. Leave any of these people out of the loop and the plan will suffer. This is especially true of the pastor. He (or in the case of a pastoral administrator, she) must at least be consulted about important decisions that are made in the parish, especially if the pastor is required to defend the decisions when confronted by questioning parishioners. The pastor does not need to be one of those deciding the issue, but the pastor's support, encouragement and consultation are critical if any success is to come to the venture.

We have worked in parishes where a committee or staff person made plans they thought affected only their own area of ministry. They knew the pastor was not enthusiastic about the project but they continued nevertheless. The plan may succeed for awhile but eventually it dies because it doesn't have the backing of the pastor.

Suppose the social justice committee is concerned about the growing use of capital punishment in the country. A number of people had been executed in their own state over the last year. The committee consulted the parish survey results and discovered that half the parishioners agreed that capital punishment was a just sentence. They decide to alert the congregation to the bishops' statements decrying the death penalty. They put together a plan for raising awareness that included bulletin inserts that would tell stories about those recently executed. They arranged for a meeting where people could talk about their feelings. They even planned to send a petition to the governor to grant a stay of execution for the next person on death row. They go to the pastor with their plan and get somewhat of a "wet blanket" response. He points out how this might hamper people's ability to worship at Mass. It will create flak among the conservatives and do more harm than good. Eventually he gives his okay, although grudgingly. The project goes off as planned but only a few show up for the discussion. The people sense this is not a concern of the pastor's. It is a pet project sponsored by a fringe group that is not in the mainstream. As a result, it can easily be ignored.

Had the committee consulted the pastor *before* deciding on the project rather than informing him *afterwards,* they might have had more success. The resulting plan of action may not have been the same but it would have had a more lasting impact. It would then be seen as central to the parish's mission and not some incidental project that can be disregarded.

A better approach would be to get the pastor, the staff and council involved in the project from the beginning. This might include an in-service with them, or doing a "dry-run" just for the leaders to see how they react as a preliminary phase before going to the parishioners.

It takes more time and the end product may not be all one had hoped for, but if you want to have an impact on the parish, attend to the fourth imperative: *KEEP THE PASTOR INVOLVED.*

## Be Creative

The next imperative is *KEEP THE CREATIVE JUICES FLOWING.* We have touched on this theme throughout this book. Without imagination and creativity there will be no future for parishes, no promise of new life. Not everyone is gifted at stiffing up this imaginative spirit. It takes prodding and a conducive environment. Once primed, however, it is hard to turn the pump off. Not only will the intuitive people catch hold and provide options for the future, the down-to-earth, practical people will jump in as well.

The following process to help people think creatively is only one of many possible options. The first step to thinking imaginatively about the future and to discovering what options lie open for the parish is to begin with the past.

To help people dream about the future, we often use a history line of significant events in the life of the parish over the last 15–20 years. Whether it happened last month, last year, or 10 years ago, any event, person, building or project people can remember is put on the history line. This gives people a sense of continuity with the parish's traditions. Whatever new ideas people come up with will have their roots in the recent history of the parish.

Once the history line is complete, each person is given an index card and asked to state in a word or a phrase how they size up the parish at the present moment. These words are listed on newsprint. A sample list might include: At a crossroads. Ready for something new to happen. On the brink. Stuck in a rut. Ready to move. Diverse. Confused. Self-centered. Needing direction.

The list of feelings about the present situation helps prepare people to take the next step, one that will carry them into the future. Before taking that step, however, one more ingredient is necessary. It relates to the essentials of parish life. What are underlying aspects that must be preserved no matter what options are chosen?

We use a group activity called *Whatsit*[2] for this step. Any similar process that helps uncover a parish's mission or purpose will do. The *Whatsit* activity involves giving every participant a deck of 12 cards. Ten of the cards have written on them different aspects of parish life. One might read, "The strength of the parish depends on the strong leadership of the pastor." Another, "The most important work of the parish is to teach, sanctify and give direction for the moral lives of the parishioners." A third reads, "The strength of the parish depends on a good liturgical program providing a variety of forms for worship." In groups of 6–8 people, each person arranges the deck of cards in order of importance, from the most to the least important. In this way, the individual has a chance to clarify what is the purpose or essential mission of the parish. Each person then displays his or her first choice and explains why this is most important.

The activity continues as the group listens to everyone's first, second and third choices. At this point, the card playing is interrupted to see if there have been any common trends or similar threads in the choice of cards. Looking at people's last choice is also revealing. For one person, for instance, the strong leadership of the pastor might be towards the top of the deck, while for another it is on the bottom as the least important. The discussion that results is often revealing about people's perception of what are the essential aspects of parish life. What are the reasons for its existence, in other words.

After people have had a chance to dialogue about the purpose of the parish, they turn to the future. What would they like to see happen a few years from now? First they agree on a target date, one that is not too immediate so as to allow time for change and planning, but not too distant so they can still visualize the parish reaching its dream. People usually choose a date three to five years in the future.

We next ask the participants to list all the "Givens" they can think of for that date. These are aspects that will affect the parish on the target date over which we have no control. Examples include the number of priests, the makeup of the neighborhood, the age profile, projected growth or decline rates in the area. These "givens" provide the framework for the next step. No matter what people plan, they must take these "givens" into account and stay within the confines of what is possible.

We then ask people to put on their fantasy hats and dream for the future. We tell them that outside the room it is no longer the present moment but 3–5 years from now. "What does it look like? What would you want to have happened in the parish by then?" The group starts to paint a picture of the parish as they would like to see it in the next few years, filling in as many details as they wish. We put no restraints on their imagination at this point. The exercise helps expand people's horizons and loosens the group up for the next step.

We then pass out dreaming sheets to each person. In the context of prayer, we send the people off for 30 minutes to work on their dreams for specific areas of parish life. Figure 3 provides an example of this dreaming sheet.

We give them only two instructions while they do this. One is to write legibly so that someone else can read their dreams. Second, if they need more space, use the back of the sheet, but stay within the same section as on the front of the sheet. The reason for this is that the sheets will be cut up and collected according to each area of ministry. The writing on the back has to correspond with what is on the front of the sheet, so dreams in the same area stay on the same cut-up piece of paper.

When all the people have filled out their dreaming sheets, they are collected and cut up so that all the dreams for worship are in one pile, those for formation and education in another, the dreams for outreach and Christian service in another.

---

## Figure 3
## Parish Vision Worksheet for 200_

As I reflect on what I would like to see parish look like in 200_, this is what I come up with:

1. *This is the way the parish worships and prays* . . . (Describe your desired outcome (goals) for parish Masses, prayer experiences, spirituality, etc.)

   _____

2. *This is the way the parish is managed* . . . (Describe your desired outcome (goals) for use of resources, communication, staffing, decision-making, etc.)

   _____

3. *This is the way parishioners relate to each other.* . . (Describe your desired outcome (goals) for community-building, activities, parish groupings, etc.)

   _____

4. *This is the way the people-old and young-learn about their faith/tradition* . . . (Describe your desired outcome (goals) in education for all areas and ages.)

   _____

5. *This is the way the parish relates to the larger community* . . . (Describe your desired outcome (goals) for outreach, service, pastoral care, ecumenism.)

   _____

6. *This is the way the parish gets involved and plans for its future* . . . (Describe your desired outcome (goals) for volunteers, newcomers, planning, etc.)

   _____

IF YOU USE THE OTHER SIDE, WRITE IN THE SAME PLACE
AS ON THE FRONT. PLEASE WRITE LEGIBLY.

These dreams are then given to the leaders for each area of parish life as a guide for their own goal-setting over the coming year. The exercise takes the better part of a day, about 4–5 hours in all. What it does is push out the boundaries of creativity and imagination. People start catching on to more than what is and explore what could be. It is exciting to watch parishioners come alive and do creative dreaming, not only for their own area of ministry and interest but for the parish as a whole.

The process does need direction and some amount of softening up. That is why we begin with the history line and the present situation of the parish. This provides the foundation and anchor for the dreaming. Defining the limits within which to dream also helps people stay inside the realm of realizable dreams.

On the other hand, the process frees people to be creative and provides a method for getting the juices of imagination flowing. Too often parish options are limited and narrow. Helping people open up to what could be provides the soil for a rich new way of being parish. As it says in Proverbs, "Without a vision, the people perish." (29:18) The Jerusalem Bible's translation is more descriptive. It says, "Where there is no vision the people get out of hand." (p. 973)

## Good Organization

The sixth imperative for "getting there" is *ORGANIZE FOR CONTINUITY*. It should be apparent by now that structure is essential to parish life. The leaders of a parish might come up with a great plan for the future life of the parish but if it doesn't have a framework on which to hang, it will fall by the wayside once the enthusiasm of the moment passes.

Getting the creative juices flowing is not enough. There must also be a way of organizing the dreams so as not to overtax the resources of the planners. This will assure the continued success of the ministries.

In working with parishes, when we come to the end of a day with parish leaders, we make sure that every committee or task group has a clear idea of what is expected of them and within what timeframe. We make sure that each group has a contact person. We establish coordinators or a steering committee to oversee the entire plan so that deadlines are reached and proposed tasks accomplished. On a few occasions, when people say they will work on a committee or task group, we have taken their name tags and stuck it on the newsprint that describes the work of that group. Once it is on the newsprint, it can't be pulled off. It says, "Hello, my name is Joe." Seeing his name on the newsprint helps him realize, "I'm committed to this job I agreed to accomplish, along with the rest of my task group.

In the long run, a parish has to find a way of dividing up the tasks so that no one person or group is overburdened. We dwelt on this when dealing with freeing structures in Chapter Six. What we emphasize here is that whenever a parish plans for its future, it must also plan ways to realize its future through good structure and organization.

The individuals who thought up the project will move on. On the average, 52% of the staffs we work with are changed from the time we start with a parish to the time we finish the contract, two and a half years later. The term of office for pastoral council members is usually two or three years. Pastors come and go much more frequently now than in the past. The era of long pastorates is over. The only way to provide continuity in the midst of this constant turnover in leadership is to create a structure that will continue despite these changes.

We worked with a military parish in which every person, pastor included, was transferred every three years. The leaders came up with wonderful plans for creative worship, religious education and community-building. The challenge was to discover structures that would keep the momentum alive despite the constant turnover. The predictability of Army life helped. What people encountered on leaving one post was repeated in another. But this chapel community had some great new insights they wanted to keep alive, even when they themselves were transferred.

What they decided to do was construct a special notebook that spelled out their dreams and the steps they had set up for realizing their dreams. This notebook became the second "Bible" for the parish. Copies were carefully passed from council member to council member, from pastor to pastor and from staff person to new staff person. Plans were changed and adapted as new people took over the reins, but the emphasis on providing continuity endured. No amount of effort and energy spent on keeping the original dream alive through good structures will go unrewarded. Names and positions will be forgotten but the process will continue.

## Ownership

The seventh imperative is *SHARE THE LOAD*. The temptation, whenever there is a new way of operating or a new plan of action, is to hang on to it and protect it from being destroyed by those who don't understand its significance. This is a noble ambition. What often happens, however, is that the plan or action belongs to just a few of the "insiders." It is not shared with others. Leaders tend to keep tight control over a pet project so that it will keep going. Unfortunately, it often dies for lack of common ownership by the parish as a whole.

This is what is amazing about the way Jesus went about founding his Church. From the start of his public ministry, he called together companions to hear the message and spread the Good News. He sent them out in pairs to heal and evangelize before they knew what this new message was all about. His ministry lasted only three years. He then put the whole responsibility for the new Church into the hands of a few raw recruits. With the help of the Spirit, they caught on to the message and went out to the entire known world, spreading the word about Jesus and about the Church he founded. Can we do anything less?

The more people that can be included in the planning and early stages of problem-solving, the more commitment and ownership they will feel in carrying out the agreed-upon plan. The more people are consulted before a conclusion is reached, the more they will take interest in it and support the result. The more concern and attention is put into informing a community before a decision is implemented, the more respect the people will show toward the leadership.

In the past, the final decision-maker for major decisions was the pastor. He was the ultimate authority. As the post-Vatican II era took hold, the pastor became more of an orchestra conductor, overseeing the harmonious interaction of staff, council, committees and ministries. This, too, is evolving so that the pastor is becoming more of a jazz musician. He is an integral part of the leadership, but not the one up front leading the band. He's part of the band. The pastor and the other leaders are listening to each other and are sharing the lead with each other.

We have worked with a number of parishes in southern Louisiana. While there we often visit the French Quarter of New Orleans, especially Preservation Hall. This provides an excellent example of sharing the load. People are crammed into a small, dimly-lit room, waiting for the Dixieland jazz musicians to appear. One by one, a number of elderly people saunter in. They sit down on rickety old chairs, pull out their instruments and start to play. One person gets them started and towards the end of the song draws them together for the final chorus. In between, they "share the load," first one, then another taking the lead. It is a wonderful manifestation of partnership in ministry. The music is electrifying. The standing-room-only crowd goes wild. The musicians take it all in with apparent disinterest. As the evening progresses, so does the music. At the conclusion everyone is exhausted but delighted by the experience. Perhaps that is what parish is all about.

## *Social Outreach*

The next imperative keeps a parish from concentrating too much on its inner life or on its own agenda. We call this Eighth Imperative, *EXPAND THE BOUNDARIES.* What this implies is that a parish must always keep its public mission in mind. The purpose of a parish is twofold, the care of its own membership and the demands of the social gospel. Placing too much emphasis on one or the other is a distortion of what parish is meant to be.

Few American Catholic parishes need to worry about giving too much attention to the outer mission of social transformation. The parishioners will see to that. Most Catholics, as our statistics in Chapter Two indicated, are reluctant to have the parish get embroiled in public issues or social concerns.

The greater temptation is to wall off the parish from the other world of everyday life. The drawbridge comes down a few times a week. The parishioners file in over the moat. The drawbridge goes up and the people interact with their God and with one another as if the world didn't exist. Once the worship service or parish function is over, people file out and go about their business, making little connection between the parish and the rest of their lives. And yet a parish without a Christian service, social justice dimension is not an authentic extension of Christ's Church on the local level. This social dimension cannot be relegated to a paid staff person and a few volunteers working on Christian service projects. It has to be imbedded in the fabric of the parish as a whole.

Every member, every ministry, every activity, every statement about parish life must reflect this broader mission. No longer is it "Me and Jesus" or "We and Jesus," but "We, The World, and Jesus." As a result, one requirement for discovering new ways of being parish in the next century is to push out the boundaries of the parish and extend its influence into the surrounding neighborhood and world beyond. This will happen when people are welcomed into the parish no matter where they live or what their background. A spirit of acceptance will permeate parish organizations and ministries. Programs and services from other churches will interact with the parish's own so that mutual resources are recognized and shared. Members are encouraged to close the gap between the parish and their everyday lives so that the two are more compatible and united. Issues in the surrounding community that cry out for attention are brought before the parishioners for dialogue, problem-solving and an action response.

As we stressed in Chapter Ten, the inner and outer mission of the parish are one and the same. The Spirit of Jesus keeps prodding us to expand the boundaries of our minds and ministry. It is the world that needs help, not ourselves. We are the apostles, the change agents, the prophets, the ones who know what is really important, the people who look beyond what is immediately obvious and recognize God at work in the world. The "we" of which we speak is not just the leadership. It is the entire membership. Don't underestimate the power of the Spirit to move mountains.

## Never Alone

The ninth imperative is *TAP INTO THE SPIRIT.* We are not alone as we struggle to envision the parish of the future. This is not all our doing. We are coworkers with the Spirit in shaping the parish for the third millennium.

The shortages, frustrations, limitations, obstacles, all have a purpose. They point us in a new direction. They wake us up to new realities. They challenge our narrow vision and open our eyes to possibilities. That is the Spirit at work in our world. Our task is to discover how best to tap into that power in our midst. We are free beings. We can turn the offer of grace and insight down, but this would be such a loss.

On the other hand, we can tap into this resource and let it be our guide to new paradigms. How can we keep this Spirit a constant companion in our search?

One avenue is spirituality. In Chapter Three we probed into the richness of this resource. Each one of us needs to develop our personal, communal and societal spirituality if we are to utilize the power of the Spirit in our midst.

One example is Mother Teresa. She talked at the 1992 National Convention of the Knights of Columbus, challenging them to wake up to the needs of the poor. She refused to share their banquet because it was such a contrast to what she was saying. They responded by adding to their original contribution an extra amount equal to the cost of the entire banquet. That is a start. What would have happened, however, if they had canceled the banquet and took the food out to the poor and homeless in the surrounding city? It would have been a logistical nightmare, of course, but the participants would not have forgotten the experience.

Exploring the possible avenues for tapping into the Spirit are often scary and demanding. Just when we think we have done our best, a new opportunity presents itself. A parish starts up small groups for scripture sharing. One group goes the next step and asks about leafleting cars during all the Masses to protest the local abortion clinic. The priests invite people to a weekly bag lunch to provide insights into next week's homilies.

The priests are glad so many "homily helpers" show up. In the process, however, they get an earful about poor delivery and cutting down the length of the homilies. The principal inaugurates a collection campaign for recycling cans and newspapers. She is soon confronted by the eighth graders who demand a stop to paperware at the school lunches. We get attacked just when we feel we are doing well. This could be the Spirit taking the parish and its leadership to the next level. It could be the start of a conversion to a new paradigm, a new way of acting.

Another avenue for tapping into the Spirit is to pay attention to what is scarce in the parish and in its ministries. This awareness often points to new abundances. Think of the story of the loaves and fishes. So little food for so many people. Jesus takes what he has, says a prayer (Taps Into the Spirit) and tells the apostles to hand out what is available. Whether the loaves multiplied in the apostles' hands or whether it prompted others to follow suit and pull out what little they had from under their tunics, we will never know. All we know is the result. Everyone was fed and there was plenty left over. There was abundance in the midst of scarcity.

The same dynamic happens in the parish. What is scarce? Only a handful of people show up for adult formation. There is not enough money in the collection basket. More teachers are needed for religious education classes. Few young people come to church. There is such poor attentiveness at sacramental preparation classes. These are the scarcities. Is there any abundance in the midst of these scarcities?

Jesus had only a few people to work with and many of them didn't show much promise. They became the heroes of the early Church. The same can happen in adult formation. Perhaps the few people who do show up become the leaven and shake up the entire parish.

The shortfall in income forces a change in priorities and creates new emphases in ministries. This brings new life and commitment to the leaders and people. Scarcity becomes the occasion for a wealth of new ideas and insights.

The Spirit works in such mysterious ways. Tapping into that power often feels like we are operating in the midst of a dense fog. Eventually, however, the sun comes out. We see the light. We understand what has been happening. It is a whole new day that is dawning. This is an abundance worth waiting for.

## Flexibility

The final imperative is *MAKE CONSTANT ADJUSTMENTS*. This includes the evaluation and fine-tuning necessary in order to keep a plan or new focus on track and productive.

Trying to figure out a new way of being parish in the next century may not be the hardest task. The more difficult endeavor may be keeping the leaders and people moving toward the desired outcome. Endurance, commitment, accountability, maintaining perspective and keeping energy alive; these are the tough steps in seeking new ways for being parish. People come and go, key leaders are transferred, pastors reassigned, terms of office are up, new people take their places on the council and commissions. In the midst of all this change, how can a parish maintain a forward momentum and keep searching for new paradigms?

What saves a parish through this turmoil is making adjustments to fit the situation. The endpoint must be constantly before the community. For example, in liturgy we commit ourselves to the goal, "When people leave the weekend Masses they are saying, 'Wow, I want to come back to that!'" How close the liturgies come to realizing that goal will vary according to who is available to make it happen.

This goal indicates that the parish is committed to vibrant, participative, life-giving, challenging, community-building weekend liturgies. A three-year plan is worked out, with intermediate stages to be reached each year. For the present year, for instance, the focus will be on greeting people and on participative music. Next year the emphasis will be on the homilies and shared prayer. The following year will stress a celebrative environment and physical improvements.

All those associated with liturgy planning are excited by the plan and give it full approval. The music ministries go to work selecting music appropriate to each Mass on the weekend. A call goes out for greeters. Only those not involved in any other parish ministry are eligible. Over 100 new people respond. A new spirit is generated the moment people enter church.

Then suddenly the husband of the music minister is transferred out of state. The entire plan is threatened for lack of direction. It is time for making adjustments. A new minister is hired, fully aware of what the parish wishes to accomplish at the weekend Masses. He turns out to be a great boon to the spirit of the liturgies. Then suddenly the lead couple that is handling the greeters complains about getting overextended. A replacement must be found. Rather than stepping in to fill the vacuum, the liturgical planners call together the greeters and uncover a team of people who are willing to coordinate this activity. Once again, adjustments are made and the process continues toward the goal.

A key ingredient for keeping any plan on track is evaluation. This should not come at the end of a project but in the middle, so that adjustments can be made before it is too late to change the plan.

Most people, perhaps Americans more than others, shy away from evaluation. "Did I mess up?" is the underlying fear. One way of overcoming this apprehension is to build into every ministry, project and parish function an evaluation process so that it becomes part of the accepted routine in the parish. Another help is to stress positive attitudes and successes as well as shortfalls and limitations.

Assessments of both ministries and individuals need to be made. The form we include here is one way to evaluate ministries. (See Figure 4) Each year, the people who coordinate an area of ministry fill out the sheet individually and then compare the results with one another as a way of acknowledging what has worked well and uncovering what more needs to be accomplished. Such a form could be used to evaluate the progress made in music and greeting people at the weekend Masses mentioned in the previous example.

---

## Figure 4
## Self-evaluation of Parish Ministries

NOTE: This evaluation form is to be filled out by the individual minister first and then the results are shared with other members of the group.

AREA OF MINISTRY:_____

1. What is the overall goal for this area of ministry, that is, what is this ministry trying to accomplish in the long run?

   _____

2. What is one specific goal that we have been trying to accomplish in this area of ministry over the last six months?

   _____

3. How close have we come in achieving either our short-range or long-range goals. Are we, in other words, doing any better now than we were six months ago?

   _____

4. How has this area ministry responded to the needs, desires and expectations of the parishioners as expressed by them in the survey?

   _____

5. In your opinion, what's still missing? What, in other words, still needs to happen so that this area of ministry is meeting its goals and responding to people's needs and expectations?

6. What, if anything, is getting in the way of progress in this area of ministry, that is, lack of organization, poor meetings, timing, environment, leadership, response, planning, etc.?

[Any other comments you may like to make about this area of ministry can be noted on the other side and used for further discussion when the entire group meets to compare notes.]

## Conclusion

These are ten steps for renewing parish life in the years ahead:

1. Ask the Folks
2. Focus the Information
3. Gain Success with Short-Range Projects
4. Keep the Pastor Involved
5. Keep the Creative Juices Flowing
6. Organize for Continuity
7. Share the Load
8. Expand the Boundaries
9. Tap into the Spirit
10. Make Constant Adjustments

These point to a new way of being parish. The Catholic Church of the United States is on the edge of greatness. The Spirit is forcing change on many levels. It can no longer be business as usual. The new ways of being church are already being tried out in local parishes and small communities throughout the country. A shift is taking place. It is right in front of our noses if we only pay attention. It is time to stop and smell the freshness of new life in our land. The Church of the Third Millennium is being conceived this very moment. The period of gestation is at hand. As St. Paul tells us in the Letter to the Romans:

> In my opinion, whatever we may have to go through now
> is less than nothing compared with the magnificent
> future God has planned for us. The whole of creation is

on tip-toe to see the wonderful sight of the sons (and daughters) of God coming into their own. (Romans 8:18–19, J.B. Phillips Translation, NY: MacMillan Co., 1958, p. 332)

# Questions for Review and Reflection

*Ask the people*

List all the ways now used for gathering information from the people. What is missing or what more needs to be done?

*Focus the information*

Can you name any priorities that focus the work of the leadership and ministers? How do needs differ from wants or solutions?

*Gaining success*

How much success do you feel the parish has made in achieving its goals and objectives? Are there any goals? Are they realistic and realizable?

*Pastor as key*

Ask your pastor to tell a story about when he felt that he had little influence over a decision. Ask others what they felt. How do the stories compare? Who else is influential in the parish?

*Be creative*

Draw a history line and name the significant events in the life of the parish during the past 15 years. What events were the most creative? Where is the parish now?

*Organize for continuity*

What parish traditions must be preserved no matter what options for the future are chosen? What new traditions should be introduced and protected?

*Ownership*

Is there one parish program for which you feel responsible? Is there shared ownership for this program? Do you feel you are working for others instead of with them?

*Social Outreach*

Does your involvement in the parish have an outreach dimension so that it serves more than just the membership? Does the parish have an influence in the surrounding area?

*Tap into the Spirit*

What evidence do you have that the Spirit is alive and well in the parish? What new, unexpected events have happened? How is the ministry beyond our own abilities?

*Make Adjustments*

Leaders like to control, to organize and have predictable outcomes. A parish is too fluid for this to happen. How flexible are the leaders, how open to change is the planning, how ready to adapt are the ministers?

## Prayer Ritual

*Music*

"Blest Are They" by David Haas. (Chicago: G.I.A. Publications, Inc., 1985)

V. Blessed are the poor in spirit.

R. THEIRS IS THE KINDOM OF HEAVEN.

V. Blessed are those who ask the parishioners and respond to their needs with sensitivity and action.

R. THEIRS IS THE KINDOM OF HEAVEN.

V. Blessed are the gentle.

R. THEIRS IS THE KINDOM OF HEAVEN.

V. Blessed are those who tap into the Spirit of the Lord and the spirit of the people, announcing goodness and new life.

R. THEIRS IS THE KINDOM OF HEAVEN.

V. Blessed are those who hunger and thirst for what is right.

R. THEIRS IS THE KINDOM OF HEAVEN.

V. Blessed are those who share ownership, who believe in others and who hunger and thirst for growth and development for all people.

R. THEIRS IS THE KINDOM OF HEAVEN.

V. Blessed are those who mourn.

R. THEIRS IS THE KINDOM OF HEAVEN.

V. Blessed are the priests, poets, and musicians who express the sorrow and hopes of their people.

R. THEY SHALL SEE GOD.

V. Blessed are the pure of heart.

R. THEY SHALL SEE GOD.

V. Blessed are those who see the scarcity of others and respond with generosity.

R. THEIRS IS BLESSEDNESS.

V. Blessed are the peacemakers.

R. THEY SHALL HAVE PEACE.

V. Blessed are those who bring compassion to suffering, who communicate the pain of the people and who persevere in solidarity with others.

R. THEIRS IS BLESSEDNESS.

*Closing*

Repeat the opening song, "Blest Are They."

1. The Parish Evaluation Project located in Milwaukee, provides helps for surveying parishoners' attidutes. It is part of a planning process for parishes called Parish Assessment and Renewal (PAR). Information about these resources can be obtained by contacting PEP: Pastoral Consultants at 3195 S. Superior Street, Milwaukee, WI 53207. 414/483-7370.

2. The Whatsit group activity can be obtained from the PEP office in Milwaukee. Address listed above.

# Bibliography

Avery, Michel, Brian Auvine, Barbara Streibel, Lonnie Weiss, *Building United Judgment, A Handbook for Consensus Decision Making*, Madison, WI: The Center for Conflict Resolution, 1981.

Bannon, William J., and Suzanne Donovan, S.C., *Volunteers and Ministry*, Paulist Press, NY: 1983.

Baranowski, Arthur R., *Creating Small Faith Communities, A Plan for Restructuring the Parish and Renewing Catholic Life*, Cincinnati: St. Anthony Messenger Press, 1988.

Baranowski, Arthur R., *Pastoring the Pastors, Resources for Training and Supporting Pastoral Facilitators for Small Faith Communities*, Cincinnati: St. Anthony Messenger Press, 1988.

Baranowski, Arthur R., Kathleen M. O'Reilly & Carrie M. Piro, *Praying Alone and Together, An 11-Session Prayer Module for Small Faith Communities*, Cincinnati: St. Anthony Messenger Press, 1988.

Bausch, William J., *The Christian Parish*, Notre Dame, IN: Fides/Claretian, 1980.

_____, *Traditions, Tensions, Transitions in Ministry*, Mystic, CT: Twenty-Third Publications, 1982.

Boff, Leonardo, *Ecclesiogenesis*, Maryknoll, NY. Orbis, 1986.

Bradford, Leland, *Making Meetings Work*, University Associates, LaJolla, CA: 1976.

Brennan, Patrick J., *The Evangelizing Parish: Theologies and Strategies for Renewal*, Allen, TX: Tabor Publishing, 1987.

Brennan, Patrick J., *Parishes That Excel: Models of Excellence in Education, Ministry, and Evangelization*, New York, NY: The Crossroad Publishing Company, 1992.

_____, *Re-Imagining the Parish*, NY. Crossroads, 1990.

Bridges, William., *Transitions: Making Sense of Life's Changes*, NY: Addison-Wesley Publishing Co., 1991.

Bridges, William., *Managing Transitions: Making The Most of Change*, NY: Addison-Wesley Publishing Co., Inc., 1991.

Broholm, Dick and John Hoffman, *Empowering Laity for Their Full Ministry: Nine Blocking Enabling Forces*, Newton Center, MA: Andover Newton Laity Project, 1981.

Burghardt, Walter J., SJ, *To Christ I Look, Homilies at Twilight*, NY: Paulist Press, 1989.

Byers, David, editor, *The Parish in Transition*, Washington, DC: United States Catholic Conference, 1986.

Callahan, Kennon L., *Twelve Keys to an Effective Church*, San Francisco, CA: Harper, 1983.

Carroll, Jackson W., *As One With Authority: Reflective Leadership in Ministry*, Louisville: Westminister/John Knox Press, 1991.

Chinnici, Rosemary, *Can Women Re-Image the Church?*, NY. Paulist Press, 1992.

Chittister, Joan D., OSB, *Job's Daughters: Women and Power*, Paulist Press: 1990.

Clark, Jean Illsley, *Who Me, Lead A Group?*, San Francisco: Harper and Row (Winston Press), 1984.

Conn, Joann Wolski, ed., *Women's Spirituality: Resources for Christian Development*, NY: Paulist Press, 1986.

Crosby, Michael H., *The Dysfunctional Church: Addiction and Codependency In The Family of Catholicism*, Notre Dame, IN: Ave Maria Press, 1991.

Dale, Robert D., *Pastoral Leadership*, Nashville: Abingdon Press, 1986.

De Mena, Henry F., Jr., *How To Increase Parish Income*, Mystic, CT: Twenty-Third Publications, 1982.

Dolan, Jay, Scott Appleby, Patricia Byrne, CSJ, and Debra Campbell, *Transforming Parish Ministry: The Changing Roles of Catholic Clergy, Laity and Religious Women in the United States 1930–1980*, NY: Crossroads/Continuum, 1989.

Doohan, Leonard, *Laity's Mission in the Local Church*, San Francisco: Harper & Row, Publishers, 1986.

_____, *The Lay-Centered Church: Theology & Spirituality*, Minneapolis: Winston Press, 1984.

Dudley, Carl S., (ed.). *Building Effective Ministry: Theory and Practice in the Local Church*, San Francisco: Harper and Row, 1983.

Dues, Greg, *Dealing with Diversity, A Guide for Parish Leaders*, Mystic, CT: Twenty-Third Publications, 1988.

Egan, Gerald, *Change-Agent Skills A: Assessing and Designing Excellence*, San Diego, CA: University Associates, 1988.

Fagan, Harry, *Empowerment: Skills for Parish Social Action*, NY: Paulist Press, 1979.

Flagel, Clarice, *Avoiding Burnout, Time Management for DRE's*, Dubuque: Wm. C. Brown Co., 1981.

Gallagher, Maureen, *Continuing the Journey, Parishes in Transition*, Kansas City: Sheed and Ward, 1988.

Gilligan, Carol, *In A Different Voice*, Cambridge, MA: Harvard University Press, 1982.

Gilmour, Peter, *The Emerging Pastor*, Kansas City, MO: Sheed & Ward, 1986.

Gram, Frances & Richard Currier, *Forming a Small Christian Community: A Personal Journey*, Mystic, CT: Twenty-Third Publications, 1992.

Gremillion, Joseph & Jim Castelli, *The Emerging Parish: The Notre Dame Study of Catholic Life Since Vatican II*, San Francisco: Harper & Row, Publishers, 1987.

Hirsh, Sandra Krebs, *Using The Myers-Briggs Type Indicator in Organizations: A Resource Book*, Palo Alto, CA: Consulting Psychologists Press, Inc., 1985.

Hoffman, Virginia, *Birthing A Living Church*, NY: Crossroad, 1988.

Hoge, Dean R., *Converts, Dropouts, Returnees*, NY: The Pilgrim Press, 1981.

Keisey, David, & Marilyn Bates, *Please Understand Me*, Del Mar, CA: Prometheus Nemesis Books, 1978.

Kelly, Maureen, M.A., *The Dysfunctional Parish Staff: Transforming Conflict Into Compassionate Ministry*, Cinninnati, OH: St. Anthony Press, 1992 (5 cassettes).

Kleissler, Thomas A., Margo A. LeBert, Mary C. McGuinness, *Small Christian Communities: A Vision of Hope*, NY: Paulist Press, 1991.

Leas, Speed B., *Moving Your Church Through Conflict*, Washington, D.C: Alban Institute, Inc., 1985.

Lee, Bernard and Michael A. Cowan, *Dangerous Memories*, Kansas City: Sheed and Ward, 1986.

Lewis, G. Douglass, *Resolving Church Conflicts*, Harper & Row Publishers, San Francisco: 1981.

Lindgren, Alvin & Norman Shawchuck, *Let My People Go: Empowering Laity for Ministry*, Nashville: Abingdon Press, 1980.

McKinney, Mary Benet, OSB, D.Min., *Sharing Wisdom: A Process for Group Decision Making*, Allen, TX: Tabor Publishing, 1987.

Mead, Loren B., *Critical Moment of Ministry: A Change of Pastors*, Washington, D.C.: The Alban Institute, 1991.

Mitchell, Kenneth R. and Herbert Anderson, *All Our Losses, All Our Griefs: Resources for Pastoral Care*, Philadelphia: The Westminster Press, 1983.

Myers, Isabel Briggs with Peter B. Myers, *Gifts Differing*, Palo Alto, CA: Consulting Psychologists Press, Inc., 1980.

Rademacher, William J., *The New Practical Guide for Parish Councils*, Mystic, CT: Twenty-Third Publications, 1988.

Riso, Don Richard, *Personality Types, Using the Enneagram for Self-Discovery*, Boston, Houghton Mifflin Co., 1987.

Rost, Joseph C., *Leadership for the Twenty-First Century*, NY Praeger, 1991.

Schaller, Lyle E., *Effective Church Planning*, Nashville: Abingdon Press, 1979.

Schillebeeckx, Edward, *Ministry, Leadership in the Community of Jesus Christ*, NY: Crossroad Publishing Co., 1981.

Shea, John, *The Spirit Master*, Chicago, IL: The Thomas More Press, 1987.

_____, *Starlight: Beholding the Christmas Miracle All Year Long*, New York: Crossroad, 1992.

Sofield, Loughlan, & Brenda Hermann, *Developing the Parish as a Community of Service*, Le Jacq Publishing Inc., USA: 1984.

Sofield, Loughlan & Rosine Hammett, *Inside Christian Community*, Le Jacq Publishing Inc., USA: 1981.

Sofield, Loughlan & Carroll Juliano, *Collaborative Ministry, Skills and Guidelines*, Notre Dame, IN: Ave Maria Press, 1987.

Spencer, Sabina A. and John D. Adams, *Life Changes: Growing Through Personal Transitions*, Impact Publishers, CA., 1990.

Swain, Bernard, *Liberating Leadership: Practical Styles for Pastoral Ministry*, San Francisco: Harper & Row, 1986.

Sweetser, Thomas R, SJ., "I'd Like To Say: Why Married Clergy and Women Priests Are Coming," *St. Anthony Messenger*, Vol. 92, No. 11, April 1985.

_____, "Parish Life in the 90's," *St. Anthony Messenger*, Vol. 93, No. 4, Sept. 1985.

_____, *Successful Parishes: How They Meet the Challenge of Change*, Winston Press, MN: 1983.

_____, "The Parish of the Future: Beyond the Programs," *America*, March 10, 1990.

Sweetser, Thomas & Carol Wisniewski Holden, *Leadership in a Successful Parish*, Kansas City, MO: Sheed & Ward, 1987, 1992.

Sweetser, Thomas, and Patricia M. Forster, "A Festschrift on Small Faith Communities," *Chicago Studies*, V. 31, No. 2, August, 1992.

Sweetser, Thomas P., SJ, "Managing The Parish," *Church*, Vol. 7, No. 4, Winter, 1991.

_____, "Parish Leadership Versus Parish Management," *Human Development*, Vol. 13 No. 3, Fall, 1992.

_____, "Scarcity and Abundance in Parishes," *Review For Religious,* Vol. 51, No. 4, July-August, 1992.

_____, The Flip Side of The Priest Shortage." *St. Anthony Messenger*, Vol. 100, No. 2, July, 1992.

Wallace, Ruth A., *They Call Her Pastor: A New Role For Catholic Women*, NY: State University of New York Press, 1992.

Westley, Dick, *Good Things Happen, Experiencing Community in Small Groups*, Mystic, CT: Twenty-Third Publications, 1992.

White, Edward A., *Saying Goodbye: A Time of Growth For Congregations And Pastors*, Washington, D.C.: Alban Institute, 1991.

Whitehead, James D., & Evelyn E., *Community of Faith*, NY: Mystic, CT: Twenty-Third Publications, 1992.

_____, *Method in Ministry*, NY: Seabury Press, 1980.

_____, *The Emerging Laity: Returning Leadership to the Community of Faith*, NY: Doubleday and Co., 1986.

_____, *The Promise of Partnership, Leadership and Ministry in an Adult*

*Church*, San Francisco: Harper & Row, 1991.

Whitehead, Evelyn Eaton, ed., *The Parish in Community and Ministry*, NY: Paulist Press, 1978.

Wilson, Marlene, *The Effective Management of Volunteer Programs*, Boulder, CO: Volunteer Management Associates, 1976.

_____, *Survival Skills for Managers*, Boulder, CO: Volunteer Management Associates, Johnson Publishing Co., 1981.

_____, *How to Mobilize Church Volunteers*, Minneapolis: Augsburg House, 1983.

# Index